CORAL SEA CALLING

Pioneer Tales of
Australia's Northern Waters

ION IDRIESS

Illustrated by Frank Norton

ETT IMPRINT
Exile Bay

This 7th edition published by ETT Imprint, Exile Bay 2025

First published by Angus & Robertson Publishers 1957
Reprinted 1957, 1980, 1981

First published by ETT Imprint in 2022
Reprinted 2023
First electronic edition published by ETT Imprint in 2022

ETT IMPRINT
PO Box R1906
Royal Exchange NSW 1225 Australia

ISBN 978-1-923205-67-3 (pbk)
ISBN 978-1-922698-56-8 (ebk)

Cover: On board a pearling lugger, Thursday Island, 1936

Designed by Tom Thompson

CONTENTS

Publisher's Dedication

For

Dr Jeremy Robert Greenwood

Who followed his curiosity

17th August 2022, Mackay Reef in the Coral Sea

Author's Note

THE full story of Australia's Coral Sea would occupy numerous volumes. Having often been surprised at how little we know about this fascinating little sea so peculiarly our own, I'll tell you a little about it; but only up to the time of the first pearlshell rush. After which, should you desire to know more it will be my pleasure to oblige-though only in a matey sort of way, for the "Big Story" must be left to pens far more capable than mine.

There may be an error or two in the earlier portion of this book, for in Australia's very early days only scanty records were kept. Indeed, no records at all were kept of many subjects, or if they were they have been lost, thus complete accuracy is almost impossible in recording many events. However, even the very early events narrated here I believe to be as accurately set down as possible - to a sweet-tempered, irritable little scribbler such as me, anyway.

But the greater part of the book is written upon my own stamping grounds, and you can confidently take the Coral Sea with me.

In days gone by, when life aboard a smelly trepang cutter was high adventure, I listened to the old-timers of the early *beche-de-mer* days yarning under the 'Tree of Knowledge" at Cooktown. Again at Thursday Island I talked with many, still hale and hearty, who had served aboard the "hell ships" in the early pearling days. And I met the hard-bitten though quietly efficient officials of that little sea of mighty reefs and romantic islets, met the pearlers of pleasant memory. At Somerset I had access to Jardine's voluminous reports and journals, and met his sons. I read Chester's records, as well as those of other Residents who in autocratic power had graced romantic Somerset and ruled as best they could the troublous waters around.

To cap all, in the Coral Sea I cruised with a quiet little man who, I believe, knows more about the islands and folk of the Strait than any man living - the Reverend William MacFarlane, "Wandering Missionary of the Strait". It was mainly through him that I was able to visit all the inhabited islands in the Strait, meet on friendly terms the last of the old island chiefs and Zogo-men, listen to their stories, their view of those long years of clash between black, brown, and white. Otherwise I would only have been able to tell you of the white man's point of view. I owe a lot to "Mac", as do others. It was through "Mac" that I first met Maino, last Mamoose of Tutu and Yam, son of Kebisu, Sea Chief of Warrior Island. But you will meet Kebisu and Maino in this book. So, step aboard the lugger, and sail with me.

ION IDRIESS

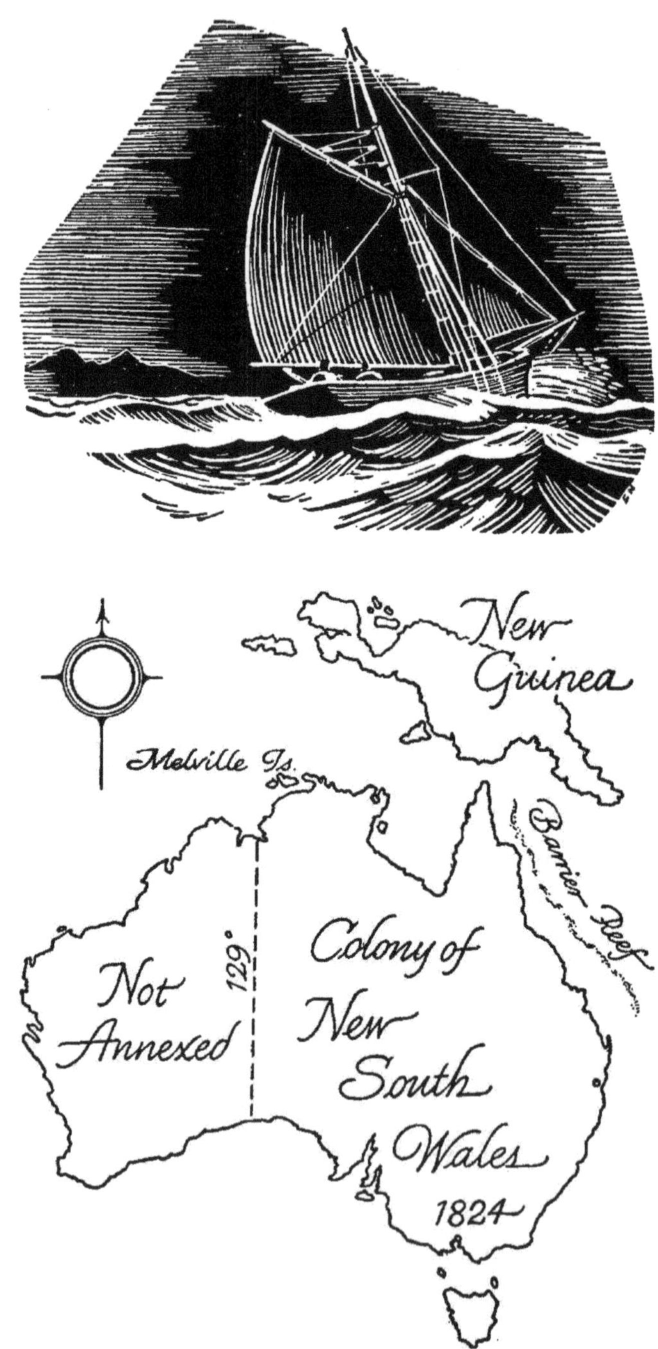
New Guinea
Melville Is.
Barrier Reef
Not Annexed
129°
Colony of New South Wales
1824

I

TOWARDS THE UNKNOWN NORTH

WHO were they?

Only the winds sigh answer.

Men in a boat. A boat with a song in her rigging, stoutly built, bowling along under jib and mainsail, foam at her bows, under Australian skies. Nearly a century and a half ago - only a sigh from yesteryear.

You could not swing a cat in that craft, a man must "monkey" his way to crawl into the bunks for'ard. She would smell of sea things, of tarred oakum and bilge and fish-baits and tough meats stowed in the brine-casks, of salt-sprayed clothes and rope, and rank tobacco smoke. Hungry brown and red and yellow cockroaches, impatient of daylight, big cheeky fellows. with ginger feelers, would poke inquiringly out from her timbers even before sunset and scuttle all over her as darkness fell. Stealthily at first, but on hot nights their creepy rustling would drown the very breath of the ship. Their sharp teeth with eerie sound would gnaw to the quick the horny toenails of the uneasy, tossing sleepers, nibble the hair above their ears, slithering back up the head just out of reach of nervy fingers, diving back to the meal as the sleeper's hand slid limply away. Just so, a hundred years later, by - the hot, murky glow of the hurricane lamp, I have watched them feasting on the toenails of our snoring crew on suffocating nights. How those diamond points of sweat used to glisten on those brown, hunched up, naked bodies!

Such a little sail, a brave sail gliding north, into the unknown north upon a great big sea. An empty sea-though presently they glimpsed a vanishing sail, by the cut of her jib a Yankee whaler from Hobart Town bound for the mysterious Islands-maybe the Sandalwood Isles, or the New Hebrides, the dangerous Solomons, the Marianas, or perhaps some Samoan Paradise, or the cannibal "Fee Gees".

They would long watch that vanishing sail, voiceless link with their fellow man. They would muse about her, for Sydney Cove was full of the whalers now, their tough crews ever ready to play merry hell among the respectable waterfront inns and the less reputable grog-shops, which did not matter so much; at times in a laughing, riotous madness, amongst screams and curses and breaking furniture, they would "clean up" a hell shop, which mattered not at all. Sydney Town's vicious hooligan gangs kept to their dens when these hardened whaler crews were on the rampage. Even the redcoats steered clear of them unless in armed squads, duty bound - which is saying a lot. For armed might and deeds of violence were ordinary enough in the rutted quagmires called streets those days. The whalers, though, were welcome, for they brought trade and spending money where money was scarce indeed. And their valuable oil was grist to the Sydney merchant's mill. For this tiny port of a few thousand people, now sprung up in the isolation of the world's last continent, was growing most surprisingly virile, not only in deeds, but in trade also, smelling out the makings of an honest pound in remarkable fashion, despite the fact that Sydney's very existence was both unknown and unheeded by practically all the far-away "world". Above all, it was growing lively in ideas, far too aggressively so, in the opinion of authority and numbers of the influential gentry.

Thus the men in the boat would discuss the events of their day as the whaler's topsails melted into the far horizon. It was nearly certain that she would sail the open Pacific just outside the "Sailorman's Graveyard", that mighty Barrier Reef so feared and so little known, which was discussed in awe when sailormen met in Sydney Town. 'They in the boat must hug the coast and thus sail nor'ward *inside* the Great Reef.

Generally the whalers fished the waters from Hobart Town to the beautiful New Zealand Isles, stronghold of tattooed Maori warriors howling defiance from their forts. Wonderful stories drifted into Sydney Town of that shadowy dependency of the Colony of New South Wales. Other whalers vanished northward towards mysterious seas and island worlds among strange peoples, where island kings and queens were brown and black, creamy and lemony, and milky white, with black manes of hair to their knees or great fuzzy, crinkly mops in which captured butterflies fluttered. Fascinating tales those whaler crews told along the waterfront as ship after ship came sailing into Sydney Town, heavy-laden with that valuable oil. Tales of beauteous isles of everlasting sunshine where Nature grew everything the heart of man could desire, where chain-gangs were unheard of, where slavery was unknown. Where there was no such thing as prison hells, the gallows and the cat-o'-nine tails, the treadmill and the stocks. Where it was blessed rest and play all day, dance and sing and sleep all night, warm under tropic skies. Where every girl was beautiful and knew it, garlanding herself with flowers, with kisses and song and laughter garlanding her lucky man, too. Where every white man in any ship's crew, be he ever so humble, was master of all he surveyed. Entrancing tales they told also of men who had deserted ship and settled on such isles with dusky queens, and ruled as real kings. Yes, they told such tales under the very shadow of Gallows Hill.

The gaunt-faced men in the boat, hunched there with backs bent from toil, their bony hands splayed from hardship, would stare out over the starboard bow towards that vanished sail, would marvel at, would sigh over such tales, so eagerly discussed in Sydney Cove. It was certain that some tales must be true, for they had seen goggle-eyed, fuzzy-headed brown and black men among the whaler crews, had marvelled at prettily dyed grass skirts, carved clubs and shells and masks and weird idols of ebony wood, had gaped at necklaces of corals and sharks' teeth, had gasped at the money those men spent with such carefree abandon, until one tough sea-dog would boastfully say, "There's plenty more - and better - where that come from! All it needs is guts to go and get it, and guts is just what you convicts and sons of convicts ain't got!"

Which sentiments, when sneered before free settlers and emancipists, now resulted in fierce brawls. For now there were just as many free men in the vast colony as convicts, and feeling was growing increasingly bitter that this strange land, which so many had come to love, should be scorned as only a dumping ground for British jails.

Why, even a Governor had declared his faith in its future greatness! Look what Macquarie had done! From a starving village of mud-and-wattle huts he had built this fine town. Just gaze at those great stone buildings overshadowing the waterfront! He had built streets, too - even a road over those Blue Mountains to the sweet-grassed Bathurst Plains. He had stopped the dog-fight between the Army and Navy, and given that detested Rum Corps its marching orders back to England. Above all, he was all for the free man, for free emigration to this new country; fiercely he fought against those of the military and civilian gentry who sought to keep this land a felon prison so they could control cheap labour under the lash. "They" had beaten him after years of bitter struggles, but not until he had built up this colony so that Time must beat *them*! So now many men in town and bush prayed so, talked so, *felt* so. For by what Macquarie had done it was plain to see how this wild bush would respond to a guiding hand. The town, the roads, the free settlements out in the wild bush, such quick response, such foundation for the ships now corning out, crowded with emigrants, free men and women! There were nearly forty thousand people in the colony now, bringing in a revenue of the great sum of thirty thousand pounds a year! This new land paying its very own way, and now-wool! Why, it was in all men's minds, the miracle of this wool and what the future might bring. There was that fightable Macarthur of Camden, as determined a man as Macquarie even, as great a worker, too - Macarthur, who but a few years ago had sworn that this new land could produce wool as good and better than any in the world and that, by God, he would see that it did! And the more the laughter of England, of Saxony, of the Old World, the fiercer he swore he *would* do it. And now, to the amazement of all men, it almost seemed he *had* done it. Despite all that work, those years of bitter quarrels here and abroad, he still had found that seemingly devilish energy, that crazy obstinacy that cared not one whit for any consequences, and that unbreakable will and time to do what he had sworn to do. He had now grown samples of wool equal to the best Saxon merino, turned the contemptuous laughter of the Old World's great Saxon wool industry to astounded silence, and set them fighting for the very life of their wool trade. The unbelievable had happened here, in an unknown land peopled only by savages until a very few years before.

That one man had produced such a miracle from this now proved good earth had born a fierce belief, a stubborn faith in the minds of men of a rich destiny in this strange new land. Men even whispered that this sunburnt earth itself had helped Macarthur. Well, then, it had responded to Macquarie, too! It would help all who treated it rightly.

Little wonder men here and there throughout the colony were dreaming of great things to come in this bewildering new land. Many were openly, dangerously growling that this land must *not* remain a felon settlement.

Why, some among the knowledgeable gentry were boldly prophesying this land might one day support even - a million people! To hell, then, with the Old World and its ideals of slavery and the lash - let it keep them! This new land so unexpectedly - it seemed a real miracle - offered a new life, and many in this truculent Sydney Town had grown determined to seize it, to fight for it if need be.

With these "mutinous sentiments" some harshly disagreed. But all imbued with the "new" beliefs were eagerly greeting each little shipload of free settlers and whispering to them of a new life as against the old, believing the day must surely come when enough free men would live here to make this a free country. In time, they might even grow strong enough to insist upon trial by civilian judge and jury!

Thus increasingly men and interests were taking sides in bitter debate in this land of yesteryear, and those men in the boat would ponder on such things to pass the hours as day and night took them farther out into the unknown. Sailing on, they would steer well clear of the up-flung spume from rollers thundering upon what seemed an obviously dangerous reef. It really was the bar at the mouth of the beautiful Clarence, but the "Big River" had not yet been discovered. With warm interest they would ponder on what was happening behind that sea of scrub-clad ranges Far away in there venturesome pathfinders had now cut a track over the Moonbi Mountains; those restless settlers ever creeping farther out called some great tableland there "New England". Deep within that vista of tree-tops, these sea roamers from Sydney Town knew, the dreamy botanist Allan Cunningham, for whom his men would do anything, was pushing on into still more northern wilds. His horses must now be sturdily plodding on through the virgin bush northward; quite likely those inland horsemen were even now riding level with this lonely speck of a boat. Across the spaces of sea and bush and sky they felt in their loneliness as if those men so slowly, so painfully toiling onwards, were toiling with them. They by sea; those invisible others by land. Whose peril would prove the greatest?

All aboard would wish Cunningham to find something great, would wish his safe return. For the sturdy botanist-explorer spoke out bravely against strongly antagonistic powers in favour of free settlers and yet more settlers, publicly stating, too, that the emancipists, those men granted freedom, were among the very best he had in all his strenuous trips. In his own quiet way he spoke up for this new, strange country when called upon, declaring that one day it would be great and free, speaking out against transportation and urging that to develop this great new land all men should be free.

Free! The botanist-explorer was one of them; this lover of plants with a quiet courage could and would speak what so many in this colony could only feel-what others feared to speak.

It could have been upon that very day in 1827 that, away inland over their port bow, Allan Cunningham rode out from the timbered bush to halt entranced at the vision splendid stretching farther away than the eye could reach, the far-flung paradise of the Darling Downs. In his excitement and enthusiasm, what visions did that man see? If only he could have seen Toowoomba and Warwick, and the magnificent expanse of agricultural and pastoral prosperity of the Darling Downs of today!

At this time the deeds of explorers and landseekers were followed with the greatest interest by all in Sydney Town, at the little bush settlements, so very few, and at the campfire. So were the fiercely debated doings of the Governor of the day, the faction fights of colonists and officialdom, of free men and Army and Navy and emancipists, the longed-for arrival of ships with news, the burning question of convictism. For the isolated thimbleful of people then battling in this huge, unexplored continent were really only one large, lively, and pretty quarrelsome family; and what affected one concerned all, often in conflicting ways. For such is life.

Those in the boat realized that the work of Oxley and Evans, Hume and Hovell, Lockyer and now Cunningham, was closely intertwined with their own lives, as with those of all in the colony, no matter how humble they might be.

They knew they would be lonely men when their little boat passed by the farthest outpost of these northern explorers.

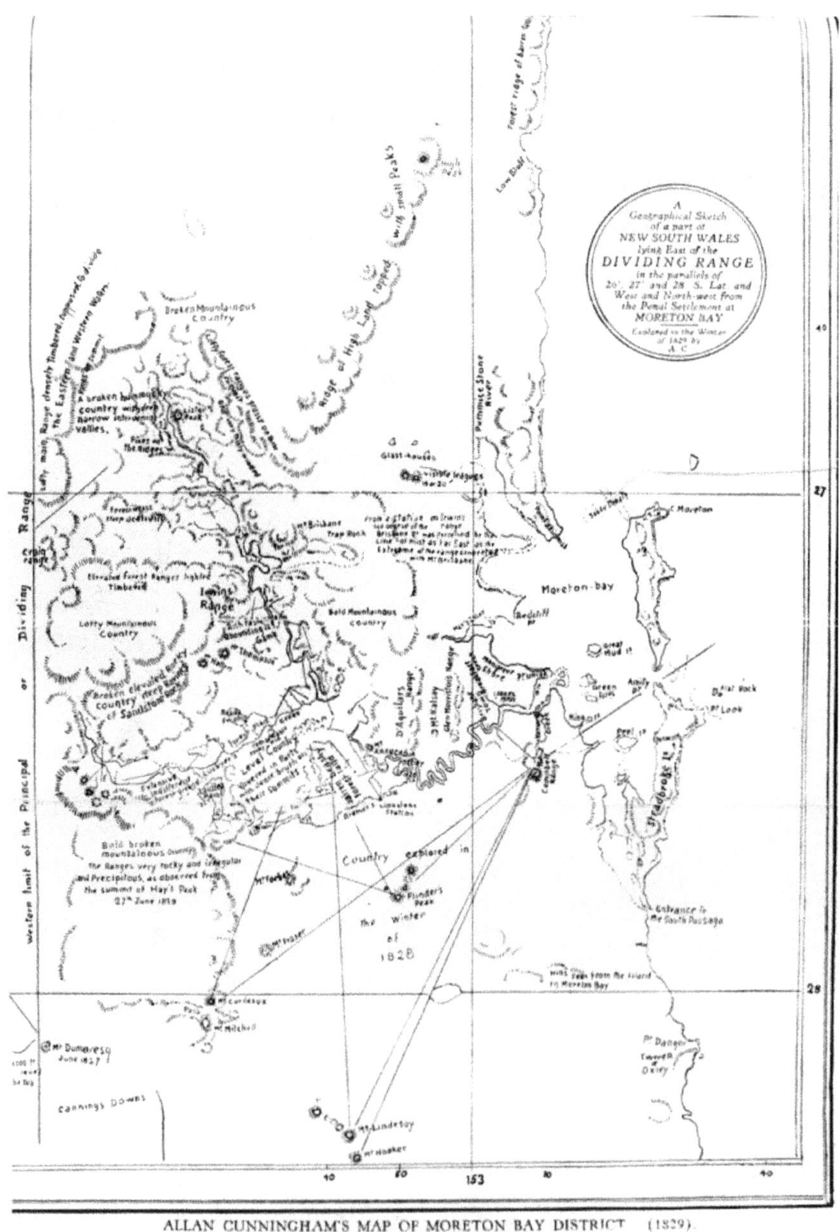

ALLAN CUNNINGHAM'S MAP OF MORETON BAY DISTRICT (1829).
By permission of the Surveyor-General of Queensland.

2

THE CONTINENT AWAKENING

EXPLORERS' and sailormen's charts and sailormen's yarns would have warned them to keep a sharp look-out for "a hill sitting on top of a range" a few miles inland. Captain Jamie Cook had named it Mount Warning as a guide to future mariners. By "following" that mountain down to the coast they would sight Point Danger. Then 'ware of breakers ahead - for the great captain named this landmark as a double warning, because the rocky "toe" of Point Danger stretched under water far out to sea, a cruelly hidden death-trap to sailormen. "Give those reefs a wide berth, mates!"

A few very scanty scraps of information such as this would be their only guide now for nearly two thousand miles.

In the surprising years to come Mount Warning would be declared the starting point from which surveyors would define a boundary that would divide New South Wales from the new Colony of Queensland.

Safely past Point Danger, these sailor adventurers would sight a big island that appeared part of the mainland itself. As the hours slid by they would gaze anxiously over the bows until, "Ah! There she be!"- at sight of a second large island, separated from the first by a narrow passage. This would be Matthew Flinders's Moreton Island; their course lay true.

They would glumly gaze at the two islands, for all in New South Wales now knew what lay behind. Moreton Bay, the new "far north" penal settlement, terrifying tales of which had drifted south to Sydney Town-tales recently fearfully linked with Logan's name. Men swore that all commandants must have been born in hell. But the story of Oxley, the explorer, and Pamphlet, the castaway, had seized all men's interest, and the men in the boat knew that the very same fate could easily befall them, yet more disastrously. Sailing past that island, they certainly would discuss the strange adventures of the castaways Pamphlet and Finnegan and Parsons. It was even declared in Sydney Town that John Uniacke was going to write a book about it; he had yarned with the two castaways every hour when free from his duties, especially with the lively Pamphlet, and had written down what they told him.

When in 1823 Governor Brisbane had sent Oxley searching that distant coast for some isolated, almost inaccessible place to build a new penal settlement, Uniacke had sailed with him in the Mermaid, a staunch little cutter nearly worn out in exploring service. Sailing in round those two long islands, they had poked into that widespread estuary of Moreton Bay, with its lake of waters densely forested with mangroves and the timbered hilltops stretching back into the unknown inland. Uniacke had been with Oxley on that sunny day when he landed on Bribie Island, and a mob of savages led by this strange white savage, Pamphlet, hairy as his black followers, had come out of the bush to greet them. And Pamphlet had told Oxley about a big new river, and sent his mate Finnegan next day in Oxley's boat to show him the river, which Oxley had named after Governor Brisbane.

This wild white man, Pamphlet, seemed to be boss of all these savage blacks. A few years ago he, with his three mates, had sailed from Sydney Town in a sturdy open boat for a camp down the coast called Wollongong, there to load with cedar for the new Sydney buildings. When almost at the camp a black storm blew them out to sea. For eleven frightening days and nights that storm raged, some days, so they declared, black as the awful night. They believed the howling winds had driven them south past the Wollongong camp. Actually, they had been driven round in the opposite direction, back north past Sydney, and blown hundreds of miles yet farther north. On the twelfth day they managed to raise sail, and for ten days steered by the clouded sun on what they imagined might be the right course back to Sydney Cove. All they could see was the rolling of waves and spray and foam, and low overhead black clouds travelling like furies. One terrifying night their boat heeled over and thumped upon a reef, but the big waves lifted her and carried her over those rocks with hardly a leak, while for awful moments they believed they were doomed at last. Suffering horribly now, they battled on as men will even in the depths of despair. Then one man collapsed and died of hopelessness and thirst. By now they could only croak to one another. At long last they saw mist-shrouded land, and sailed straight for it, desperately praying for shelter as yet another storm came threatening. They gained a narrow inlet among mangroves and crawled ashore as the new storm broke. And this time the great waves smashed the boat, leaving them stranded they knew not where. Actually they were on this unnamed island five hundred miles north of Sydney Cove, hundreds of miles from the nearest white man. Westward for three thousand miles there lived not one white man. Yet, as they huddled under trees from the fury of the rains, they planned they would crawl to the beach when the weather cleared and seek shellfish, anything that seashore and bush might offer them to eat. Then they would start to walk to Sydney Town - northward!

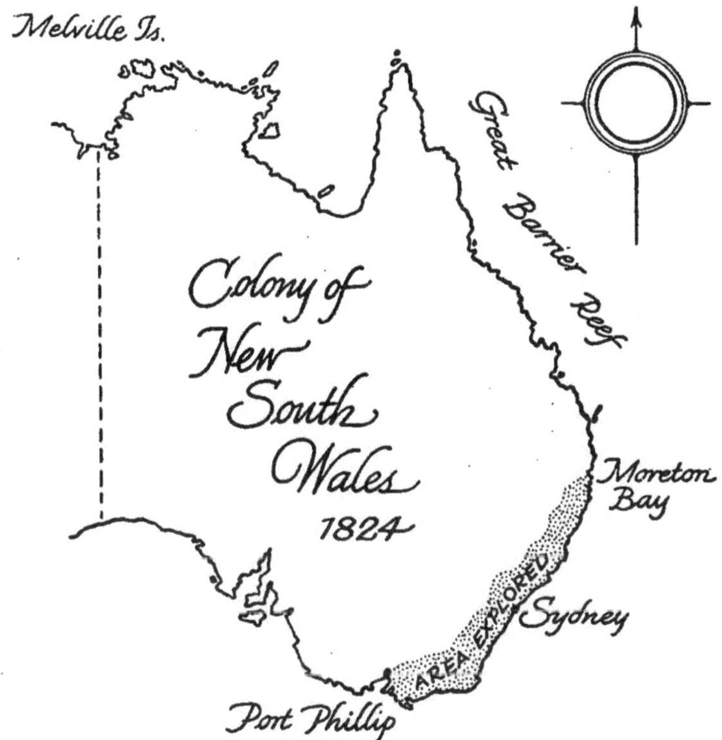

Northward for fifteen hundred miles, right to the waters of Torres Strait and beyond, there was not one white man. Had they only known the plight they were in!

The colonists far south, always hungry for news of "local" happenings, were also keenly interested by the fact that the savages who found and nursed these castaways back to health, treating them with the greatest kindness, had fiercely attacked Matthew Flinders. In years soon coming they were to attack whites again.

As soon as the castaways recovered strength Pamphlet and Finnegan "took to the life" in an amazingly short time, accompanying the tribesmen on the hunt as their feet grew tough as leather, and even planning war forays. Pamphlet, especially, quickly learnt the "lingo" and the use of spear and nulla-nulla, and was "great on the war dance"; soon he was "bossing the tribe about". The inquiring Uniacke learnt that the tribesmen actually put up with a lot from these soon so confident castaways, and were extraordinarily patient, excusing jokes that grew very rough at their expense, at times even laughing contempt and ridicule away. These two castaways undoubtedly "had something".

Their adventures were indeed passing strange. And it was this Pamphlet who had met Oxley in the bush, and told his mate, Finnegan, to take him next day to that new river, on the banks of which the new penal settlement was now being built.

Under Commandant Logan! Coincidences being part of life, it could easily be that on this very day, while they were discussing these very events, at an exclamation all eyes in the boat would glance astern. And their faces would be clouded, their mouths set grim, as the frigate fast overhauled them. Not that they were runaway convicts, not that they had stolen the boat, not that they had any cause for fear. But the coming ship was a symbol of the shadow that clouded most men's minds, she and the redcoats and the Governor's men were symbols of the power that meant ill-paid labour, a constant struggle to make a home and live, a denial of human rights, with behind it "the System" of the musket, the lash, the gallows.

Yet the frigate with all sail set made a lovely picture bowling along before the strong sou'-east breeze, crested foam at her bows, sunlit canvas gleaming white against blue of sky, rolling green of sea. Contemptuously she passed them by without speaking, doubtless knowing why they had left Sydney Town.

In silence they watched her leaving them gradually astern; they knew where she was bound for - Moreton Bay.

The frigate was H.M.S. *Rainbow*; her captain was Henry John Rous who would eventually become an admiral. He was the second son of the Earl of Stradbroke - which was fortunate for the Earl, for by having a lively and warm-hearted son he would have an island named after his noble self.

This dashing naval officer had a way with him. A favourite with the ladies, of course, he and his officers were a prized asset to the closely knit social life of the jealous little town. But he was a man's man also, and destined to do his little part in this great adventure of opening up the last continent. Two years later he was to discover the mouths of the Tweed and Richmond rivers. Also, during this very year (1827), he would think out and with enthusiasm organize the first sailing regatta held in Sydney Cove. Who would have thought, a few years before, that this despised collection of tents and wattle-and-daub huts stared at by blackfellows would quickly grow to a town that could triumphantly hold a sailing regatta?

Even so, little Van Diemen's Land, but two years now separated as the Colony of Tasmania, had beaten the big continent by holding the first Australian sailing regatta in Hobart Town a few months earlier.

This Captain Rous could handle a horse as well as a ship, and was enthusiastic enough to take the very big risk of importing a racing stallion he aptly named "Emigrant". Racing men, like seamen, often set great store by omens. Is it strange then that Emigrant, in this strange new land destined to develop so amazingly, should become the sire of many good racehorses?

For a hundred years and more, much more; folk of many parts would take a share in Australia's Great Adventure.

3

THE MELTING POT

ON board H.M.S. *Rainbow* was an aggrieved, moreover a much harassed, man. Stiffly determined to do his duty as he saw it and to hell with all dissentients, Governor Darling, of this Colony of New South Wales, was on an official visit to the new penal settlement at Moreton Bay, the locality discovered through the indomitable spirit of explorers, the settlement founded by His Majesty's officers backed up by the force of men in this practically inaccessible bush barely three years ago.

Lieutenant-General Sir Ralph Darling was a worried man, declaring the troubles the chain-gangs laboured under were as trifles to the chains he wore.

Thus, during those few heaven-sent days of respite at sea, he let off steam, pacing the poop with the respectfully listening commander. He, representing His Majesty's Government, set upon by this Wentworth leading a handful of native-born *Australians!* Just fancy that-calling themselves Australians as if they were breeding a new nation! Australians and all emancipists and new settlers howling for the abolition of transportation, howling for freedom and equality and free political and judiciary systems, demanding a legislative assembly, if you please, trial by civilian jury, and God knows what else beside! Demanding the right, too - nay, actually taking up land wherever they found it under the hooves of their wretched horses, claiming wide areas of bush despite the fact it was expressly forbidden to cross the boundary beyond the Nineteen Counties! Five million acres of land - not enough for these greedy wretches! Just because they felt a continent under their feet they thought they could take what they liked, against strict orders creeping out beyond the Hunter northward, driving their flocks beyond the Lachlan and Goulburn plains southward, riding out beyond the Bathurst Plains westward even to the Wellington Valley! A crime against authority, defying every effort of concentration of settlement. Well, they would find they could not ride beyond the Governor's control!

As he paced the deck with the attentive captain beside him, the Governor's hands, clasped at his back, were nervously twitching. He continued to pour out his complaints. While these settlers were riding out to the forbidden plains and ranges, he in Sydney Town was being hounded by a scurrilous local Press - so-called Press in this God-forsaken wilderness, a Press that he certainly would suppress and throw their blasphemous writers in irons! Upsetting even the discipline of the military, let alone the convicts!

That cynical Justice Forbes, against him and Imperial Authority! That swine of a libellous Hall! Educated gentry such as they playing into the hands of those wolves of settlers howling for the very land upon which they trod! And here he had come out to these barbarous shores prepared to do his very best for this country, for these conceited, quarrelsome, snarling, backbiting gangs of would-be opportunists that made up this truculent Sydney Town!

Thus the brooding mind of the most powerful man in all the South Pacific. But after a couple of days at sea the strain gradually eased under the steady roll of the frigate, the restful freedom of sea and sky, the respectful cheery companionship of this so-human captain. Over a soothing glass of port in the captain's cabin, with the twinkling stars of heaven above, the Governor relaxed, though he was still unable to resist letting off steam in this sympathetic atmosphere, so rare to him. Sipping his port, he mused ruefully. Yes, no matter what he did they fought his every move. Not only the Australian born, the free settlers and emancipists and convicts, but even some among the military, even among the landed gentry, the judiciary and officials. And yet his first act had been to proclaim the separation of Tasmania from New South Wales, to give Van Diemen's Land a separate administration under a lieutenant-governor. He was trying to open up roads into that interminable bush, he was establishing an inland postal service, so that the outlying settlements could receive letters and news when it did come, was even trying to light those awful Sydney wagon lanes - "streets", as they called them! Far more than that, he was even now fighting with the Colonial Office to authorize him to lay claim to the whole of the continent before the French could take the western half of it. "And, by God, I will claim it, too!"[1]

Chewing over his wrongs, the grudges of this thankless colony, the Governor was certain he was doing his best for these truculent colonists. Consistently he had encouraged exploration - Cunningham, Lockyer, Oxley, and Logan. And it was through him that this very Moreton Bay, now over their bows, was being opened up, that Oxley and Lockyer had explored this Brisbane River upon which Captain Logan was now building that "inaccessible" penal settlement those confounded Sydney colonists had howled so much for, declaring their wretched Sydney was too good a town to be debased as a convict dump. An end to transportation, indeed! This country to be for free men! They will clean up Sydney Town, will they?

"It would seem they are winning," said the Governor with a grim smile to the attentive commander, "for they have the worst of their felons transported to Norfolk Island, which they are pleased to call Hell on Earth" The second worst lot are to be isolated here, far from their Sydney Town. Out of sight, out of mind - but it certainly looks like the thin edge of the wedge. And yet more certainly these wretched felons will not hurt the tender feelings of the good citizens of Sydney from *this* wilderness!" And when he spoke thus it was beautiful morning again and they were on deck, gazing at the wild shore now hemming the frigate in. Silently now each gazed. Surely no poor wretch would even think of escaping from here, to perish miserably in the bush or agonizedly from the spears of savages! But some among those wretched slaves ashore would risk even that. Where life is hell on earth the human spirit will risk escape to anywhere, to anything.

Little wonder that this Governor - like others, actually a conscientious and painstaking man with his big job and this new land at heart - should be bewildered and often furiously angry at the savage undercurrents working against him as he sought to carry out what he believed to be his duty.

Neither he nor the Home Authorities realized that the hoary traditions and cruel injustices of older lands when transplanted here would come into the melting-pot under the untainted skies of the Southern Cross, that in this last continent a happier way of life was to be born.

After the inspection of Moreton Bay the Governor, grown human again in the comradeship of the ship as she sailed back for Sydney Town, named the larger of those two islands Stradbroke Island as a compliment to the commander's father. For the hale and hearty seaman had been good medicine indeed to the Governor's furrowed brow. But the men in the boat in the wake of the vanishing frigate had growled very different sentiments from those of the harassed Governor.

"Moreton Bay, a penal settlement of the damned! Captain Logan!" one growled and spat overside. At the System, even more than at the hated Commandant who, after all, was but a part of the System.

The energetic Logan, apart from his ruthless brutality in exercising the discipline of the day, was an organizer and worker, a builder, too. From that primitive bush he wrested and shaped materials with the sweat of the convict gangs, building the settlement so staunchly that some of his buildings have stood until fairly recent years. Many remember the old Observatory that was Logan's windmill; the old Treasury was his military barracks; his commissariat store was the State Store in William Street of the fine city of Brisbane of today. A tireless explorer also, he would have gone a long way in helping to build up this flew land had not his path in life been that of a military officer in charge of a mercilessly isolated penal settlement. Brave, cool, and ever resourceful, fascinated by this strange land, he spent every day he could from the growing settlement in exploration by land, sea, and river. At a distance from the settlement he had now stationed an outpost of soldiers to protect toiling convicts against aborigines while they were quarrying limestone for cement, and this was the beginning of the busy town of Ipswich. While the men in the boat would be sailing on to work out their own little share in this new country's destiny the ever restless Logan would be discovering rich areas suitable for pastoral lands, the Logan Valley, the Logan and other rivers. Yet when not on exploring trips he would be doing a soulless job, breeding frightful misery and fiendish hate - which in time must surely catch up with him.

Those in the boat sailing on into the unknown felt freedom in the majestic blue sky, breathed it in the sweet night air, saw it above in the passionless stars. Only thus did it feel good to be alive. Vaguely, restlessly, inquiringly, they, like many others in the vast colony, realized they had never felt this way in the old lands from which they had come.

And now a real loneliness settled down over this lonely boat upon this lonely sea. For now the invisible company of the lands-men explorers was being left far behind, not for years to come would any pass north of this Moreton Bay.

They sailed on now in the vanished wake of phantoms, who yet had left their records for a guide and a warning to those who came after. So next day they were watching anxiously as they sailed along a picturesque coast, which they took to be the mainland but was actually the largest sand island in the world. Sunlight glinted on its far-flung hills and wind-blown valleys, on countless precipitous ridges falling abruptly down to the sea or sloping to a beach running for many miles. A bold-looking coast indeed, to be the scene of shipwrecks when Moreton Bay was no longer a penal settlement. Little wonder the great captain had not discovered this was an island, for it was separated by a strip of water only a few miles wide, and the *Endeavour*, wary of lurking reefs, had skirted it well out to sea. The valleys and ridges of this island shielding the unknown mainland were beautiful under giant kauri pine, towering blackbutt, red stringybark, red satinay, tallow-wood, mahogany, and numerous other rich timbers, which, to the watchful men in the passing boat, might shelter packs of wolves, perhaps even more fearsome beasts in this unknown land, certainly wild men. As they sailed by they stared towards the dense undergrowth, in places ablaze with wildflowers, noisy with innumerable birds, its shores teeming with fish and marine life.

No wonder it was a favourite hunting ground of virile savages, of whom the voyagers were understandably afraid. Yes, ruggedly beautiful, and a "queer" island, with its creeks and swamps and lagoons and strange lakes into which no stream flows - lakes four hundred feet above sea level, the waters of some crystal clear, others whitish, others reddish. To those in the boat all this coast for a thousand miles and more would be mysterious. What would they have thought could they have gazed upon the strange lakes of this island alone? And its buried forests? For just here and there you can see the long-dead logs where a fierce storm or heavy wet season has gouged out a new valley, thus uncovering logs that were healthy trees drinking in sunlight thousands of years ago.

But no white man as yet knew of all this, and of other strange things ashore there. Wretched castaways in deadly fear would first see part of it, then Andrew Petrie, sailing down Moreton Bay from Brisbane, would land there within another fifteen years. But now the men in the boat were staring at a long bluff growing ever bolder, stretching out from the headland; presently they heard it in full song as the rollers boomed upon its basaltic cliffs.

"Must be Indian Head!" suggested the helmsman uneasily. "Give it a wide berth!" One voiced the thoughts of all. "The muskets are ready primed, ain't they?" Without answering, all hands knew the muskets were kept ready day and night. Now plainly silhouetted upon the bluff were numerous dark figures of warriors, women, and children, staring out towards the strange vessel that kept well out of reach of the chase.

Exactly thus Captain Cook had seen that bluff and named it when sailing past in the *Endeavour* some fifty-seven years before. To the early voyagers the natives were "Indians". Not until years after would the original inhabitants of this strange new land be distinguished as Aborigines, the island inhabitants far north as Torres Strait Islanders, the nearest New Guinea men as Papuans. All were thought of as "Indians", akin to the scalp-hunting Indians of North America. Not until Indian Head was far astern did those in the boat breathe freely.

Some ten years later a miserable white woman would crouch upon that very headland staring hopelessly out to sea. Naked, her terrible blisters burnt black from the sun, her body fiendishly scarred by firesticks and beatings, she was the slave of the blacks. Her husband, Captain Fraser, had been battered to death before her eyes. Things yet more terrible she would be forced to endure. From then on, men would come to know this great sandy island as Fraser Island Many tragedies were to darken this strange sea where the boat sailed steadily on - north!

4

THE GREAT REEF

MEANWHILE Governor Darling, returning from .his inspection of Moreton Bay, was sailing south.

The frigate made a lovely picture, sailing in through the Heads, the harbour hills dull green under their scrubby bush. They would sight a fishing boat here and there, a native canoe, as they sailed up the big harbour playful with white-caps. There was little else but the bush-clad shores and hills as they rounded the Sow and Pigs. They passed that grim rock Pinchgut, and now upon the hills appeared quaint things so useful in their day, the slowly turning arms of windmills. And then over the port bow a few buildings showed among the trees. The Governor squared his shoulders, frowning towards the little waterfront settlement as the Rainbow glided on. Half a dozen ships moored in the Cove, the few stone buildings that Macquarie had built standing out bravely in the sunlight, the Barracks commanding the centre, the Government Offices towering as a pyramid above the pygmies of the straggling town buildings, intersected by quagmire roads, closely surrounded by thick bush. A hotbed of intrigue lay there, thought the Governor bitterly, a hotchpotch of faction fights and discontent, jealousies and disloyalties and fierce hatreds - mostly centred upon him. Well, he would do his duty as he saw it. They wanted a fight. They could have it!

Squaring his shoulders as he stepped ashore, the Governor took the salute from the military guard awaiting him with all ceremony as the representative of His Majesty King William IV. With arrogant dignity Sir Ralph Darling thus again took over the governorship of this turbulent Colony of New South Wales, while reading in the cast-iron faces of the military, the suavity of officials, the enigmatic smiles of the gentry standing by, the silent wondering curiosity of the sightseers, that trouble awaited him.

It did. And plenty.

But in those days there were troubles to spare for everybody, and the Governors of the day simply had to put up with their share. Governors and toilers alike would sink like falling leaves to their graves while the opening up of this continent went steadily and surely on.

Yes, as surely as that little boat now vanished in the wastes to the north, her apprehensive crew quite unaware of the wonders below and around them. A wise man long ago declared that a mouse was a mighty marvel of Nature. Far beyond all human comprehension are the countless marvels that make this Coral Sea the most fascinating sea laneway in the world. As they sailed due north the coastline was ever to port, on their westward side. Eastward, to starboard, the Great Barrier Reef guarded them from the open Pacific, its mighty bastions walling them in for a thousand miles and more; it would end within sight of that dark island of mystery - New Guinea.[2]

The Great Barrier Reef, itself a natural Wonder of the World, so deceptively peaceful now, laced with its curtain of spray where the lazy rollers from the Pacific broke against it in murmurous song. Stretching away as far as the eye could see, that misty veil; on some days you may catch little rainbows playing within it, that spray flying up, drifting down, spouting up, raining down, as the rollers rumble against the Reef to lazily crumple and surge forward in torrential hissing, to gurgle back, back, still back, to pause as for breath, to gather new strength, to swell and grow, to grow bigger then swiftly bigger as they come surging in swelling might, yet again to smash upon the rampart in broken thunder, hurling aloft that hissing curtain of sun-kissed spray. Thus day after day, while lands have sunk under its waters, other lands have risen up reborn from its bosom - for how many thousands upon thousands of years! Under the stars, a deep murmur crooning to Mother Moon; in peaceful weather just a murmurous song, that slumber song of the mighty Reef kissed by the ever importuning sea.

But when the wind ruffles the Sea Lord and the Reef refuses him entry the roar of his anger is the rising thunder of a cannonade rolling on for those hundreds of foaming miles, pounding and breaking in thwarted fury against the walls of the unshakable Reef.

That Great Barrier now protected the men in the boat from the wrath of the mighty Pacific, making calm, except in the cyclone season, the thousand-mile-long sea lane between the Barrier and the mainland coast. Safe from the open ocean, yes. But within this sea laneway lie a thousand smaller reefs, keeping ever anxious the look-out in the bows, who must watch for the sudden appearance of light-green water, of a yellowing patch that would betray lurking death, the teeth of a reef that would rip through the bottom of their precious craft as easily as the shark rips open the belly of a swimmer.

A coral reef just under water is often fantastically beautiful.

Strange that beauty can bring death!

Within those warm inner waters the great Mother Reef has scattered her children with lavish hand, reefs of every size and kind: smaller barrier reefs rising parallel with the shore-line, fringing reefs which enclose islands, cays, and "just reefs" - a bewildering maze. And then there are the coral islands, and islands that are "specks" from the mainland, of granite and basaltic sandstone - hundreds of islands.

This mighty Reef, to which the Pyramids are less than a pebble, has been built by the coral polyp, a tiny sea-water thing which scientists[3] declare to be an animal, a real live (when it's not dead) coral animal. Being far from a trained scientist and thus fancy free, I've often wondered if maybe it is part fish, part plant, part animal, part insect, part something else. Quaint fancies come to you after years in those waters, when on lazy days you lie peering at the innumerable strange things living out their busy lives just below the sunlit surface. This wee coral animal, which varies in size from a pin-head to a very small button, is born, lives, and dies to build. Actually, it really lives to eat and grow fat and go about its business, as we all do. However, absorbing its life from Mother Sea, it also forms its skeleton of lime, which is left behind when it dies; (Food and drink, acted upon by the oxygen we breathe from the air and the metabolism of our own "innards", build us our own skeletons also.) And ceaselessly on these minute skeletons grow countless more baby coral animals, leaving their skeletons in tum, being cemented together throughout countless centuries into vast masses of limestone, thus building up a buttress of such might as to withstand the storms of ages.

Happily that buttress protects also our north-eastern coastline from the ever hungry Pacific, saving for man the precious land.

The men in the boat would know nothing of the tiny builder, though they would see its works for a thousand miles and constantly marvel.

Not seeing the tiny creatures, often they would gaze at giants, the largest living things in the world, a school of whales effortlessly sporting their way southward, some chasing friends in lithe, majestic play; occasionally a baby rainbow would sparkle within the vapour they spouted up. The men would fear as some mighty one passed them by so close they could see his little eye regarding them in curiosity, see the barnacles growing upon his hide as the water glided off his glistening bulk. Itchy indeed and irritable becomes a big old-man whale when his hide is plastered with barnacles like fleas nipping the skin of a dog. Hard and fast "fleas" these, twitch and shake and roll much as he likes, he cannot shake these burning parasites off. But he can rub the pests off, if only he can find something to rub against. Herein lies possible danger for any boat sailing through a school of whales. For if lousy Old Barnacles happens to see the boat, if his itch instinctively works his tiny brain in time, he changes course, dives, and in effortless, beautifully timed movement comes up just under the boat to feel its keel so delightfully, so thrillingly scraping, crunching off those tantalizing shelled creatures from his back as luxuriously he cruises his whole vast mass and length from starboard, scraping the keel until he emerges away at port. At such a moment you hold your breath, believe me! You feel the lift of the entire vessel under your creepy toes, feel the shiver in her timbers as that vast bulk scrapes past underneath while the masts sway and the blocks agitatedly rattle. I know for I have been aboard a lugger when it happened.

Native crews are wary of such possible danger and leap to cans or buckets and bang them and dance and yell and hammer the water in a shrieking attempt to scare off any such "amorous" intention. Sound and vibration have surprising effect under water if the surface is viciously smacked, and Old Barnacles generally hesitates disappointedly or sheers off while the boat and his chance passes by. But should those tons of bovine stupidity get under a boat, and should something frighten it at the moment it is using the keel for a scraping comb, then there is one vast upheaval as the sea erupts. A cutter would be swamped, a lugger could be capsized. I've long felt certain that an occasional small vessel has been lost that way.

As the boat sailed north so the leviathans sped by to the south, school following school, the puffs of their water vapour stretching north and south as far as the eye could reach. These mighty things, and the thunder of the devil-ray, and shoals of big fishes, often in such packed numbers that they appeared as a passing cloud upon the water, would hold the interest and wonder of the men in the boat, as such things have held mine. But the greater wonders within one drop of water below their keel the eye of man cannot see.

A sea now of sunlit loveliness, slumberously lazy under the steady trade wind. The distances slipped by as thus for three weeks more she sailed, bowling along with jib and mainsail filled; they felt the life in her as she rose to the waves with slap of spray from the bow, gurgle of foam hissing astern under the counter. But when the shadows close in the sea grows lonesome, the coast a serrated black mass under a vague sky, those worlds of stars so hopelessly far above. And maybe the breeze would die with the light, whispering away from the softly complaining sail, to the murmur of lapping tide down under in the darkness, lit only by the sudden streak of molten green phosphorescence as a big fish sped by.

One on bare feet would move to the galley. When the fire lit up its rosy flames would crackle cheerfully, but, alas, they must carefully shield it lest fierce eyes from that black mainland note their presence. Even a lighted match on a dark night can be seen miles away. They must cook and eat of their rough fare, to live. When under those beautiful stars sleep would come, one must ever watch throughout the silence of the night - and haply maybe for a fleeting instant feel the breath of God kiss past his cheek from the fathomless depths of Space.

Now and then when sitting there they quietly wondered what strange things, beasts and birds and wild men, might live and die and rave and love and fight deep within that unknown land ever reaching northward beside them. Far back in Sydney Town it was vaguely thought that lions and tigers and elephants, perhaps animals and reptiles unknown by white men, might exist there, surely kingdoms of wild Indians, too, surely lakes and inland seas.

No man knew.

They sailed doggedly on, risking everything to reach land's end. For there, awaiting them in the "Lost Strait", Torres Strait, lay fortune, ruinous failure, or death. This strait, discovered by Torres in 1606, was doubted by mariners of the day, and as time passed it was disbelieved in, and known as the "Lost Strait", until Captain Cook rounded the Cape York Peninsula, thus finding the "Lost Strait" allegedly separating Australia from New Guinea to be there in fact. The men in the boat were sailing in the long-vanished wake of the Endeavour, and of Flinders and King, and the fisherman-convict William Bryant, and, soon now, of Bligh of the Bounty. Each historic adventurer had been so urgently anxious to reach that once lost strait which would lead them into the open Arafura and civilization beyond.

Yet, just as overlanders far south were opening up new lands, as in another twenty-five years prospectors would be opening up new mineral fields, so they and others in little boats to come after them would open up a new sea.

5

THE LOST STRAIT

THEY would open up a new sea-by seeking-a sea-slug!

Just the lowly "sea-cucumber", otherwise *beche-de-mer,* the trepang of the Malays, a humble thing that crawls along on the bottom of the sea. They were risking their lives for a sea-slug that they could not even be sure of finding in these little-known waters. Dismal were the tales brought back to Sydney Town by survivors of shipwrecks of the cruel reefs, of hunger and thirst two thousand miles from help, of death from the spears of the mainland savages, from the clubs and the bamboo knives of the island headhunters.

They would have heard of castaways being cut up and salted like hunks of salt pork, of men and women deliberately fattened for the pot, and of terrors even worse.

It was the befeathered headhunters[4] of the far north they would fear most, for these roved the sea in huge sailing canoes, raiding island villages and unwary fishers for heads, and in seasonal cruises sailing far down the Great Barrier Reef and back up along the coast of the Great South Land. Living under a savage yet fiercely efficient organization and disciplined culture, these sea-going warriors were far better armed, far more dangerous than the primitive savages of the mainland. The men in the boat would have heard tales of these and of their lust for heads - human heads. And one late afternoon they very nearly lost theirs. For they sighted a wreck high upon the Great Reef, masts fallen by the board, bows pointed skyward like the beak of a broken bird. They gazed apprehensively, then one growled, "Yes! She's alive with the black swine!"

Swiftly they lowered sail and wallowed in the lazy sea, ready to turn about and fly for their lives should they have been seen. But the savages swarming over the wreck were too crazily excited at the treasures all around them to notice the distant boat - or so it seemed. That wreck was a bedlam as befeathered warriors. smashed casks and chests and sacks, and littered deck and hold with wonderful things, to shouts of amazement as others snatched armfuls of loot, only to throw it down for fresh treasure. Greedy stampedes at the yell of, "*Toori! Toori! Toori!*" as some found axes and things of iron, to them more valuable by far than gold is to us. Far too excited were they to bother about that little boat, motionless well astern. Very fortunately so, for these were the Sea Chief Kebisu's men from Tudu, called by white men Warrior Island; they were great sailormen and headhunters, and death to white men.

The looting went on in a laughing frenzy as they rushed to the sides to throw down armfuls of treasures into the huge canoes. Until across the calm sea, in the dying down of the wind at sunset, came a sudden roar of voices, then a flame shot up and black monkeys were leaping across the broken deck and into the water.

The wreck was afire.

We know this, and how it happened. For many years later old Maino, son of Kebisu and last Mamoose of Tudu and Yam, under the palms on a beautiful tropic night, told me the reason why.

Down below a ship's lantern, still alight, was hanging from a beam. These islanders had never seen a lighted lamp before, and when an islander saw something he did not understand he would either run or hit it with a club and see what happened.

Bogo, who was the bravest, so Maino told me, crept up close to that strange light-thing, then swung it a mighty blow from his club.

Shatter of flying glass, darkness, breathless silence, then from the littered hold reached up oily little tongues of flame that grew, then suddenly leapt and blazed, as with terrified yells the warriors fought up to the deck. Thus the club of Bogo smashed the Eye of Light, which in revenge bore innumerable fire demons that in a few moments blazed into an inferno.

The men in the boat stared with mixed feelings as the yelling savages leapt down into their canoes and paddled swiftly away into the north, brilliantly illuminated by those now roaring flames in the darkening sunset. Unaware of the great good fortune, though thankful indeed that the "Indians" had not seen them, they were angry that this treasure trove of the sea should be denied them through ignorant, murderous savages. What wealth to them would still have remained aboard that ship, even after the savages had looted her and sailed away! And now every precious thing was roaring skyward in smoke and flame, shooting up clouds of dazzling sparks that illumined the calm sea as with the glare of a fallen star. Unknown times similar scenes were to illumine this often beautiful, so deceptive sea.

What gave those men in the boat the idea that in the "Lost Strait" they might find *beche-de-mer* we can only guess at. Maybe it was a lingering rumour in Sydney Town that Captain Park believed he had recognized the sea-slug in the shallows by the Caso[5] wreck while Flinders made his open-boat voyage back to Sydney in his successful bid for rescue. But the all-powerful Governor of the day had frowned upon that rum our, as later Governors were to try to smother the rumour of gold. Perhaps one aboard the boat had even read a copy of Flinders's recent book and staked all on the great navigator's account of meeting the Malay fishers in the Arafura Sea three thousand miles away. Maybe one among them had been a shipwrecked sailorman and, surviving both the bloody kris and slavery, had seen those same queer Malay proas returning home to their piratical islands, laden with smoke-dried trepang. It happened in those days, too, that an occasional - a very occasional - lucky castaway, made a slave of by the Malays, by quick wits rose to great influence among the numerous native sultans. Such a one could easily have made a voyage on a proa, and thus would learn the value of the sea-slug, how to look for it, how to clean, boil, then cure it when found. Such a man, if Fate returned him to Sydney Town, may well have suggested to his mates that since the trepang slug lived in the Arafura that washed the northern shores of this strange continent, then perhaps it might also live to the east in those waters somewhere within the Great Barrier Reef that mariners were beginning to call the Coral Sea. Why not? Stranger things by far had happened there!' Anyway, the whalers were making fortunes in oil from Sydney to the "Fee Gees"; the sandalwood ships were reaping wealth in the Sandalwood Isles. The Chinee merchants would pay fancy prices for the wood and oil-fortunes out of just a tree! There'd be other fortunes, too, in those Spice Islands for a hundred years to come. Why should there not be fortunes awaiting men with guts in that queer Coral Sea where the Lost Strait meets the Arafura?

Thus some dreamer among them could easily have spoken and fired the others to risk all. We can only guess; but for some years even before this voyage it was vaguely believed among sailormen that if there really were any wealth in that queer sea it would lie "right up near the Indies", particularly in the Lost Strait since found again by Cook and Flinders and King. That was where wealth of sea might lie, in Torres Strait where the waters of the Coral Sea merged with the Arafura. Perhaps the "meeting of the

the waters" hemmed in by the southern coast of mysterious New Guinea and unknown North Australia, lashed by those fantastic tides and currents and feared islands, may have given birth to such belief. A weird belief, maybe, but how true it was to prove!

Even stranger theories in the minds of men have come true in the past, and will come true again.

Sailing past Captain Jamie Cook's Cape Tribulation, near the beginning of the huge Peninsula, surely then the voyagers would soon recognize the mouth of the Endeavour River where the great captain had so thankfully put his stricken vessel ashore to repair her. And far away up the Peninsula coast, by the rough chart of the day, they would recognize Princess Charlotte Bay, in my day the haunt of the Australian "Sandalwood Kings". Knowing they were drawing near journey's end, they would keep a sharp look-out for Bligh's Cape Direction, his so-longed-for first sight of the Australian coast after he had found a passage through the Great Barrier Reef. Eagerly they would gaze out over the bows for Restoration Island and, sighting it, voice their conviction that after two thousand miles they were now in the very wake of Bligh. His journal would tell them: "This day, being the anniversary of the restoration of King Charles II, and the name not being inapplicable to our present situation (for we were restored to fresh life and strength), I named this Restoration Island."

On this tiny, rocky little isle Bligh's exhausted men scrambled ashore in famishing haste, searching the rocks for shellfish. Those in the boat would see it exactly as Bligh's men saw it, with the low-lying mainland shore but a few hundred yards distant, and natives standing there beckoning them ashore - exactly as a lighthouse gang of us saw it many years later when building a warning light on Restoration Rock.

Sailing on, they would know beyond all doubt now that they were closely sailing in. the very wake of Cook, of Bligh, of Flinders, of King, and that fisherman-convict of the lion heart, Will Bryant, and his desperate wife and children. For such names and deeds would be household topics throughout the colony; in Sydney Town especially many were still fiercely taking sides in the aftermath of those turbulent events of Bligh's day, but a few years past. Thus, following those who had gone before, they would reach journey's end where the choppy waters of the Strait cut their course, just where the survivors of the frigate Pandora had sailed on their open-boat voyage to Timor, through the Lost Strait that had seen so much of despair during the short time it had been found again.

Doubtless the men in the boat would growl angrily at the fresh memory of the Pandora's four boats, which carried chained wretches in uttermost misery, and which, coming at last to Timor, brought despair and death to Will Bryant's unfortunate wretches who had safely survived a terrible voyage a short few months before.

Those in the boat would not cross Captain Edwards's wake because of sailormen's deep superstitions, and also because to them fortune, poverty, or disaster lay in the waters adjoining the Strait itself. Doubtless, as is the way with almost all forlorn hopes, now that they were at journey's end they had probably come to doubt their sanity in chasing such a will-o'-the-wisp.

Not until years afterwards would they, or those who were to follow them, learn that they had already sailed over many and many a patch of the sea-slug they desired so eagerly, and of sea wealth far greater. For the Coral Sea, mothered by the mighty Reef, has sown her treasures with wanton hand.

Young Aboriginal boys with *beche-de-mer*, or sea-slug.

6

WHERE THE SEA-SLUG FEEDS

THEY found their *beche-de-mer*, so beloved of the Chinese mandarin, and of the Powerful Ones in mysterious Tibet, believed by the few who had ever heard of it to be a fabled land floating upon the "Roof of the World". That the sea-slug could be traded to such a place, barred as it was to all the world, makes us think that in those days men used more brains and energy than we generally give them credit for. Yes, the sea-slug was eagerly bought by the hundreds of Sultans of the Indies and the seas beyond; like the bird's-nest it was obtainable only by those who had the money to pay. And thus on this day, in a new sea under Australian skies, the men in the boat, in laughing delight, found a rich patch of the slugs sluggishly browsing along the sea bottom, sucking in the sand in which live the tiny things they eat.

Up there towards the tip of Cape York Peninsula, by the Strait itself, at that season of the year there would be blue sky, calm blue sea among the maze of reefs and shoals, sunlight glinting on the mainland bush, the dull grey-green of a mangrove-girt islet upon some coral reef, and in the distance the grassy brown hill-slopes of small islands sparsely clothed with weeping casuarina and pisonia, hardy vines and scanty tea-trees. An immensity of air, salted with the very breath of life, and corning with a "swoosh" overhead and a bedlam of piercing calls, a whirling cloud of sea-birds diving in splashes of foam as they chased a dense shoal of herring, while the snakelike head of a turtle peered unconcernedly at the fuss. The boat with loose sail would be resting there motionless, just before the tum of the tide. The water would be warm to the sunburnt bodies of the men wading and bending, wading and bending without pause while the tide was out, each with a basket on arm, bending to grab a sea-slug and throw it into the basket, bending to grab another. For in rich patches on new grounds the big sea-slugs lie thick upon the shallow bottom, especially during the spring tides. Those toilers would be workers with the steady, concentrated energy of men digging up gold; and in those days, when a shilling was so valuable, they really were picking up gold, for these sea-slugs would find a rich market indeed if only the catch could be brought back to Sydney Town. Besides, they must slave while the weather held good. And they did not know when they might be chased away by "Indians".

Within the Strait, a few miles to their north, would be visible the forested hills of Murralug in the Prince of Wales Group, inhabited by the fierce Kowraregas. From there, the Torres Strait chain of islands stretched a hundred miles to New Guinea shores. Eastward, across the open reef-strewn waters to the Great Reef itself, a water-spout might shoot up, a strange happening giving them momentary pause.

They would not venture anywhere near those dreaded isles to the northward; daily they would keep uneasy watch, gazing into the dim north for sight of the big mat sails. Relief must have been theirs night after night to feel their heads still firm upon their dead-tired shoulders. They must keep watch, too, for the signal smokes on the near-by mainland and adjoining isles, though against these savages who could only venture out towards them paddling dug-out canoes they would feel they had some chance with sail and musket, even against vastly superior numbers.

They would have been anxious indeed had they known the fiercest sea-going warriors of the Strait knew all the time they were there, and were puzzling over what they were doing. We know this because the men of Warrior Island, only seventy miles to their north, kept a record of the incident by portraying it in their dances, and in the tales handed down from generation to generation by their story-tellers of marvellous memory. It was told to me and to others, with many an expressive chuckle, by old Maino, as yet unborn when those anxious waders daily added to their pile of precious *beche-de-mer.* If these men were not the first to seek *beche-de-mer* in the Coral Sea they were the first to be recorded by the islanders of the Strait.

The boat of these Lamars,[6] these "ghost men" as the islanders believed all white men to be, had been seen, then forgotten in the panic of fire in the looting of that wreck down the coast. And now, informed by smoke-signal and swift canoe[7]; the Warrior Island men studied what these unwelcome strangers appeared to be doing. From the look-out hills on both Albany and Mount Adolphus Island, they were watched daily. That the white men seemed to be so eagerly seeking the despised sea-slug that "crawls upon the belly of the sea" intrigued the islanders immensely. But when word came that they were actually cooking it the head-hunters were filled with disgust; they spat upon the coral strand with screwed-up faces of utter loathing. To think that those filthy beasts of Lamars would actually eat those crawling things of the sea!

Fat old Maino used to chuckle mightily when retailing the story. When word first came of the cooking, his father's tribesmen were solemnly engaged in the serious task of cleaning heads, prizes secured during a recent island foray, eighteen grisly trophies. The eyes and tongues had just been carefully cut out. These, with a few other prized organs of the body, would be expertly sun-dried. They would shrivel up and remain in a state of preservation for years if need be. I have seen such a tongue. Hard as rock, it looked like a shrivelled, thoroughly dried-up walnut. The eyes would be kept as a prize for young lads who had shown especial ability while undergoing the Spartan-like initiations to warriorhood. A lad, keeping the eye in his mouth for hours, thus slowly moistening and warming it until it "bloomed inside", would then swallow it. It was believed that this would give him night-sight, so that in the darkest night he could plainly see to creep upon his enemies. Other organs imbued the eater with other virtues. It was under the palms of Eroob that old Maino told me how his father gave him as a great favour his first warrior's tongue to eat, and various other organs also.

Thus the warriors were cleaning the heads preparatory to the drying and painting of the skulls when word came that the white strangers were cooking the sea-slug to eat it. The very thought of such a thing made several of those tough-stomached warriors walk away to be sick. Old Maino, squatting comfortably on his big fat hams, would fairly roar and roll with laughter in telling this.

They planned at their leisure to swoop down and take the heads of these beastly eaters of sea-slugs after the very important seasonal Turtle Ceremonies should be over. Those heads were a pleasure that could wait.

But the white men had not been cooking *beche-de-mer* to eat; it was far too valuable for that. They were boiling it in the big iron pot preparatory to smoke-drying it; thus it is preserved for market.

Time came when they had gathered as much as the little craft could hold. Luckily, they slipped away in dead of night. Probably those watchers outlined on the island hilltops against the skyline had sharpened their uneasy wits, for a dawn came when they were gone.

What relief must have been theirs when by day and night they safely sailed that thousand miles, then left the Great Reef astern! They must have felt at home when sailing back past Moreton Bay with a golden cargo, five tons of *beche-de-mer* worth £140 a ton in Sydney Town. That we also know from a sparse old record here and there. And we know that a few hundred pounds meant fortune when a penny, nay, a farthing was of value. What tales they could bring back, too! What a chance to boast in their relief, yet know they could offer to any inclined the promise of real wealth awaiting in that strange northern sea! Along the waterfront at least they would be nearly as much thought of as the explorers returning to Sydney Town. And truly they had taken greater risks than the explorers.

They would not be greeted by the Governor, of course; there would be no band or soldiers parading stiff as ramrods at the salute, nor cheering citizens with smiling ladies; there would be no speeches and no grand ball in their honour; they could not hope to see their names in the Gazette, the Australian, or the Monitor. But sailormen all would be eager to hear their story, while those canny merchants who dealt in ships and produce of the sea would quickly scent profits.

Yes, it must have been a homecoming bright with golden dreams. They had earned it all.

They could not have dreamt, though, that they were the pathfinders to the thousands of square miles of three Australian seas upon which time would bring fleets of vessels to reap ever richer harvests.

7

THE COCKROACHES

THE news brought to Sydney Town would cause men to pause a moment, to wonder yet again at this strange land, now with this strange sea. What other wonders might this new continent yet hold? At this time and for many years later all the interior and the north past Moreton Bay was one absorbing mystery. But this Coral Sea, so far away, could only be explored by such hardy sea-dogs as sought a living from the sea. Doubtless a few venturesome ones, with some merchant interested in the China trade, would combine to fit out a ship or two to exploit this new discovery. But it would be a risky venture for both seaman and merchant. Wasn't it away up there somewhere that all those Malay pirates were so murderously active, hovering round? Why, only a few years ago, in 1824, hadn't all Sydney Town given a grand farewell to His Majesty's ships and troops sailing to take possession of all that unknown coast, up through that same Coral Sea? Port Essington; the new settlement was to be called. And the pirates had captured H.M.S. *Lady Nelson*. and cut the throats of all her crew, every man jack of them! And now it was strongly rumoured that others of those fiendish cut-throats had captured the supply brig *Stedcombe,* too, looted her, then burnt her and made her crew slaves or slit their throats as a butcher does a pig!

'Why even now in the harbour H.M.S. *Success* and convoy were being fitted out, and more soldiers were training to sail and hold that place somewhere away up there. Lucky men must be those *beche-de-mer* fishers to come back to Sydney Town still breathing through their windpipes! And, yes, a lucky merchant and a game one who would buy their produce and sail his ship up through that same pirate-haunted sea to China - and be forced to risk the Chinee pirates, too, on the way, by Gad! But then, so it was rumoured the profits of a successful voyage meant fortune.

And many sighed, wishing they were sea-dogs, for countless humans have risked a cut throat on a mere chance of fortune.

Thus Sydney Town in its lonely isolation discussed this strange news. It was linked with that dim and far-away place called Port Essington, about which all had been vaguely uneasy for these two years past. At long intervals only hushed whispers of trouble and tragedy drifted in from those far-away northern seas.

The colonists, of course, knew nothing of the geography of their own north, let alone the far north, simply because those vast areas had' not been explored. Neither did most of them realize that to reach the Arafura you must first sail the Coral Sea, then "round the Point" - Peak Point of Cape York Peninsula - and that the fever-stricken hole now called Port Essington lay some seven hundred miles farther on along those coastal wilds. But the tragic news that very recently had come to Sydney Town was quite correct.

The *Lady Nelson,* seeking supplies for the struggling settlement, was captured off Barbar Island two hundred miles east of Timor and every man of the crew slaughtered. Soon afterward the supply brig *Stedcombe* ran into a pirates' nest off Timor Laut. All the crew were cut to pieces except the two terrified ship's boys, young Edwards and Forbes. These were kept as slaves and many a time were to wish they had died in that holocaust with the crew. Young Edwards, being "broken in" at the very time our boat was finding its *beche-de-mer,* would survive ten years of slavery, then die. Forbes, a broken wreck, would last out four years longer, to be almost miraculously rescued in 1839 by Captain Watson in a schooner called, of all names, the Essington.[8] Thus this poor crippled wretch would be the one survivor of two ships' crews attacked by Malay pirates, ships able to put up a fight for themselves, too. This, like the grass-covered graves at Port Essington, is a forgotten episode in the early exploration of our northern coast.

But Forbes would have to live out another eleven years of slavery before these events would be fully known. All that Sydney Town now knew was that the two supply ships for that far northern settlement had been captured by Malay pirates and the crews' throats cut, and now this hardly little boat had come sailing back to Sydney Cove from those very same waters[9] loaded with precious cargo called *beche-de-mer,* which, all put together, for a time gave welcome cause for discussion and for wondering what would be done about it all.

But with a fresh eruption between town and Government House, Sydney returned to its own back-yard in the relish of energetic gossip of the all-in fight again raging between the Governor and the "Voice of the People", those red-hot newspapers the *Australian* and the *Monitor*. The exclusionists who wished for cheap convict labour were heatedly taking sides with the Governor; the free settlers and emancipists who wanted the convict system abolished were as fiercely siding with the newspapers; while the troublesome land-seekers were still pushing out over range and plain, defying the edict of the Governor that they must keep within the Nineteen Counties. Men were crying out for women, too, shiploads of women. He-men though they were, whiskered and all, they realized something was missing. Many had left their troubles behind them, but man is never satisfied. There was trouble among the convicts, too, even rumours of discontent among the soldiery, those two smart regiments the 39th and 57th, though no one would ever dream it while watching them on parade, or changing guard at the guard-houses, or in the band playing at the Barracks before the fashionable throng, or smartly marching on duty bound through the town thoroughfares, or escorting long, footsore convict gangs on the road to Parramatta. Few strangers would ever dream it who, greatly privileged, might enviously watch the lordly officers preening their feathers before the ladies at a Governor's ball.

The Governor, meanwhile, was concerned with making roads to the rapidly growing country settlements. Why, on the Hunter River, that village called Newcastle had fifty private homes built and a population of two hundred with ships carrying hewn coal to the Indies and Calcutta: and Bombay at ten shillings a ton. Yes, this wild country was developing prodigiously fast these last few years. And no doubt, in between fights, the Governor was looking ahead to overcome any future water shortage, now that the Tank Stream was failing to meet the demands of the increased population. He was going to give Sydney a permanent water supply by tunnelling to Busby's Bore. With all these new hands coming out, it was no joke carting water from Blackwattle Swamp and Botany Swamp when the tanks in Hunter and Pitt streets went dry.[10]

And now a hundred street lamps were to be built and lit so that you could walk down the main streets at night and even see your way about without falling over a cow or a blackfellow's dog or squelching up to your knees in a bog. Many of the worst ruts had been filled in by the convict gangs. You could see these poor wretches every day, harnessed like animals, straining to pull their heavy, creaking, stone-laden carts down the streets. How their muscles and the lash weals on their backs stood out as they strained like bullocks when the cart bogged!

Of course, some of the daily fun was lost by these improvements. It had been great sport to watch a fine lady crossing the street with those dainty mincing steps, one scared eye on the puddles, the other on the expectant populace, one little hand trying to manage her voluminous skirts, the other occupied with her dainty parasol to shield her complexion from the bold sun's rays - great fun to watch her in her inexperience suddenly flop piteously down in a hole of mud. Of course, there would always be some gallant to jump from his horse or leap to her rescue, and if haply he, too, slipped in the clay it made a good day's fun for those citizens lucky enough to see it. Yes, a little innocent merriment was being taken out of a hard life by these modem improvements. But then, we must expect to pay for progress.

The Governor was even trying to clear this plague of fighting, snarling, snapping blackfellows' dogs - and citizens, too - from the streets. Loud was the wail from the blackfellows, but they, too, had to pay the price of progress. And as for those riotous and bawdy ones who brawled and caroused in public, they must mend their ways. Why, it was almost safe to walk the streets at night!

There was much excited talk of weird new inventions in the Old World when a ship arrived. Puffing Jinnies drawing wagons on land; steam, the same as the steam from a kettle, driving a ship at sea; and now a gas to make a light! Some said its glare was so powerful it could blind you if you didn't take care. What was the world coming to with such frightening inventions? Ah, but these clever men had better look out lest they set the world alight! And what would be the good of it to us all then, when we'd all be a-roasted?

Yes, there was plenty to talk about in lively Sydney Town.

What really was the strength of these fellows in a boat who'd found a Coral Sea that grew grubs for which Chinee mandarins would give real money? Could such a thing be true? Were there really such things as sea-grubs? Who'd ever think of eating sea-grubs! Why, they must be as savage as these blackfellows chopping grubs out of dead trees along the foreshore. Just as bad as those Frenchies eating snails - ugh!

And then this rumour among the settlers and landed gentry that Allan Cunningham had found a track over the mountains - Cunningham's Gap, some said it had been named away inland from that new settlement along the coast at Moreton Bay, a track to those great lands he'd found. And now settlers could land their flocks by sea, and drive them overland to new pastures, then ship their produce through Moreton Bay back to Sydney Town.

And now a new hullabuloo was raging because the Governor declared that no settler would be allowed within fifty miles at least of

Moreton Bay. If any settler did, then he'd find himself in Moreton Bay - with a chain round his ankles hewing limestone!

To hell with the Governor and the System and all it stands for! Now those lands must lie there away out in the wild bush - a paradise, the explorer's men called those great plains - and be useless to man and beast, just because the Governor was determined to cage his convicts at the only port that could give access to them. To hell with this convict system!

To Cunningham's chagrin and the settlers' anger, "the System" kept those wonderful lands rigidly bottled up for another twelve years, till in 1840 Moreton Bay was disbanded as a penal settlement and the district was thrown open to settlement. To burst such bonds as these, our great-grandfathers had to fight long and bitterly, till at last the increasing numbers of free settlers forced the abolition of transportation.

Eagerly now throughout the colony all hands were discussing the exciting rumour that a whole shipload of free women were to be sent out. Not poor unfortunates branded for some trifling misdemeanour or even for none at all, but free women who could become wives to the colonists if they wished, and of course they would wish - these love-starved he-men never doubted that! Probably, at this exciting news, our sea-slug adventurers invested in new shirts and scissored their whiskers also. Lording it now with real money in their pockets, they would feel as good as any. And their luck was in. Who could tell?

Yes, there was plenty to talk about these times - if a man was not too dead tired o' nights and, above all, if he were free.

While trying to run the country, and incidentally making quite a fair job of it, the angry Governor, with these constant quarrels and development work in town and bush on his hands, had no time whatever to ponder on the rumour that a lowly boat had returned to Sydney Town loaded with five tons of dried *beche-de-mer,* perhaps a marketable commodity in the East, which might lead to a new industry - a sea-slug which these men said they had found two thousand miles away in a coral sea. Meanwhile the men had found a merchant willing to try to market their trepang in Asian markets. Next year three little boats would sail to the Coral Sea, three little brigs, now sailing past Moreton Bay, praying for good winds and that their luck would hold true.

8

WHEN IRON IS GOLD

LUCK was drawing to a close for the unfortunate Commandant Logan, energetically building in that still inaccessible bush north-ward at Moreton Bay, now to be called Brisbane Town.[11]

To that settlement of human misery, strangely enough, Governor Darling in 1828 ordered Charles Fraser, botanist of Sydney Town, to make a Public Garden. And the energetic Fraser started to make a wonderful job of it, laying the foundations of the beautiful Botanical Gardens of the City of Brisbane today. Thus, even in those harsh days, a Governor fighting bitterly against bitter enemies could still think of a garden in far-away bush where chain-gangs slaved. In the same year, Captain Rous, whose company had been such balm to the harassed Governor, had dis-covered the mouth of a river which he called the Clarence, but which we now know as the Tweed, and also the mouth of the Richmond. This event naturally gave officers and crew of the lively frigate an excuse to celebrate right royally on their return to Sydney Town. During that year also the first gas actually was lit in Sydney, in a chemist's shop, to the gaping admiration of the citizenry. Meanwhile those stubborn ones continually crying out for a free land and free laws now won a small triumph, just one more little step ahead: the

Legislative Council of New South Wales was enlarged. But the iron hand of court martial still gripped the colonists; there would be years of struggle yet before they forced the authorities to give them trial by a jury of their own civil citizens.

Very soon after Captain Rous had sailed across the estuaries of the coastal rivers, Sturt, plodding on inland, far to the westward, discovered a big river and named it the Darling.[12] Step by laborious step, by sea and land, a continent was being opened up and a new people was coming into being. One year later, in 1830, Fate, which in this case was "the System", claimed the Governor's officer, Commandant Logan of Moreton Bay. His regiment becoming due for relief, he reluctantly prepared to hand over his post. Still deeply interested in exploration, gripped like many others by the spell of this new land, he determined to make one last journey and complete a map of the district. During a last painstaking trip, after a skirmish with hostile blacks, he did so. Ruefully returning towards the settlement with the knowledge that he would never make another exploring trip, he absent-mindedly rode aside from the party alone, following the tracks of a straying horse.

They found his body a few days later in a shallow grave. He had apparently been clubbed to death by aborigines.

The fact that the aborigines rarely buried a victim gradually aroused suspicion. Many of the convicts went nearly crazy with delight at the news, having suffered dreadfully under the System. Several gleefully declared that the hated Commandant had met with a party of wild blacks led by a "wild white man" who had sooled them on to the killing.

This may have been true, for it is known that in rare cases an escaped convict survived to live with the blacks.

In whatever way his death happened, I think the unfortunate Commandant was himself a victim of the System - with many, many others.

But far from all this turmoil the *beche-de-mer* fishers now toiled regularly year after year. Three little boats now, and three small brigs-cockleshells really, but considered staunch enough vessels in those days, sailing into the Far North through the lonely waters of that mighty sea lane walled by the Great Reef.

How long it took them to learn local conditions and environment we do not know. The winds, the squalls, the calms, the gradual shifts of the wind, the spasmodic veering, the steady periods, the tides, the currents - in a lifetime they would not learn all the changing mysteries of these alone. To learn to sail north with the beginning of the south-east trades, to weave their way among those countless reefs, to find their patch of "fish" and garner it in the eight months of good fishing weather, then sail back with the strong nor-west behind them. Tiny vessels went down in loneliness before they learnt the right time to fly the perils of the cyclone season; others were trapped by natives.

As for the work, once find a patch and the rest was easy-when they knew how. Just straight-out toil from dawn until long after dark, picking up the slugs from the sea-bed, working at the gutting, at the boiling pot, at the smoke-house, then bagging the dirty-looking, leathery, shrivelled-up fish. And that sea offered them unlimited riches, though the finding would appear to a landsman something like searching for a mob of sheep lost in trackless bush. It would take them time and experience to learn that even a lowly slug crawling along the sea bottom likes to "travel" with its mates, that it definitely prefers certain conditions and areas for its grazing grounds, that it is subject to change of weather, tide, and currents, even to the pull of the silvery moon that cold lady seems to have quite a lot to do with all of us. In short, they must learn that even this humble slug is a part of Life, abiding by the particular laws that govern its life, and is not to be just picked up anywhere. And until the searchers ruefully learnt these strange secrets they would fish many and many a day in vain. And water-salt and sore would their eyes be, tired their lungs, weary their bodies, from constant diving to find only a bare sea bottom.

So very strange, the sea. As strange as the land, for in years coming prospectors would say with a sigh, "Yes, there's gold somewhere here all right - but there's plenty of earth mixed with it", just as before them the *beche-de-mer* fishers would have said, "Yes, there's plenty of *beche-de-mer* in the Coral Sea - but there's plenty of water mixed with them!"

This *beche-de-mer*, this "sea-cucumber", this sea-slug is like an ugly bloated sausage, about a foot in length, sometimes crinkly, sometimes prickly, crawling very slowly in the shallows, its wee, so much alive tuft of tentacles scooping the sand to its mouth, sucking in the food from the sand. We do not know what long experience was necessary before the adventurers came to class them as brown fish, black fish, prickly fish, and red fish, teat fish and curry red, Manna teat, chalk fish and tiger, lolly fish and mainland black, and yet others. Some classes, being more succulent than others, command better prices from the connoisseurs of that delectable soup. Not for many years to come, until they learnt about deep diving, would the fisherman find the most valuable of all, the deep-sea black, which lives only in deep water. On good feeding grounds within the eighty thousand square miles of the Barrier Reef waters the *beche-de-mer* grows to be the largest and best-conditioned of its kind in the world, doubtless because of the limitless foodstuffs in that little "Sea of Plenty". But on poor grounds a dinghy-load of the slugs might boil down to one disappointing bagful.

Once a patch was found in shallow water, then at low tide - especially during spring tides - the men had only to wade and bend and pick up the slugs by hand and throw them into basket, canoe, or dinghy. They would soon have learnt that the slug has a nasty habit of ejecting long strings of beastly gelatinous stuff, which looks like its intestines, over the man who handles it. If one among them had seen the Malays at work he would know of this, and with practice would be able to handle the slugs less distastefully. (All the same, the Malays I have watched were by no means as touchy as we were if a slug did squirt its innards, or whatever muck it is, all over him. It gave his friends a laugh, and there was plenty of water to wash it off, anyway.) The best thing to do was to split the slug open immediately before it could play its unpleasant trick, but precious time often did not permit this to be done.

Gazing overside from the dinghies, with sparkling sunlight beating down on the still, crystal-clear water, the fishermen would be able to see plainly the sea-cucumbers on the bottom. If the water were too deep for wading they would have to sink down, snatch a slug in either hand, rise to the surface, throw the catch in the dinghy, take a deep breath, and sink again. These early adventurers, unlike the native divers who were soon to follow, would not have been expert enough to collect and scoop up an armful swiftly, then rise to the surface hugging the ugly things as a woman hugs an armful of loose parcels. So they would toil on until the tide came swirling in again or the sun went down in darkening crimson far over the western coast. Sunrise over the Great Barrier Reef in good weather, sunset over the distant mainland, are glories that no words can picture.

The next stage of their work was the curing of the slugs they had gathered. They would cautiously spy out some small, uninhabited island girt with mangrove, red mangrove, from which they would cut the wood that, slowly burnt, would smoke-dry the *beche-de-mer*, and the strips of bark that' would be boiled with it in the cauldron, not only helping to preserve it, but also giving it the reddish colour that enhanced its value. (Fishing enthusiasts may be interested to know that in my day we always threw our new fishing-lines into the pot; the fat from the boiling slugs or the tannin in the bark, or both combined, gave them a beautiful smooth finish, took the annoying kinking quality out of them, and made them water-proof, as it were, thus preserving them and adding strength.) If the slugs had not already been gutted it would have to be done at this stage; often they would be thrown into the boiling salt water for a moment, then taken out, slit open, cleaned, and thrown back to boil for a further eight or ten hours.

The smoke-house had also to be built, and the trays and mats erected and made correctly. The slugs were kept open by means of bamboo pins while they were being smoked on the trays. When they were thoroughly cured the hard, shrivelled-up, leathery-looking things would be bagged and stored in the hold. Care had to be taken lest the bags got damp, for then the decaying fish would have to go over the side, and all the time and labour would have been in vain. Alas, what heart-breaks. there have been!

The whole tedious operation took time, especially for in-experienced men, and time was so very valuable. In those early days there was the constant risk of ambush on land, unless the fishermen were lucky enough to find an isolated island growing the right wood. Otherwise it was better to load up with the wood and bark and put to sea again, building the smoke-house as best they could on the tiny deck. Then some would fish by day while others on board attended to the cleaning and boiling, smoking and curing, all through the day and night. This was done even in my day, so many years later, when "the pot" was half an iron tank, sawn through. Apart from the constant risk of fire, life aboard such a tiny vessel during the hot calms was hell - the heat, the toil, the eye-smarting, throat-burning, suffocating smoke, the shell fishy smell of the bubbling slugs, and the handling of the beastly, slime-spewing things. And the tucker, rough as it was, for the crew must be cooked. There were seasons when even the one luxury of being able to toil in our bare, sunburnt hides was denied us by the maddening swarms of sandfly or trochus fly, until a heaven-sent strong breeze blew up.

These were the bad times, of course, but only by knowing the conditions of life aboard a *beche-de-mer* cutter of only forty years ago can a man have some idea of what the adventurers of a hundred years before put up with. Within comparatively recent years, of course, conditions have improved rapidly. The introduction of the glass-bottomed box was the first big step forward, then came water goggles, the lead weight with embedded barbs, and deep-fathomed cord. The development of the seaworthy, efficient cutter and lugger of today, with such improvements as small, compact smoke-houses, has made life aboard much more bearable. But the early adventurers had to do everything the hard way, the monotonous, slow way-and time was everything. Time before the nor-west squalls should come!

Could not some at least of the mainland aboriginal "savages" be induced to work for them? To do the fishing, or the time-wasting curing of the fish, the chopping and collecting of wood, the gutting, the boiling, the smoke-drying?

But how? By tempting them with gold?

They would have been contemptuous of gold, neither knowing nor caring what gold was. Some among them indeed had seen it, away back in the hills on the mainland. Some had picked up a dull-yellow, "ironstoney" looking nugget, gazed curiously at it a moment, then chucked it contemptuously away. Gold is only a name, only valuable when it can buy things.

It was hope for gold that had brought these adventurers at the risk of their lives into these wild seas-gold of the sea. The slimy old sea slug meant big money. But to the aborigines *toorook* was *gold - toorook,* that to the white man was simply iron!

Iron, which could be fashioned into spear-heads so immeasurably superior to wood, stone, or bone. Iron, which could be ground into knives that were everlasting, compared to those of stone and bone. Iron, so infinitely more efficient when made into a tomahawk than the clumsy axe-head of stone. Any old iron at all - waste from the staves of casks, worn-out horseshoes, rusty nails, worn-out shovel blades, broken chain links, any rusty old scraps at all were to these savages *toorook* - their gold!

Yes, and they would even work for it! Which one among the white adventurers first guessed this and decided to take the grave risk, and which one gained the partial confidence of some small group of natives, then cautiously tried to trade iron scraps for labour, we do not know. By rough sign-work he would have made them understood that if they gathered a certain number of sea-cucumbers their reward would be a precious piece of *toorook,* while a big catch would gain a wonderful knife of *toorook,* and a small canoe loaded with the slugs would bring that thing above all price, an iron tomahawk!

And so began, just here and there, in isolated localities, an armed neutrality in which the natives traded their skill and labour in return for the strange goods they ardently desired. With this came the amazingly rapid development of a pidgin English, often known as "*beche-de-mer* English". Just the very beginning of the process which with time would develop into the second phase of the clash between white, black, and brown in the opening up of Australia's northern seas.

For some years only the local knowledge of small groups of the coastal aborigines was sought, or of small sub-tribes and families of natives on adjoining islands. To trade with a large tribe meant taking the chance of being clubbed and losing boat and all which would not matter to dead men, though the early hands did not look at it in quite that way. They also naturally avoided, as they would the plague, the far less numerous but far more dangerously armed sea-going headhunters of the Torres Strait Islands, a few of which were within sight to their northward.

Soon then, the "Indians" here and there were "working" for the white strangers - when and as they liked, to be sure, but satisfactorily - and were being paid in the eagerly sought iron. The gathering of the slugs was child's play to them. They would simply nick them up from the bottom with a fish spear at low tide - no laborious bending for them. In deeper water the diving was fun, with many a sarcastic joke at these evil-smelling, ugly-looking, clumsy strangers who would give precious *toorook* for useless sea-slugs.

Soon the white adventurers learnt the value of a fragment of broken glass, and when next season their little boats returned they carried grimy collections of broken bottles and glass chips as well as fragments of scrap-iron. This was not by any means as easy as it sounds, for in those days scraps of iron and glassware took a great deal of collecting.

Dazzling payment, this, to the natives - to be given a bottle for a few useless sea-slugs! A bottle was a marvellous thing, for when broken it was already a knife, and a handy spear-head maker could easily chip it into twenty sharp-cutting spear-heads. Then there was that magic thing that when you looked into it showed you another man. A young warrior could win a smile from a desired girl with that magic thing, because when she looked into it she saw a girl just like herself! And that girl would smile at her, too, and giggle and laugh just as she herself was laughing. And the awed piccaninnies could gaze into it, too. and see other piccaninnies, and scream and race howling to their mothers for protection.

Thus a cautious co-operation was built up, with the whites ever ready with arms by their side against treachery day and night, but an understanding of mutual advantage all the same.

When those natives thus contacted here and there realized that the dreaded white men did not wish to use their thundersticks against them but to give them these wonderful things in return for despised sea-slugs, then the fishermen's troubles in regard to native divers and peace on land while curing their fish were practically over, so far as those particular groups of aborigines were concerned - so long as vigilance was never relaxed, of course. Inevitably, some among the white men presently believed they had the natives "eating out of their hands", and generally paid for the error with their lives. But it all went to the experience which had to be built up over those so many adventurous years. There were other painful lessons to be learnt the agony, the nearly certain death that came of treading upon the hideous, moveless, so perfectly camouflaged stone-fish; the poisoned foot, the swelling leg, a thousand miles from aid, caused by the needle-like spike of some poisonous shellfish.

To the increasing numbers of white adventurers this wary co-operation with the natives was a pleasant surprise as well as considerable gain and relief. Hopelessly outnumbered, completely isolated as they were, to have shot down the natives wholesale on sight, as it is often believed they did, would have been fatal to them. It was to their great advantage, in safety, time, and monetary gain to be friend1y with as many natives as possible. True, only in those few areas near the coast did this understanding develop, and even then terrible things were to happen - treachery, murders, massacres by both white and black. But the guarded friendship that quickly developed with a tribe here and there was. all to the advantage of the white invaders.

In the coming years, the aboriginal was to lose everything - his country and his life. But the end was to come from future "civilization" and disease, not from the bullets of the whites.[13]

9

FIRST WITH THE NEWS

THOUGH for yet another thirty years the farthest north and the Coral Sea would live and roll in primitive life, practically as the first *beche-de-mer* adventurers had found it, very different would be the rapid change in the far south. Growing into a lively hive of industry now, this quarrelsome Sydney Town in 1830, with fifteen thousand inhabitants, was claiming itself a city; another fifteen thousand settlers, now widely scattered, were pushing on over the Bathurst Plains, discovering the Liverpool Plains, crossing the New England mountains, settling along the Hunter Valley. Sturt was voyaging down the Murrumbidgee, Mitchell outfitting to ride north of the Liverpool Plains. The *Patmelia* had sailed the first settlers' to the Swan River three thousand miles to the west, to make their homes in a vast, unexplored area, in itself larger by far than many a European country. For now this last, new continent was definitely all under the one flag.

The colony was recovering from a depression, and its wide-awake merchants were doing marvellously well, despite their isolation from the Old World that barely knew the continent, let alone the colony, existed, and cared less.

Buildings going up - a great boom for the fast-developing building trade - more and classier carriages being built for the gentry, but, alas, chains still being forged for prisoners. Stock increasing at a rate undreamt of, such flocks and herds as had never been thought possible by the amazed yeomen of the old lands. Why, a man, be he ever so humble, who toiled here for a few years might find himself with such a flock as would send many a noble, many a proud baron green with envy. Yes, there was magic within this earth for a man who would toil, arid he could feel himself growing with the results of his labour, a new life, an unfamiliar independence, a pride in himself as a man. Aye, this was a good land, a land to hold and love, a land worth fighting for.

It was understandable, then, that wherever men gathered in city, settlement, or bush there was now one demand, one unbreakable resolve. "To hell with the Convict System! Freedom for all, freedom for us and our land!"

The popular pastime of "Governor-baiting" went on as furiously as ever, the victim fighting back with gusto. Loud agitations for more ships and yet more ships, but-loaded with free immigrants! And still the loud wail for "more women"! That call seemed quaintly popular throughout the land in those days, about the only burning question, apart from freedom, that all hands seemed agreed upon. In time fast coming they would be prepared to fight bitterly "government by musket" if necessary, yet they were quite prepared, nay anxious, to accept government by petticoat.

However, within this lively colony all now seemed set, and was set for years of active expansion and prosperity.

The year 1831, in which Governor Darling met his Waterloo; brought other excitements to Sydney City, the arrival of the *Sophia Jane* attracting marvelling throngs to the harbour to cheer the arrival of the first steamship from England, though she arrived under canvas. As if this were not wonder enough, the S.S. *Surprise* was launched in Sydney, being the first steamship built in Australia. A surprise indeed, and a remarkable achievement for this tiny population so completely isolated from the long-established shipyards and industrial advantages of the Old World. An omen of things to come, maybe. At Clarence Town, too, they built a steamer, the *William IV*, the timbers being the sturdy ironbark and flooded gum from Australia's own shores. The resource, ingenuity, and initiative of the colony's early ship-builders indicated that a virile race was being born in a new land. Many small ships were built long before this, the first, the *Rose Hill Packet* for the Parramatta River trade, was launched in 1789. Others followed, the industry handicapped by the deadening government restriction that no vessel of any sort might be built capable of sailing to China, India, or "the Islands". In other similar ways the shackling hand of the Old World sternly sought to hold back progress by the early colonists. Despite this, a surprising number of small vessels were built in Sydney Cove alone, even before 1800. Then in 1819, at the village of Richmond on the Hawkesbury, the brig *Glory* was built, followed by others. John Grono, from wild bush near Pitt Town, carved out a ship-building yard that for years was to tum out many a goodly ship. Brigs, sloops, schooners, and barques were built from native timbers in most of the coastal rivers, as also in Sydney Cove. In numerous other ways this new land responded to the initiative and work of the colonists, whose increasing confidence and hope were expressed in the cry for a free country, for the breaking of chains not only of iron, but of tradition, restrictions tenaciously holding progress down.

This year of Darling's downfall saw the first shipload of assisted immigrants boisterously welcomed to Sydney Harbour. For the first time, too, Crown lands were thrown open to the public for free competition. Slowly but surely chain after chain was gradually being weakened-broken.

The discontented factions of Sydney City, combining, at last drove Governor Darling from the colony, that enraged martinet fighting a bitter rearguard action all the same. Except for those interests siding with the Governor and the System, Sydney indulged in the wholesale horseplay typical of the period. At night bonfires round Sydney Cove lit up the shipping and the dancing figures round the barbecues, in beery song chorusing the red-hot verse of the day to the fuming Governor, now aboard the ship *Hoogly* which would sail him back to England. At one notable feast a bullock had been roasted whole and the head, be-decked with ribbons, was rowed out to the *Hoogly* by a roistering party of "gallants", who then serenaded the Governor's wife and daughter, silently watching from the *Hoogly's* deck. Not too complimentary a way of farewelling the representative of His Majesty King William IV. But, after all, that farewell attracted quite a lot of attention, the singing voices in the balmy evening air and the riotous laughter echoing merrily out over the water. Differently, on that very day, had screams rung piercingly across that very water from the prison hulk Phoenix anchored just down the foreshore, screams of the poor wretches mercilessly flogged with the cat-o-nine tails. But few took active notice of those screams; they were a daily part of the System.

Sir Richard Bourke took over the governorship of this problem child, the world's last continent. Not that he would know *beche¬de-mer* if he saw it; he would have other things to attend to - and plenty!

Also arriving with the Steamship Age to the now virile colony was a lusty infant of a different kind, eventually to outshout its rivals and take a lively past in the troublous future, destined to grow with the coming new nation into one of the world's great newspapers - the *Sydney Morning Herald.* Thus there were now four squabbling little sheets to add loud voices and ginger to the turbulence and tribulation and expansion moves of the colony.

These "rags" of the day went at it hammer and tongs. Every scrap was all in, whether they were fighting the Governor, or one another, or one of the various factions, or barracking for the advancement of the colony arid its own interests as each saw fit. Each little sheet, with its Tom Thumb staff more often than not up to its ears in fight and difficulties, was lively with the spirit of the times. "First with the news, and devil take the hindmost!" was the practical and zealously carried out slogan often acted upon at risk of drowning or a broken neck from a galloping horse, as we know through scanty reminiscences left by the old-timers of the day.

Ships from overseas were few and far between, and Sydney went months at a time without oversea news. Three and four months without outside news was ordinary. Now we take as a matter of course fresh editions of big papers pouring out into the streets each day, with news brought in a flash from overseas by wireless, telegraph, and cable. But in those days, which were only the dawn of the Steam Age in these seas, the colonists not only waited long months for news from friends in the Old Dart, but often were not sure whether they were at peace or war. (Perhaps they were better off than we are, with our almost hourly news of war or cold war or threats of war from some "hot spot" or other.)

So, at long intervals and always late, the news of the outside world had come to the colony through its early years - momentous news of the Nile and Trafalgar and Waterloo and that arch-devil "Old Boney", the clash of Greeks and Turks and of revolutions and inventions. The colonists of the Last Continent were ever on "pins and needles" for news! And the Sydney papers of those energetic days were there to give it to them! A successful "rag" of those times could at a pinch support two reporters on its staff, maybe a compositor while the editor was in or out of jail or the court as the case might be. Editors those days appear to have been particularly harasssed men, and to survive the vicissitudes of newspaper work had to be slippery as eels. The shipping reporter was the boy, the honour and glory of the paper rested upon him, and all the world knew it. Among his numerous jobs - one of which seems at times to have been keeping a sharp watch for the bailiff - he had ever to have his eye upon the distant flagstaff away up on the hill. Immediately a ship was signalled he yelled and was gone as if the devil were at his heels. Leaping on a horse always kept ready saddled, he went tearing down the "street" hell for leather for the Cove, where at a strategic position a six-oared whaleboat was pushed into the water at the sound of his Red Indian approach. The boat was moving as he jumped aboard. Those "paper" boats were specially built and manned by a highly skilled crew, ever ready. And they took to sea in all weathers when called upon. So the race was on. First to reach and board that still-distant ship would get the very few papers captain or passengers had saved, would get "the news"!

Our hero would be praying that his rivals, grown weary of constant looking towards that flagstaff for months past, had missed the signal flag, or that they might be suffering excruciating thick heads after the night before, with consequent clouding of alertness and eyesight, or just simply that they'd fall down and break their necks.

The agonies of greeny seasickness that reporter went through in stormy weather were nothing if only, even at the actual risk of his life, he could board the ship first and get his claws upon those precious papers, leaving to his heartbroken rivals an "empty ship". What utter joy when, as his crew with powerful machine-like strokes sent the swift craft racing back to port and honour, he would catch sight of another "paper" boat, in a spume of spray emerging from the Heads! No matter how agonizedly seasick he was, he would leap up to send a yell of derisive laughter towards his too late, woebegone rival.

Racing across the harbour, he would tumble out on shore, mount his horse, somehow, and gallop madly back to the office, where all hands and the cook were feverishly waiting to rush their man's triumph into print. Meanwhile the citizens would be rapidly gathering to rush that lucky paper first out with the news. During the Crimean War years yet to come there would be near-riots outside whichever newspaper office was frantically printing news.

It is difficult in these days, in this great city, to realize the isolation of the colonists, as the tough yet ever progressive phases of settlement and industry went on - yet still it was nothing compared to the isolation of the little boats now yearly sailing the Coral Sea.

Fine old journalists like Finch, Heney and Brewer and others tell us that in the Sydney of the early 1830s there were barely a score of houses visible in the bush of the North Shore; there was no such place as Pyrmont or Woolloomooloo, Darlinghurst or Surry Hills, for these now long-since densely inhabited suburbs were simply bush, as was even Hyde Park. Residents of one fabulous suburb might not be flattered to know that King's Cross was not even thought of. In all of William Street there were but three little houses. Who, today, could imagine that Oxford Street was sheer bush, wild bush all the way to the Heads? So that often a reporter, after having no easy job securing his precious material from a lumbering little old ship at sea, would have to race it back along a bridle track to the office. Those reporter hounds began to play the dirty on one another, on the principle that all's fair in love and war. Sneaking down to the wilds of Watson's Bay, some smart alec would camp there with the boat all ready and an eagle-eyed look-out "up top", gazing through the night for lights to southward. At first blink the reporter would leap aboard the boat and be racing for the Heads and his distant quarry while his rival was blissfully snug under his blanket - if the poor wit owned a blanket. Often the wide-awake one would have to race as far as Coogee or even farther before the boat could pick up the ship. And many a fine job was done on dark, stormy nights by boat's crew and reporter; the poor devil's heart was probably in his boots a many and many a time. Have you ever tried to board a rolling, plunging, overwhelming juggernaut of an old-time sailing ship during a wild night at sea, with wind and waves and faint shout and faint light mistily above that lumbering bulwark, a dangling rope and a towering bastion of water, gleaming woodwork swaying down upon you, to lurch away and down under canvas-bulging masts at the last critical moment, while you go down, down into the troughs with the rollicking waves and your stomach rushes up to choke your throat?

That's how the news was brought to Sydney Town many a time in those days - while far away out in the bush a blackfellow might be running for hours, holding a cleft stick with a note in it, to carry a message from one settler to another. Even in my day, in the farthest bush, I have seen such an aboriginal messenger racing through the scrub. Yes, we progress fast these days. Tomorrow we shall be taking trips to the moon.

The new Governor soon proved to be a wary bird, a good listener who did not talk too much, but when he did he apparently meant what he said. Probably Sir Richard Bourke's training had taught him a human understanding of the difficulties and troubles of men, their capabilities and their failings, their deceits and bravado and cunning, their staunchness to a belief or cause, their pettiness and bravery, and imbued him with the patience and initiative so vitally necessary in overcoming the difficulties of a vast enterprise in a strange country. For he had been Assistant Quartermaster-General of Wellington's hard-pressed army in Portugal, and had later been responsible for supplying the desperately fighting, often wearily moving army with all supplies from Corunna until the war's end.To have successfully carried out such a job under the hostile environment and heart-breaking conditions of the times would have forged his talents for his present job. Anyway, he quietly carried on as he saw fit, listening to the arguments of conflicting parties, drawing his own conclusions, then making decisions as he thought best for the country. In the six years of his governorship he gradually grew into the colony's most popular Governor as yet. Also, progress bounded ahead.

One of the wisest things he did was to abolish the "Nineteen Counties". Henceforth the overlanders could legally push out over the absurd boundary line and legally take up the lands beyond.

Numerous venturesome ones - Authority had called them rebellious ones - had already chanced it and done so. They had battled on to far-away areas whose names would later be well known - Gundagai, the Murrumbidgee, the Namoi, Tamworth, Armidale - under constant threat of confiscation of land and flocks, of fines and even imprisonment.

Thus the colonists at long last had burst yet another chain. And the effect of that event would be felt, in years coming, even in such a far-away place as the Coral Sea, even in the lives and environment of a few humble *beche-de-mer* fishermen, a few little vessels sailing quite unnoticed each year from Sydney Harbour to return - those that did return - a year later. For the bursting of that boundary line immediately turned men's minds to those northern lands Oxley had discovered twenty years ago. They gazed out over the mountain-tops, those wild valleys, unknown gorges, those rocky razor-backs seemingly without end stretching into the northern mists that only Cunningham and his men had as yet trod. Far away on ahead there somewhere lay that paradise of Allan Cunningham the botanist, the Darling Downs! Men's feet itched, reflectively they glanced at the hooves of their horses, then stared again out over the mountains into the northern mists.

That northern trek would come. Nothing would stop it now. What of Moreton Bay? Still blocking the way into and out of the rich interior, that penal settlement must go. And then a town could form five hundred miles north of Sydney. Ships would come, then would sail yet farther north again in the very wake of the trepang fishers, loaded ships bound for China, India, and the Indies.

And now men toiling overland had found the Big River, the mouth of which had already been discovered. News came to Sydney Town of magnificent lands and timbers on this beautiful Clarence; a prophet already had arisen prophesying that mighty ships would be built from this river's timbers alone, settlements would spring up from its jungle-clad banks.

So, another step to the north.

10

SKULLS AND SHIPWRECKS

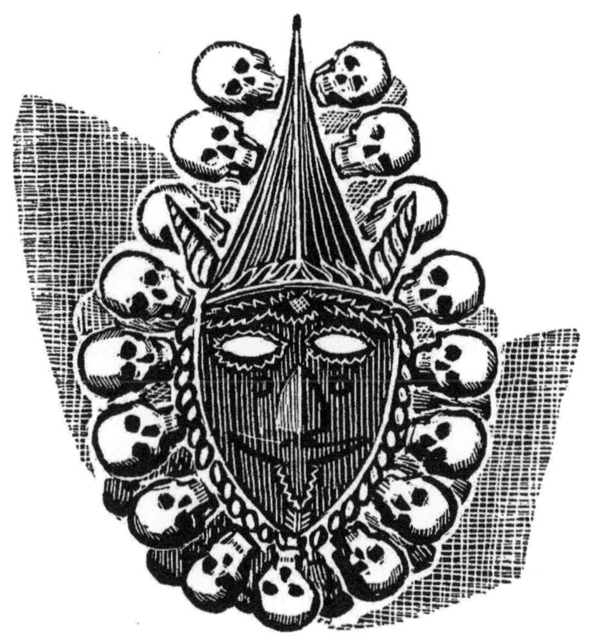

SO SLOW at first, unnoticeably sure, then with steadily growing momentum was the opening up of the Last Continent, as the seed unfolds to the plant, the sapling, then the young tree taking shape.

Governor Bourke's regime saw a romance of movement westward. Volumes could be written on the achievements of that brave period. Port Phillip district was eventually thrown open to settlement in 1836, and thus Melbourne was born, fifteen years before that fortunate area became the Colony of Victoria. During the same year a settlement called Adelaide was formed still farther westward, and a great area of New South Wales was now called the Colony of South Australia. Whimsical fate then played a lone, tragic card in a totally different direction, our direction, two thousand miles away under the unknown skies of the far nor'east. For in October of this year the attention of all Sydney was drawn at last to the farthest north, to the continent's Coral Sea. Not by the toil or adventures of those few trepang fishers still quietly sailing away on their seasonal voyage to that sea of perils, nor by any great exploring discovery was this immediate, keen, awed interest brought about, but by - *skulls.*

A pathetic necklace of human skulls.

That enterprising - some called it very different names - young newspaper the *Herald,* now sharpening its claws to tear into Governor Bourke and all who sided with him to keep this land a convict settlement still, now with boisterous acclaim brought out its very first illustration - the very first illustration, I understand, to appear in any Australian paper.

This triumph of journalism met with immediate applause, maybe more for the subject matter than the actual technical achievement, which in fact was good.

The illustration was of a hideous idol necklaced by twenty-four skulls of shipwrecked white people eaten by the savages of the "South Sea Islands". The Government rescue schooner *Isabella* had just brought the gruesome relics to Sydney. Today they lie buried in old Bunnerong cemetery. The tragedy had actually occurred in the Torres Strait Islands in the Coral Sea, two thousand miles north of Sydney. And Sydney *beche-de-mer* fishers, manning several small brigs, were warily fishing within sight of the very island, Aureed Island, when the enthusiastic newspapermen were working on that illustration.

Strange that of all localities and subjects in the busily expanding south the first illustration should portray an incident from that lonesome Coral Sea!

The ship was the *Charles Eaton,* wrecked on the Great Barrier Reef in August 1834, on a voyage from Sydney to India. Leaving the wreck on rafts, the crew and passengers, excepting five who escaped by boat to Timor, fell into the hands of the Torres Strait Islanders. Only four boys were spared; the rest were clubbed and beheaded. Their skulls were then necklaced round the Great AuGud.

But what a story the newspapermen would have had, had they only known the facts - facts which would not be known until well after the great pearlshell rushes had tamed the Coral Sea! The victims had not been cooked and eaten, only certain parts of them. They had not been killed merely because the islanders hated white strangers, but because they dreaded spirits-ghosts - with a fanatical fear. To the islanders, those castaways on the raft were not human beings, but spirits in human form come down from the skies. And such spirits, they superstitiously believed, could do them deadly harm. The four boys - only two were eventually rescued - were spared because the islanders believed they were reincarnations of dead island boys, and were claimed as such by their "parents".

Yes, the Herald scored a scoop over its pugnacious rivals, but the whole story could not be known for fifty years to come.[14]

Still year by year the little boats sailed to that Coral Sea, with each voyage taking the same risks as those unfortunate ones upon the raft- as did any big ship of the day, should she meet with disaster during the time in which she crept through the Coral Sea on her way from Sydney to China, the Indies, or India.

Such a disaster struck the *Stirling Castle* when she crashed upon the Swain Reefs,[15] a death maze out at sea opposite the Mackay of today. The ship was soon a total wreck, and the survivors took to the longboat and pinnace. Close beside them to the eastward sounded the warning thunder of the rollers upon the Great Barrier. Captain James Fraser knew that nothing layout there beyond the Reef but the vastness of the Pacific. Northward was the Coral Sea, with two thousand miles of savagery all the way to Timor. Captain Fraser ordered the boats to steer southward. Only there lay the nearest civilization upon all this wild coast, Moreton Bay penal settlement. He should make it, with ordinary luck and care, within five hundred miles. But luck was against them.

The pinnace eventually drifted to land at Laguna Bay by Noosa Heads, north of Moreton Bay. Only one of its crew had survived the awful voyage. Of the longboat, now in a sinking condition, the exhausted, starving survivors crawled ashore in a tiny inlet walled by giant trees, overtopped by great sandy ridges upon which towered lofty pines. And from these wild men, fierce-eyed, looking hairy as gorillas to the helpless people, descended upon them.

The castaways had made land, not on the mainland but on what was vaguely believed to be "a Great Sandy Island", ever since known as Fraser Island, not far from Captain James Cook's Indian Head.

The captain's wife, Mrs Fraser, was among the castaways. For some strange reason, she, the captain, Charles Brown, the mate and staunch friend of the captain, and an unfortunate poor devil of a seaman were singled out for particularly savage treatment, though all hands were badly knocked about and in naked misery forced to become slaves to this unusually vicious tribe. It is difficult to imagine the horror and degradation of such a fate. Within a few weeks Captain Fraser was brutally speared to death before his wife's eyes. Charles Brown, the mate, was roasted alive and eaten, according to a survivor's account. So was the seaman. Three others, so physically hurt and weakened that they could no longer stagger along carrying the spears and game of the savages, were speared to death as useless. Of the crew of nineteen originally in the longboat eight half-mad wretches would eventually be rescued.

How the woman endured such horrors without going stark staring mad and jumping into the sea will never be known. She clung to life, often staring out from Indian Head, hopelessly praying for a miracle; twice she saw a *beche-de-mer* lugger like a distant sea-gull sailing past, bound for the Coral Sea, manned by men who knew they had every reason to beat well clear of that Indian Head, favourite look-out of the "Indians". Those white men, passing so swiftly, never dreamt that away up there among those chuckling "Indians" a tortured white woman was gazing out towards them with agony in her eyes.

As a knowledge of their language was quickly forced upon her she realized with broken heart that her husband's course had been right, that the Moreton Bay Settlement of the hated white men was but three days' walk down the mainland coast. Oh, if only they had been able to keep going in that sinking longboat!

The dusky captors taunted her with the knowledge. They were at war with all white men, they declared, white devils who had come to steal their lands. They and all the tribes would rise up and kill them all.

Trudging along with them, heavy-loaded, urged on by the biting firestick jabbed against her trembling legs, the woman forced her heart and mind to cling grimly to the south. White men lived away down there, through that great, unfriendly bush. She yearned for Moreton Bay penal settlement as if there lay Paradise.

Doubtless it was such a mad hope taking full possession of her that made her cling to life.

Then, at first with utterly unbelieving ears she heard them talk of "Wild White Men"! When she did really understand she realized that three escaped convicts were actually living with different tribes just across on the mainland, three white men, now "white natives" accepted by the tribes, and possessing a great influence over them. Occasionally they visited this very island with their tribesmen. Oh, if she could only meet one!

Then she began to realize there would be difficulties balancing life and death. With wits sharpened by her extreme suffering she was comprehending more than they knew. Lying there in the ashes of the campfires, like a dog perishing of exhaustion, she was listening - listening - thinking - thinking!

And a day surely dawned when she met her 'Wild White Man", in a near madness of hope on her side hidden by terror lest she make a false move, a mere sign before all those suspicious, wolfish eyes. Misery and terror and torture had taught her a lot within a very short time.

The white savage was Wandi; not for another seven years would it be known that his "whitefellow name" was Bracefield, an escaped convict from the terrors of Moreton Bay during Commandant Logan's early command. And now, through "his own" tribe, he had been invited across to the island to see the new captives. And he understood full well that any false move on his part would mean death for him as well as them.

No wonder we have but the barest scraps of information as to all that happened. A terror-crazed woman at the mercy of primitives fierce with hate of these occasional white strangers. An escaped convict whose bitterness against his fellow men was voicelessly explained by the weals of the lash upon his back, a hunted man who had gained freedom against frightful odds, who now drew the sweet breath of life only by gift of these same savages of whom now he was willingly and truly one. But what must have been the struggle of his sternly masked feelings to now see a battered white *woman* in this position!

They were nearly three days' march away from the one outpost of civilization, Moreton Bay penal settlement, itself five hundred miles north from Sydney; and in that period there only the barest of Government records were kept. Similarly, throughout the great colony countless most interesting happenings faded into the limbo of forgotten things because no soul present at the time had the knowledge or inclination or materials to jot down a few notes on paper. No wonder then that we have but the barest outline of what happened in this savage setting, of this episode so brimming over with drama and the extremes of fear and doubt, of human hope and terror. Had it not been for the energy and curiosity of Tom Petrie and Stuart Russell, who came upon the scene some five years later, the fate of the survivors of the *Stirling Castle* would long since have been forgotten.

One sunlit morning, far down through the bush on the outskirts of Moreton Bay Settlement a group of soldiers glanced up to stare and listen at sound of a faint, "Coo-ee! Coo-ee!" Presently they saw running towards them a naked black-gin, screaming some gibberish or other - Mrs Fraser, wife of the late Captain Fraser of the ship *Stirling Castle.*

When she was safely within the settlement, and brought before the Commandant, she seems, naturally enough, to have gone to pieces, explaining incoherently that Second Officer Baxter and six or seven seamen were still held captive by the blacks, that a "white savage", an escaped convict, had sneaked her away from the blacks by night, guided her through bush to within sight of the soldiers, and then vanished back into the bush. For long afterwards she easily became hysterical. and confused.

A rescue party set out and, greatly assisted by an escaped convict, Graham, [16] eventually rescued Baxter and his starving mates.

Mrs Fraser was shipped to Sydney and eventually returned to England. There is a record that Stuart Russell, then on holiday in England, saw her at a theatre where she was "starring" as "The White Woman held Captive by Cannibal Savages", though this seems unlikely if, as another record states, she married the captain of the ship on which she returned to England. Strangely enough - or was it naturally, for after all these unfortunate women who had undergone such shocking trials had to make a living on return to civilization - other women who had undergone similar experiences went "on the boards" also, including Barbara Thompson, after her rescue from the Kowraregas tribesmen on Prince of Wales Island in Torres Strait. At the time Mrs Fraser was rescued Barbara Thompson was a young girl in Scotland, soon to start out with her parents on a very great adventure - a voyage to far-away New South Wales, all unaware of the tragedy awaiting her in the loneliness of a Coral Sea.

Mrs Fraser being saved from "Cannibal Savages".

The Augud trophy with the skulls of those that survived the shipwreck of the *Charles Eaton*.

Andrew Petrie in his later years.

11

STILL THE WILD NORTH

MEANWHILE, at the settlement on Moreton Bay, now called Brisbane, the north's farthest outpost of civilization, Governor Gipps, on a visit from Sydney, had met a lively young fellow very fond of "walkabout". This energetic Andrew Petrie, who had a genius for making friends with the wild blacks, had discovered the wonderful bunya-bunya pine forest while on "walkabout" in a locality to be called Kilcoy.

Petrie described how he had found the forest by the bank of a stream just north of a river the blacks called "Maroochidor", which means "the river of swans".

The Governor had just received news that a sample of the cones shipped to London realized as much as £10 a cone - a fabulous price. Petrie explained that the pines were sacred trees, and that at the "Season of the Pines", once every three years, a huge concourse of natives from far and near gathered for the ceremonies of the "Feast of the Pines". The Governor, who had a soft spot for the aborigines, then determined to preserve these strange pines for them if he could. So before he returned to Sydney he ordered the delighted Petrie to organize a party and proceed to the "river of swans", the river of the pines, to make a full report on the trees, the locality, and anything of interest appertaining thereto. Also, to try to find and bring in that escaped convict "Wandi", who some years ago had helped Mrs Fraser to escape from the blacks, and to bring in any other of these "wild white men", if he could. And to make every endeavour to discover the burial spot, if any, of Captain Fraser and all murdered members of the *Stirling Castle* crew.

Petrie was delighted, yes; not so the "wild white men", who knew nothing of his preparations. The news of the abandonment of Moreton Bay as a penal settlement, joyously hailed throughout all the colony, struck terror into the hearts of those secretive denizens of the bush who had fled the settlement and taken refuge with the blacks. Almost all such fugitives had found the death they preferred to the wretchedness of chains and the lash, but these few hardier ones had become as the tribesmen themselves, jealously protected by their wild brothers. As very slowly the news percolated into the wilds these few simply could not believe it; they were certain the story was spread to lure them back to the settlement and the noose. More fearfully still they avoided the fringe of settlement lest they be shot on sight. The exception was one Baker, known as Boralchow to the blacks with whom he had lived for some years past in the Ipswich district. As a guide, he helped Gilbert Eliott find a route for drays from the Downs to the coast.[17]

Andrew Petrie, by his own capabilities, enhanced by one of those strange coincidences which seem inseparable from life, was the ideal man to seek the last tragic relics of the *Stirling Castle*. As a young fellow he had sailed in her to Sydney. By lucky chance he decided to stay ashore and seek a job, later to thank his lucky stars he had not sailed farther north in the doomed ship. Eventually he got the job he sought, in the Brisbane to be, as Superintendent of Works, and sailed for Brisbane in the first steamship to sail Queensland waters, the James Watt. Yes, the colony was progressing by leaps and bounds, and now the Steam Age came panting and puffing into the north.

Petrie and his party set out for what lay before them in a rowing boat loaded almost down to the gunwale with stores; friends doubtfully watching expected her to sink any moment. But the Argonauts set sail, an enthusiastic crew of eleven. It was the adventure of their lives to two young new-chums, Stuart Russell and Joliffe. That trip of Petrie and Russell is a book in itself, packed with romance and adventure, surely known at least to all Queenslanders.

However, the two men were the first to prove definitely that Great Sandy Cape was really an island, the largest "sandhill" island in the world-Fraser Island. And there they did find Wandi, "whitefellow name" Bracefield, with his mob of blacks, as black as they, as distrustful of the whites as they, he who had guided the distraught white woman castaway to the penal settlement seven years before. He had done so at peril of his life from his black friends, too, for they regarded such a deed as the deed of a traitor. Only with his white man's brain added to all his "blackfellow" skill had he been able to get her safely away to a good start and just elude the pursuit. It was some time before the wild man could tell his halting story coherently, for by now he had almost forgotten his native tongue. She had implored him to rescue her, she had cried, she had softened his fears by promises of the great things she could and would do for him, she, Captain Fraser's wife, in dire distress and at peril of her very life; the Commandant would surely pardon him, recommend to the Governor in Sydney Town a free pardon for him, a free grant of land! She was so crazy, she promised so wildly he had to shut her up lest she scream entreaties and bring enemies upon them. In terror of what they might do to him if once again they got their iron hands upon him, in fear of his native friends, reluctantly at last he had consented. Whichever way he turned, he knew he must burn his boats.

They just made it - that wild run night and day through the bush, the woman apparently beyond exhaustion, enduring everything in the extremity of her hope and terror. When they were near the settlement, every step forward increasing his fear, he had halted and asked her to repeat her promises. But she turned on him and threatened she would complain of him, she would denounce him.

Poor woman, feeling now with every step nearer and nearer to safety, her heart must have stopped beating when this white savage halted and demanded again to hear her wild promises! She did the very worst thing she could do in threatening him, but she must have been nearly crazy then.

However, they stared at one another a long, long time. Then silently he walked on. Presently he pointed out to her the very fringe of the settlement, that Heaven to her, that Horror to him. She had screamed and raced down towards the soldiers. He wheeled round and vanished silently back into the bush.[18]

It took Petrie and Russell patience and time to convince the white savage that this country now was for free settlers, that the chain-gang and the lash had really gone for ever. Eventually he consented to travel with them. At Brown's Point, so called because it was said that here Brown, the mate of the Stirling Castle, had been roasted, Bracefield pointed out an aboriginal friend who knew of a large river some distance away. Thus the Mary River was discovered by white men, and large tracts of valuable land which would presently lead to the settlement of the rich Maryborough lands. If the shades of "Wandi" and "Durramboi" could see Maryborough now!

Bracefield led the party to yet another tribe, a headman of whom was Durramboi, another escapee who had almost forgotten that his name had been James Davis. As a lad in Glasgow he had been sentenced to transportation at thirteen years of age; he had eventually escaped and now lived with the blacks these seventeen years past.

"I shall never forget his appearance when he arrived at our camp," writes Petrie in his reminiscences. "A white man in a state of nudity and actually a wild man of the woods, his eyes wild and unable to rest a moment on anyone object, he had quite the same manners and gestures that the wildest blacks have got."

As with Bracefield, Durramboi's first sentence when finally he could mutter a little English was a fearful inquiry as to the penal settlement. He took even longer than Bracefield to believe the penal settlement was a horror of the past; it was longer still before he could be persuaded to join the party.

Here, as elsewhere, the "wild white men" who had lived with the aborigines for any length of time became very attached to their primitive companions.

Thus at this period (1842-4) settlement north of Sydney was barely past the fringes of Brisbane and the Downs. Though the first steamship had anchored in Moreton Bay, all lands north for 1400 miles to the tip of Cape York Peninsula was still unexplored bush. Still the trepang fishers fished alone, unknown to the world, during eight months of the year hearing nothing of the world, with the rare exception that one might be fishing in the course of some passing ship that, momentarily becalmed, gave them a chance to board her eager for talk with their fellow-men. But they began to notice now that with each passing season an increase in the occasional ships beating in from the open Pacific to negotiate some dangerous passage through the Great Barrier, to cautiously sail on round Cape York Peninsula, through the Strait, then thankfully spread full sail in the Arafura, bound for the Indies. Often the lone fishers' gaze would tum to that dark line of mainland, often they would speculate on what manner of wild men lived deep "away in there", what strange animals, almost certainly fearsome reptiles. They already feared, when seeking fresh water, the man-eating crocodile lurking by the river mouths, and wondered if there might be lions and tigers and beasts still more fearsome in those thousands of miles of unknown land stretching to the farthest west.

Piercing cries, one in particular to make the blood curdle, and eerie sounds might be heard on nights when weather or distress forced some lonely little vessel to anchor close inshore anywhere along that dangerous coastline. Particularly within those dark river mouths the fearsome sounds of water and land creatures would cause a man's hair to stand on end. No man yet knew what lay deep within that country.

But constant activity in working and loading their vessels, in bartering for and managing this primitive native labour while guarding their own lives, occupied most of their thoughts. For very good reason, as this known instance will show. Three cutters were fishing in company one gusty afternoon, the sun breaking through low clouds to fill the empty sea with brilliance in which grim Adolphus Island stood out as though carved from living rock. Just farther south the grassy sheen upon the bare hills of Albany Island showed clearly against the dark green of scrub-clad ridges on the Cape York Peninsula mainland. Then the sunlight was drowned by flying cloud as a cold, misty squall came flying across the sea. So it had been on and off all day, but this was a larger squall that came whistling to smother boats and sea and all thereon. And out of this haze burst great war-canoes, alive with befeathered warriors shrieking, "Lamars! Lamars!" as they raced down upon the startled boat-crews. An instant of paralysed horror, then the aboriginal helpers dived under water as the whites frantically snatched up muskets. With an animal roar of voices the canoes were upon them; only an isolated musket-shot replied as brown warriors leapt down upon them, smashing with clubs in a maniacal fury. It was over in moments, and the opei knives were whipped out as the snarling warriors in packs fought to hack heads. Canoes and boats rocking on the waves, headless bodies in grotesque attitudes, triumphant warriors holding aloft in shrieking triumph their gory trophies. A mad scramble then for loot, savage wrestling for precious iron, the smashing of muskets to seize the iron barrel, exultant howl at finding of a sheath-knife, mad struggles for possession of an occasional tomahawk, bitter fights over rusty nails. In such small boats, swarming with panting men, the smallest piece of iron was seen within moments as everything movable was smashed. The squall passed on, and in the brilliant sunlight a warrior spotted a black dot upon the surface towards the mainland coast. As the dot disappeared the warrior yelled and pointed, and on the instant, with exultant yells, they were leaping back into the canoes and paddling with amazing speed towards the mainland.

That black dot was the head of an aboriginal crew boy, gasping to fill his lungs with air, then sink and swim under water for his life to put distance between the canoes and himself while the sheltering squall should last.

Alas, it had so swiftly come and gone! Other heads here and there bobbed up for a breath of despair as they broke surface into sunlight. None knew better than they the eagle eyes of the headhunters.

A yell from the leading canoe as their look-out spotted a black head, then each canoe was chasing heads to the accompaniment of exultant laughter, speeding on where the head had vanished to peer down into the clear green water and spy the under-water swimmer. Beautiful each ebony-black body looked in its powerful action down there, speeding with bursting lungs in its hopeless race against death. On the fighting platform of each big canoe stood two bronze warriors, they had thrown off their headdress and ornaments. They had wonderful physique, these brown Torres Strait headhunters, chests and shoulders magnificently developed by their seafaring life, sturdy legs surprisingly different to the thin shanks of the aborigines. They spied their prey and were overboard like streaks of bronze, all graceful beauty swiftly gliding down above, then beside, their agonized prey. Screams of laughter from all the warriors peering down as the frantic prey twisted and turned in a hopeless attempt to evade the grasping hands, knowing he was doomed to die yet fighting while life was left. More howls above as he squirmed and lashed out to defeat a hand snatching at that most sensitive part of man. Then, when he felt the agonizing clutch, he reared over to sink his teeth into a death grip with his tormentor and drag him deep below. But the other islander had his claws in his hair and was dragging him upward, while the grip between his thrashing legs was driving him mad as he sped to the surface. At the great gasp from his roaring throat the men in the canoes screamed with delight, as his legs whipped round his tormentor in a crazed attempt to crush his ribs to pulp. A warrior leapt overboard with the opei knife, and the tormented wretch was made to "dance" in that thrashing water as the knife whipped round his throat and neck.

Exultant yells from the other canoes told that they, too, were enjoying similar sport. They won sixteen heads in this playful chase, besides the highly prized Lamar heads back in the boats. What a wonderful day's sport!

Gaily shouting sundry pleasantries of the chase to one another, they paddled back to the drifting boats, threw everything of value into the canoes, set fire to the vessels, and swiftly sailed north, leaving the pyres drifting towards the sunset, with the sweet, full-throated island canoe song for requiem as the breeze died with sunset and the paddles were whipped out.

They were heavy-loaded with turtle and dugong meat, but now what a triumphant homecoming would be theirs, with seven Lamar heads and sixteen of the savages to hang round the neck of the Great Au-Gud in the Zogo House.

Lamars - these dread beings in human form from the World Beyond Death!

How amazed the early white adventurers would have been, had they known of this belief, so implicitly believed that for a long time yet it was to play its part in the developing clash between white, brown, and black! Few of us realize the many factors, varied and strange which all played their part in the opening up of our continent and the seas that wash our shore.

12

THE PATRIARCHS MOVE BY LAND, THE EXPLORERS BY SEA

THE fate of the *Stirling Castle,* when eventually known in Sydney, and months later in London, caused uneasiness among shipping men. Too many fine ships had been wrecked in those dangerous waters, while still others, sailing on into the unknown north, had simply vanished -"presumed lost".

Could not something be done about it?

Men of vision also now realized that this continent was steadily "growing". Not only so, but there was a "new" people being bred here, a thing quite unthought of in the early years of settlement. A few men even began to wonder whether a new nation was in the making. Whether or no, a generation of the lusty native born had grown up, while increasingly ship-loads of emigrants were sailing out from the old country. Inevitably shipping, trade, and commerce must grow with the development of these vast lands, a trade that increasingly would wish to sail north round this continent to the Dutch Indies, to China, then to India and home, thus tapping rich Eastern markets, gathering yet more trade.

And trade has kept the world alert and busy ever since the days of the venturesome Phoenician merchant-mariners, since the building up of Tyre and Sidon, of Baghdad and Babylon, since the days of lusty King Solomon, of Cleopatra, of the trading cities of Greece and Rome. Those old merchant princes and their seamen adventurers have long since vanished into dust, the stones of many a trade-built city have crumbled into the sands of the desert. But trade itself never dies.

So now a few far-sighted men clearly saw the weaving of a net round this last continent. Surely then, something could be, *must* be done about this mysterious northern sea!

And a day came[19] that the sunburnt crews of two little *beche-de-mer* brigs fishing off Cape York Peninsula stared southward in growing incredulity. For there, looming up under a lazy sou'easter, appeared no less than *three* ships, sailing in company - a beautiful picture under the bluest of skies upon the bluest of seas towards the end of the sou-east season, sunlight glinting from billowing sails snowy as a sea-gull's breast. As plainer grew the foam boiling from the lazily rising bows so grew the amazement of these lonely trepang fishers.

Men-o-war! No doubting *that* rig!

With a shout from brig to brig they voiced their concern and wonderment. Had the Frenchies come to bombard Sydney? Or was it the Rooshians? Were these ships coming to meet an enemy sailing down through this back door of Australia?

They marvelled thus as the three ships sailed past to anchor off near-by Mount Adolphus Island, to the intense curiosity of the natives gaping down from the scrubby hills.

The ships were H.M.S. *Alligator,* Captain Bremer, with a detachment of Marines under Captain J. McArthur, the brig *Britomart* under Lieutenant Owen Stanley, and the transport *Orontes* with troops. Their mission was to sail through Torres Strait and re-annex Port Essington on the far Northern Australian coast, to immediately erect barracks and fortifications and hold that coast against any enemies that might come. For rumour had reached London that a French Expedition was fitting out in Toulon to take possession of part of the unoccupied Northern Australian coast. As if to make sure the squadron would have no idle time on its hands, an added duty was to encourage the "expected" trade with the "adjacent" islands of the Dutch East Indies. Above all, they were to hold that northern coast, three thousand unexplored miles of it - a real man's job that, for three very small ships.

No such thing as a foreign landing must be allowed, of course, for this so recently despised "colony" now showed signs of amazing value, what with this remarkable wool they were growing, and one thing and another.

To the intense interest of the *beche-de-mer* fishers and crowds of sight-seeing natives, the men-o-war cautiously nosed their way along those risky channels among the Prince of Wales Group for several days, there also watched with avid curiosity "Indians" from the wooded hills. The ships' companies, the "sojers" gazing at the strange scenes from the bulwarks, might not have felt very happy had they known those "Indians" were waiting and wishing with all their might for one of the Lamar "war-canoes" to strike a reef and stay helplessly there. What untold loot would then be theirs!

But an amazing luck hovered over the ships, or else superb navigation preserved them from the amazing risks they ran. For within a few days, majestically the three ships sailed through Cook's Endeavour Strait on their remaining seven hundred odd miles west to Port Essington.

What would the feelings of those aboard be when finally their ships would anchor in that port? Just a bay, surrounded by the wildest bush, with the nearest white habitation, Moreton Bay, nearly two thousand miles away as the crow would fly. But while they were cruising in the Strait, what a sight it would have been for both islanders and trepang fishers had the fighting ships caught "Frenchie" or "Rooshian" ships hiding among those islands!

These nations had been at one another's throats for a very long time, asking nothing better than to hurl ironmongery at one another on sight. What a rattling little scrap they could have staged among those tricky waterways, those hide-and-seek islands! And what magnificent loot of burning wrecks would have fallen to. the terrified islanders when they crept from their hide-outs after the thunder of the guns had rumbled away, and the surviving ships withdrawn to lick their wounds! Fortunately, it was not to be, and the expedition sailed on to the miserable existence of that fever-stricken[20] spot called Port Essington.

Strangely enough, shortly afterwards - and you can imagine the consternation - they learnt of the presence of two French vessels anchored under the French flag near by. These were the corvettes *Astrolabe* and *Zelie* under Commodore Dumont d'Urville, whose voyage was to prove famous in the annals of scientific discovery and exploration. So there were no fireworks. Much better, indeed, the leaders of both parties were soon dining together on friendly terms, probably exchanging a risky joke or two under the stars, within sound of the bull crocodiles coughing their love-grunts under the black shadows of the mangroves at the water's edge.

That meeting of the two rival nations in the extreme, unexplored north calls to mind the meeting years before in the extreme south, when another famous French navigator, La Perouse sailed into Botany Bay just as Governor Phillip was sailing out with the First Fleet for Port Jackson, to form Sydney village. Both in the south and the north, we very nearly had French fathers!

The following year, 1839, was to be a great year for that untamed northern continent. When the news came that the penal settlement at Moreton Bay was to be abandoned, rumour spread like wildfire that this was the beginning of the end of transportation to this colony of New South Wales.

A certain Patrick Leslie, a settler of the tough breed who already had pushed out to the wilds of the Cassilis district, decided to risk all on a big venture. He had been trying to find a track over the tangle of the New England ranges down to the Big River, along the jungle-clad banks of which the Wilsons had now found wonderful land. But when this Moreton Bay whisper came he decided to risk everything and trek north to rediscover this Darling Downs paradise of the old botanist-explorer, Allan Cunningham. He was determined to get there. Then if, when he succeeded, Moreton Bay was not thrown open to let produce out and supplies in by sea, it would be just too bad.

A dogged personality, but a thorough, was Patrick Leslie. Once determined, he planned ahead, organizing his resources step by step. When all was ready, an Australian Abraham with all his flocks, he moved out into the wilderness.

A dogged personality, but a thorough, was Patrick Leslie. Once determined, he planned ahead, organizing his resources step by step. When all was ready, an Australian Abraham with all his flocks, he moved out into the wilderness. For those days, this dour patriarch had already amassed a goodly flock. In steady, methodical, bushman-like precision he moved off from the camp, droving 4000 breeding ewes in Iamb (they would drop their lambs on the march and thus his flock would be increased, even while toiling towards his objective), 100 ewe hoggets, 1000 wether hoggets, 100 rams (nothing to prevent the flock breeding on the way and thus increasing again), and 500 wethers. There were two well-loaded wagons, each drawn by twelve bullocks, two strong drays with their horse teams, ten sturdy saddle horses, well-trained dogs, and, as helping hands, twenty-four ticket-of-leave men. And of these Patrick Leslie often afterward said, "As good and game a lot of men as ever existed."

Leslie found Cunningham's "paradise" in due course, and then came the one puzzle he had not foreseen-to make his choice of land from the bewildering richness of this far-flung vista of a settler's dream.

His choice finally was a magnificent stretch of country from Toolburra to the headwaters of the Condamine. And soon the chimney smoke of the first settler's hut in the famous Darling Downs of Queensland was warmly rising into a welcoming blue sky. Leslie's young wife was to be the first white woman to see and greet the overlanders soon following along their tracks, to see them emerging from the bush, as Cunningham twenty years before had come, to rein in and gaze in awe upon the Promised Land. Next time when you are spinning along in your cosy car at sixty miles an hour on the good coastal road, or over the pleasant New England Tableland, just gaze a moment across that sea of ranges. Then try to imagine that country in Cunningham's and Leslie's day, when there were no roads, let alone towns, no stations or farms, when all that cleared country was dense timber, not a bridge over those turbulent rivers and creeks, not a sign-post, not a track excepting here and there that of the wild aboriginal. Shut your eyes a moment and imagine vast distances of ranges and gorges, rivers and plains ahead, over which you hear the murmurous waves of a sea - the wind sweeping up a gorge to sigh out over the range, swaying the sea of tree-tops of unknown miles of virgin forest.

Thus you may glimpse some faint picture of what the Leslies of Australia's pioneering days set out into with their horses, their flocks and drays, their hopes - and, if they were lucky, with their women trudging beside them.

Leslie's tracks were soon followed by Hodgson and Elliott, King and Sibley. When in 1840 Moreton Bay was actually to be abandoned, and the district thrown open for settlement, overlanders were already toiling through the bush to the Downs; their names were to become household words in the pioneering of Queensland's vast unexplored lands.

But this new land was a continent in area, and the population was measured only in thousands. It would be yet another ten years before the north-bound march of development pushed past Moreton Bay. But came a surprise by sea. For from that energetic Port of Sydney again came bravely sailing, in full panoply, a "man-o-war".

A picked crew, all keen on their job, were expecting an unusually interesting voyage, spiced with high adventure. They were to get both, and a bit more than they bargained for. Yes, they were well fitted out, scientifically equipped for those days, sailing on past Moreton Bay and on into the Coral Sea, guns all ready for action if need be. The object of the cruise was a surveying voyage along the unknown northern coast, as far as the ship could make it, and particularly to define a safe route, if possible, for the increase of shipping through an inner route within the treacherous Coral Sea.

So came the "Mighty Atom", H.M.S. *Beagle*, a tiny stickybeak of a vessel which for the next three years[21] was to poke around thousands of miles of the continent's unsurveyed coastline, sailing completely round the coast in the course of the job, only to return again to nose into the most dangerous out-of-the-way places. She was to do a mighty job, out of all proportion to the size of the crew and vessel, a job that would not only tell the southern folk of thousands of miles of coastline and vast areas of new country but would also save many a future vessel from leaving its bones within the Coral Sea.
Her commander was Captain John Clements Wickham, a first-class sailorman with a love of exploration growing into a love of this strange new country which he was going to cherish all his life. Second in command Captain J. Lort Stokes (he would discover Port Darwin) as keen a sailorman-explorer as Wickham. The complete crew made a wonderful team; otherwise, of course, they never could have accomplished the work they did.

Both Wickham and Stokes were wounded by the spears of the blacks in the course of their explorations. When Wickham had eventually to be invalided at the end of the first cruise, it was Stokes who took over and completed the job. Exploring the great Gulf of Carpentaria, he found many new rivers along the coast and ascended some in small boats fifty miles inland, in the almost feverish hope that he might find some river deep enough to sail the *Beagle* and thus discover what "might be within the mysterious heart of this continent". His parties even walked inland when the boat was blocked by river bars - what risks they took! Thus, one day, they penetrated inland from the Albert to gaze out over vast plains: He named them the "Plains of Promise".[22] He wrote in his journal that ere long the now monotonous horizon would be broken by a succession of tapering spires rising from the many Christian hamlets that must ultimately stud this country. "Alas, to speculation alone was I reduced. All I could do was to give one lingering look to the southward before I returned to the ship."

Thus the little vessel sailed on, the tireless crew charting the coastline and discovering vast new areas which we today call the Northern Territory, for three thousand miles, seen only by the wondering aborigines, and once by a fleet of suspicious Malay proas fishing for trepang along this "no man's" coastline.

As with numerous other episodes that went to the opening up of the Coral Sea and far northern coast, half a dozen books could be written of the work of the *Beagle* alone.

Thus, for nearly three seasons, just now and again, the little *Beagle* became almost a familiar sight to the sea-slug fishers as steadily she and her boats' crews did their wonderful survey job through and away past this dangerous sea they had now come to know so well. The little *Beagle's* charts would soon make that perilous "Inner Passage", nearly one thousand miles long, between mainland coast and Great Barrier Reef, incomparably safer for the ships now being increasingly sighted by the lone toilers of the sea.

And, just about the time those charts were being printed, tiny Brisbane, coming alive now under the influx of free settlers, gladly saw her last Commandant replaced by Captain Wickham, R.N., recently of the *Beagle* and now first Police Magistrate and Government Resident of Brisbane, an understanding man with his sympathy all for this country. And transportation was finished. At last, all was well for the north. And there was a change, too, for those distant Isles of New Zealand, from which there came to Sydney vague, uneasy rumours of Maori warriors threatening a war. In 1841 New Zealand was proclaimed as a separate, a Crown colony.

13

AND A TOWER IS BUILT

BUT now[23] something startling was happening to enliven the loneliness of the trepang fishers. It was first sighted by the amazed crew of the *Nellie Bly,* gliding like a sea-gull over the deep blue waters lapping the lovely Hinchinbrook Isles. For there, her reflection beautifully mirrored, a ship lay at anchor. Or was it a picture motionless upon azure blue reflecting sunlight, framed by soft green of hills of wooded islets a stone's throw beside her, background of dark green of jungle range towering over the lonely lands of Innisfail as yet unborn?

On such a morning on those waters by Moarilyan a bird high in the sky, a fish in those transparent depths, glide like jewels of sky and sea. A laugh can ring from isle to isle, and you smile at the trill of content.

And on such a morning the *Nellie Bly,* gliding north among those isles, suddenly came full upon the picture of the man-o-war. It was H.M.S. *Fly,* commanded by Captain Blackwood, a capable mariner with his heart in his job. A wonderful job-to follow on in the wake of Cook and Flinders, King, Wickham, and Stokes, and to add to their good work; to carry on with the increasingly urgent job of surveying a safe sea-lane along this wild coast, to link up such a course with the few known passage-ways from the Pacific eastward, through the Great Barrier Reef, those passage-ways which offered a ship entry from the Pacific Ocean, through the Great Barrier Reef, into this Coral Sea. For with the surprising expansion of those distant colonies more and more ships were sailing northward from

Sydney, seeking the short cut through Torres Strait to India, the Indies, and China. And more and more ships were being lost in the perilous waters encompassed within that great Barrier Reef and the unexplored coastline north of Moreton Bay.

To this even the tiny vessels of the sea-slug fishers could bear grim witness. But as the *Nellie Bly*, last away from Sydney and in a hurry to rejoin her mates, sailed on, her wondering crew wondered still more as in Rockingham Bay they saw a tender, the schooner *Bramble*, and sailing towards her a busy little pinnace, the *Midge*. Three vessels in company, and obviously naval, obviously in working trim, too. The crew of the *Nellie Bly* would have great news to tell their mates, already cautiously fishing near those savage isles some hundreds of miles farther north.

For another two seasons to come a lonely *beche-de-mer* vessel here and there would catch a glimpse of the three vessels-and, on the second cruise, of the revenue cutter *Prince George* - as they did that wonderful survey job right up along the coast, then across Torres Strait to New Guinea shores. The charts they made were to save many a ship, but the details of their experiences would long since have been lost in the dusty records of the Admiralty Office, had it not been for the naturalist, J. Beete Jukes, who set them down in his Narrative of the Surveying Voyage of H.M.S *Fly*.

One particular job was to erect a guiding beacon on Raine Islet, away out on the Great Barrier Reef. To the amazed sea-slug fishers. this was an undreamt-of development, the erection of a signpost upon their wilderness of waters.

Raine Islet lies opposite the northern end of the Cape York Peninsula,[23] and near it is a clear passage through the Reef. The beacon would mean that ships voyaging from the far south could sail northward in safety in the deep Pacific for a thousand miles outside that grim wall of the Great Barrier Reef. Then, as they drew near the northern end, that beacon could be seen from a masthead many miles away. The ship would change course towards the beacon, as you would pull the guiding rein of your horse when turning from the open road into a dark, dangerously narrow lane.[24] Expert seamanship was needed now, and prayers that the wind would hold right, that she did not miss stays, that treacherous current and tide would be safely allowed for and guarded against as all hands most anxiously sailed the ship through the narrow passage-way that actually is the jaws of death to any ship that makes false move. Nay, the most conscientious captain, the most willing crew might suddenly be struck helpless. For in those days of sail it needed but the change of wind, a veering, a sudden puff, or failure of the wind at a critical moment, then instantly the current would sway the ship - "Crash!" But, once through, every soul aboard would sigh with relief as the Great Barrier was left astern and the ship safely glided on into the Coral Sea. Plenty of perils ahead, of course, of shallows, of sandbanks and lesser reefs. But with a sharp look-out from the masthead, constant swinging of the lead at the bows, and alert seamanship, the good ship would round Cape York Peninsula, sail through Cook's Endeavour Strait, and then the tension would ease at last with a smile on every face as she dipped her bows into the Arafura.

Away eastward out of sight of land, a dismal place is Raine Islet, lonely plaything of the winds and sea. The deafening clamour of countless sea-birds that nest upon every inch of its space make it yet wilder with their piercing shrieks and cries. Upon that waste of waters it stands but a thousand yards long, a few feet above high tide. A tough, unlovely shrubbery fights for life from its coarse sandstone and pebbles and dead corals.

Upon this dismal bastion the three busy ships' companies began to build a beacon which in that wide waste would be visible by day to any anxious ship approaching from many miles away out in the open Pacific.

Those old-time sailormen built to last, mainly from primitive materials to hand. That beacon tower still stood as late as my day, a lifetime later; it had defied the sea, winds, storms, and cyclones, a titanic test indeed. It was designed by the *Fly's* carpenter, Moore - a circular stone tower forty feet high, thirty feet diameter at the base, five feet thick, quarried from stone on the islet. A wooden dome was built upon it, covered by painted canvas, and this raised the height of the tower to seventy feet above low-water mark. There were three stories inside the tower, connected by stout ladders. A tank taken from a wreck was built in by the base; pipes led from the roof so that the tank would fill with the first rain, thus precious water would be available for shipwrecked people. Pumpkins, corn, and other vegetable seeds were planted in a "garden". Yes, a good, solid, lasting job.

Come to the scene a moment with the naturalist himself, he can show you a scene upon the Great Reef far better than I can:

... I spent a night on the wreck of the Martha Ridgway *.... We had a heavy pull of a couple of hours, dead to windward. . . .* [the wreck] *lay with her bow to the sea on her starboard bilge. She was still pretty perfect above, her deck, forecastle, and poop, and even the bulkheads of the cabins remaining. The foremast was still standing, but the tide flowed in and out of her below .... The reef was about a quarter of a mile wide, and ran nearly due N. and S. for several miles. It appeared indeed to stretch to the horizon in several directions, the breaks in its continuity being so*

narrow as to be barely perceptible. A fresh breeze was blowing from the S.E., and rather a heavy sea running outside. The water was perfectly clear, and of great and almost unfathomable depth right up to the outer slope or submarine wall of the reef.[25] *The long ocean swell being suddenly impeded by this barrier, lifted itself in one great continuous ridge of deep blue water, which, curling over, fell on the edge of the reef in an unbroken cataract of dazzling white foam. Each line of breaker was often one or two miles in length, with not a perceptible gap in its continuity. After recovering from this leap, and spreading for some distance in a broad sheet of foam, the wave gradually swelled again into another furious breaker of almost equal height and extent with the first, and then into a third, which, although much less considerable, yet thundered against the bows of the wreck with a strength that often made her every timber quiver. Even then the force of the swell was not wholly expended, two or three heavy lines of ripples continually traversing the reef and breaking against those knobs and blocks of coral, that rose higher than usual. There was a simple grandeur and display of power and beauty in this scene as viewed from the forecastle of the wreck (about thirty feet above the water), that rose even to sublimity. The unbroken roar of the surf, with its regular pulsation of thunder, as each succeeding swell first fell on the outer edge of the reef, was almost deafening, yet so deep-toned as not to interfere with the slightest nearer and sharper sound, or oblige us to raise our voices in the least. Both the sound and the sight were such as to impress the mind of the spectator with the consciousness of standing in the presence of an overwhelming majesty and power, while his senses were delighted by the contrast of beautiful colours afforded by the deep blue of the ocean, the dazzling white of the surf, and the bright green of the shoal water on the reef ... this had a bright grass-green hue when viewed from a distance, and when looking down at it from the poop of the wreck might have been likened to a great submarine cabbage garden.*

Before it got dark we had righted the old coppers of the ship, which were lying on the deck, in order to cook the men's suppers. After a little trouble we rigged a table in the cuddy with some of the bulk-heads, and established ourselves for the night. ... As I was walking the poop of the wreck before looking out for a "soft plank" to sleep on, I could not help being struck with the wildness and singular nature of the scene. A bright fire was blazing cheerfully in the galley forward, lighting up the spectral looking foremast with its bleached and broken rigging and the fragments of spars lying about it. A few of our men were crouched in their flannel jackets under the weather-bulwarks, as a protection from the spray which every now and then flew over us. The wind was blowing strongly, drifting a few dark clouds occasionally over the star-lit sky, and howling round the wreck with a shrill tone that made itself heard above the dull continuous roar of the surf. Just ahead of us was the broad white band of foam which stretched away on either hand into the dark horizon. Now and then some higher wave than usual would burst against the bows of the wreck, shaking all her timbers, sending a spout of spray over the forecastle, and travelling along her sides would lash the rudder backwards and forwards with a slow creaking groan as if the old ship was complaining of the protracted agony she endured. . . there mingled perhaps some speculations as to our chance of leaving the old Fly *in some similar situation with the highly-wrought feelings which the mere character and aspect of the scene sufficed to impress upon the mind. The place was so far removed from civilized life, and so far even from any dry land ... the reef, also, upon which she stood, was one of nature's mysteries, its origin equally wonderful and obscure, its extent so vast, and its accompaniments so simple, so grand, and appropriate; - altogether, I shall not easily forget my night-walk on the weather-beaten poop of the wreck of the* Martha Ridgway.[26]

The *Martha Ridgeway.*

14

TOWARDS THE PENINSULA AT LAST

THAT lonely tower built upon the sea fresh in their minds, the trepang fishers, scudding back to Sydney with holds loaded with *beche-de-mer*, found other exciting news to talk about. For that much discussed explorer Leichhardt, long since given up as lost, had returned. Battling his way overland, he had actually reached the base of that mysterious Cape York Peninsula, the land that for years past they had wondered so much about. Turning west when Gilbert was speared to death, struggling doggedly along with Calvert and Roper wounded, he had reached the shores of that Great Gulf of Carpentaria where, they knew uneasily now, those piratical Malay proas came occasionally, seeking trepang. Captains Wickham and Stokes, too, had explored there, they knew from the *Beagle's* sailormen. And now Leichhardt by land had pushed west from the Gulf, he might even have crossed Captain Stokes's "Plains of Promise", which they had heard so much talk of along Sydney's waterfront. He had ridden on far into the westward, discovering a great vista of strange new lands. Eagerly indeed was this news discussed in the Australia of that day.[27] They of the sea-slug ships, however, wished the explorer had carried on for the remaining three hundred miles of that unknown Peninsula, and discovered the mysteries inland along the east coast opposite which they fished, instead of turning away to the hazy west.

A cheerful Christmas over, then several months later the little vessels sailed north again, carefully outfitted for the new season. In company, too-the barque *Peruvian* in full sail on her voyage to China.[28] A touch of boisterous weather came, the little boats hugged the coast, the *Peruvian* glided on into the mists, never to be seen again. Nor heard of for another seventeen years, not until the settlers had crept as far north as the Burdekin.

Then one morning a settler, opening his hut door, stepped back alarmed as a strange voice shouted, "What cheer, mates!"

"Bring the guns!" called the settler over his shoulder. "There's a wild blackfellow up on the fence!"

"Don't shoot, mates! I'm a British subject!" shouted the figure wildly.

For hours and hours the wild white man had hidden in the bush, scrubbing himself over and over again with sand and water, trying to wash his smoke-burnt, sun-tanned hide as near white as possible, muttering feverishly for hours on end, trying to muster together bits and pieces of his forgotten language. For the greatest event, the greatest ordeal of his life lay before him, and a mistake might well mean a bullet.

This trembling relic was the lone survivor of the *Peruvian*, wrecked seventeen years before. An Essex lad, James Murrell, usually known later as Jimmy Morrill, he shipped before the mast at the age of sixteen, seeking adventure. He got it.

Parting company with the trepang fishers so many years ago, the *Peruvian* had sailed on into a hurricane. When well past Brisbane, opposite where the city of Townsville stands now, she sailed bows on into a reef. Masts crashing, sails thundering down, she was a total wreck within minutes of fearful confusion. Both mates were washed overboard when struggling to lower boats. The damage done, the storm quickly subsided. The sun shone out strongly, the great waves flattened to a long, oily swell.

Captain Pitkethly, though an able man, was tragically unfortunate. He kept his head; he had to, with women and children aboard a wreck, his own wife among them. He set all hands to constructing a raft, a job that held together for forty-two days - such days, such awful nights.

Tragically, before they could fully provision the raft, a giant swell came rolling, lifting high the raft as the hawser ropes tautened, then snapped, and the raft was wallowing adrift from the wreck. Rising and falling to a merciless swell, those crouching aboard heard -felt- the spars and casks under them lingeringly groaning, shuddering, sighing, as the knotted lashings strained to hold together against the rolling might of the sea.

Those aboard then made a breathless compact, while they were still in their full senses. With the sun now beating down fiercely, with the sea-gulls' call forlorn in their ears, they whisperingly promised that if death must come, no matter how it came, not one soul aboard would eat meat from the body of another! Grim? Yes. And that frightful promise must have strained the hearts of the women, put startled fear into the eyes of the children. But in the long roll-call of ships that have vanished in that Coral Sea grim things - grimmer things - have happened.

Tide and currents carried them towards a misty blur that grew into the wooded hills, then the beaches of the mainland coast. Wild men prowled there, they knew, but they prayed at least to land. Again and again tide and current hauled them back, to carry them forward again, to slowly die down when they could plainly see the very trunks of the trees ashore, then fiercely drag them back. For one terrible month, under blazing skies and through chilly nights, they crouched and lay and prayed in misery upon those rough spars, feeling them moving to the restless water, ever striving to wrench those lashings apart. Came hunger, pitiless thirst, then a benumbing hopelessness. One by one they died, and were gently lifted overboard.

After forty-two days the raft grounded on a beach by Cape Cleveland, and seven poor wretches crawled ashore. Wilmot and Gooley just managed to reach the shade of trees near high-water mark. In that shade, which must have felt as the breath of heaven, they stretched lingeringly out, to die at last in peace. Another went seeking food, and perished. Four were left, among them was the captain's wife. And she was the first to see the wild men coming.

This aboriginal tribe gave the sick castaways very good treatment, far different to the torture and slaughter meted out to Mrs Fraser and the castaways of the *Stirling Castle.* These natives fed the stricken people, then took all their clothes from them, clothes being things to be puzzled over and laughed at and fought for. In the days following they sent word to surrounding tribes to come see these fantastically strange white people - for a price! Thus they were jealously exhibited, just as our showmen would stage a sideshow if they could only grab one of those flying-saucer men from Mars. The captain's wife was the star of the show, the wild women mauling her with guttural expressions of curiosity to prove she was in every way a woman, so strangely like themselves. But some tribesmen ran from the exhibits in fearful alarm, refusing to believe them human, believing these strange white people were spirits, reincarnations of dead people - practically the same belief as that of the Torres Strait Islanders far to the north.

When all the curious ones from "outside'; had traded in their few precious possessions to the lucky tribe and the excitement died down, the castaways had to settle down to live as the tribe lived, or die. Their one lingering hope lay in a glimpse of the coast, to look for a sail that would never come.

The boy Wilson had been very sick on the raft, yet under these frightful conditions he lingered for twelve months. He died where the town of Bowen stands today. The endurance of the woman was extraordinary. She never gave up hope while her husband lingered on. Naked under all weathers night and day, season after season, her feet cut to pieces, driven mad by mosquito and sandfly bites, tortured by the sun, eating food thrown on the coals and merely singed, putting up with the laughter and fierce, fighting quarrels of the camp, moaning in sleep by the coals of a blackfellow's fire, she struggled on. She had to. For when the tribe is on walkabout, it is follow on - or perish.

The black warriors gave her rough help, and never interfered with her. They showed her how to cover her body with thick, clayey mud when the mosquitoes were very bad, and with a grunt would warn her to watch her feet when they were in bad snake country.

Captain Pitkethly died some months after the lad Wilson. His wife then gave up hope. Jimmy Morrill was left all alone to live out his seventeen years with the blacks.

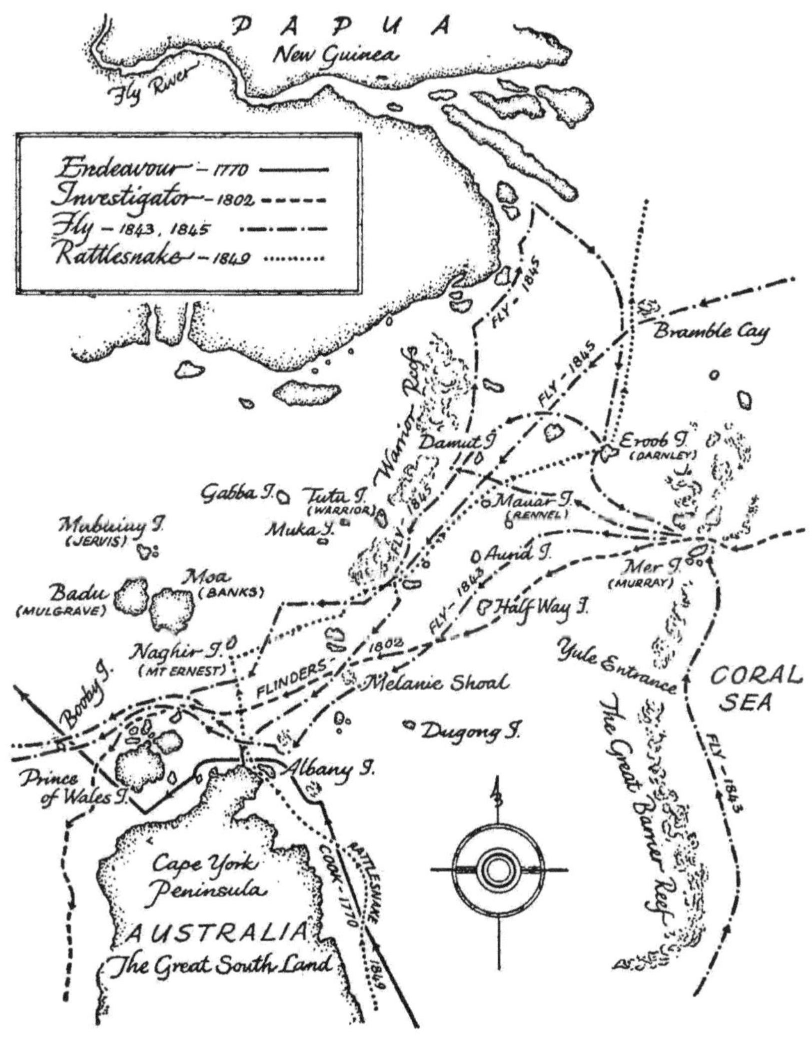

15

GREAT EVENTS IN THE CORAL SEA

THE season after the trepang fishers had sailed with the *Peruvian* the crews were again eagerly discussing Leichhardt as they cleared the Heads for the coming voyage. For that enthusiastic explorer was setting out on his fourth expedition northward, with a party of six white men and two black boys. From Birrell's station on the Condamine River found by Allan Cunningham, Leichhardt would attempt to cross overland to the farthest north-west. Greater news still! The Government was fitting out Edmund Kennedy with a grand expedition to explore all "their own country", to solve the mystery of Cape York Peninsula. This exploring expedition was to land at Rockingham Bay, well north of Moreton Bay, then travel right up through the Peninsula nearly to its northern-most point.

At last all the colony and the trepang fishers, too, would learn what lay within that mysterious land, that farthest north. Surely then, with time, towns might spring up, and loneliness vanish from the Coral Sea.

Thus the trepang fishers spoke and argued the pros and cons as they saw them from the seaward side, according to the weatherbeaten old shellbacks I heard many years later yarning the evening of their lives away as they puffed ancient pipes in the cool of Cooktown evenings, by the placid, starlit waters of Endeavour Bay. They would gather down by the tough old stump of the tree-trunk, still standing, to which Captain James Cook had so thankfully tied the *Endeavour* when he beached her to repair her broken timbers.[29] Starlight would be glinting on the monuments to both Cook and Mrs Watson, within their shadowy sepulchres of tree and vine, on the masts of *beche-de-mer* cutters and pearling luggers, and always on some "mystery craft" or other anchored near by. A bushman's song would sound from up on the balcony of the Sea View Hotel overlooking the bay, musical laughter of frizzy-headed Papuans from a black-painted brig, full-throated chant of some primitive devilry from that Solomon Islands schooner farther out in the bay. Her mast-head lamp needed cleaning, badly. A fat lot they cared about the danger of being rammed by an incoming craft in the night! Such was many a Cooktown evening; what fitter setting for a young listener to store up youthful memories as the old-timers yarned on?

And so, in full knowledge of the coming expeditions of Leichhardt, and particularly of Kennedy, the trepang fishers sailed past Cape Cleveland that season, totally unaware that somewhere. deep within that scrub one of their own seafaring mates - a captain, too - was staggering along on the tracks of a native tribe, teeth clenched to hide exhaustion, bowed down by the weight - alas, so pathetically light - of his wife upon his back. For at this time Mrs Pitkethly's feet had been so cut by jagged rock that it became impossible for her to walk, and her husband, hiding the fact that his end was fast coming, carried her pick-a-back when he could, for any who could not keep up with the tribe must perish. We know this passing scene as fact, for young Morrill, forced to scout ahead with the hunters, was to describe it himself in years coming. When the *beche-de-mer* boats would come sailing back at the close of this season the captain's miseries would be over, his wife lying in a blackfellow's gunyah dying of a broken heart.

Great interest was taken in Sydney and Brisbane in the organization of the Kennedy Expedition. The wanderings of Leichhardt, the mystery of the farthest north, had at last caught public imagination, a public now steadily increasing, eagerly welcoming expansion, with the freedom attained after so many battling years. Along the waterfront, too, particular interest was taken for this big exploring venture would be by sea as well as by land.

But those trepang fishers who sailed that shadowy sea began making grim prophecies as now they pondered upon that wild, unknown coast they claimed as their own, yet dreaded. They knew the seaward side, they were in their element upon the water, despite its many dangers. And, given wind, they could travel over water; the conquest of distance took only time and good weather. But now they saw a vision of those hundreds of miles of timbered ranges and rivers and innumerable creeks alive with wild men, and a few explorers slowly plodding along with horses ....

Still keener grew the interest when it was finally decided that Her Majesty's man-o-war *Rattlesnake* was to convoy the expedition north of Brisbane to Rockingham Bay, then sail farther north between the

Great Barrier Reef and mainland in the wake of the *Fly* and the B*eagle,* particularly keeping to the Inner Passage, charting a yet safer sea laneway for the certainly increasing shipping. The *Bramble* was to sail farther north still and, while surveying the seaways, keep a sharp look-out for the explorer Kennedy when he should emerge from the bush.

What a difference to the lonely *beche-de-mer* fishers, constantly in dread of attack from the mainland natives, and still more from the sea-going islanders, it would make to have a great man-o-war cruising in those untamed waters! Proudly they gazed out on Britain's might anchored in Sydney Cove - H.M.S. *Rattlesnake* of 28 guns, Captain Owen Stanley, 154 officers and men, and to accompany her, H.M.S. *Bramble,* Lieutenant Yule, 36 men. Not to mention the *Asp,* in charge of a very important young lieutenant. True, today we would call the *Asp* nothing more than a decked-in boat, but in charge of young Lieutenant Dayman, with several muskets and half a dozen cutlasses at command, she was not to be sneezed at. Let headhunters beware!

One by one the trepang vessels slipped away from Sydney Cove to catch the sou'-east trades to help them to the Coral Sea by March. That, to them, signified the end of the rainy season, though by now they were uneasily aware that occasionally the Terror of the Coral Sea comes howling down in cyclonic madness even as late as April. Some tiny vessels had already learnt the fact in a fury of waters, their crews going down helpless as mice clinging to a chip in a storm-water channel.

It was in March the same year, 1848, that Leichhardt set out from the Condamine, never to be heard of again. The Kennedy Expedition was to sail a month later aboard the barque *Tam-o'-Shanter*.

There was excitement in the city and Sydney Cove on a sunlit day in April. H.M.S. *Rattlesnake* was setting out on her second northern cruise. Such a fleet had never sailed for that far northern sea, now for the first time upon everybody's tongue. "A majestic sight", folk declared, as the ships sailed out of Sydney Heads, northward bound for Rockingham Bay, all hands gay with the spirit of high adventure.

In time, the convoy anchored under the lee of the Family Islands. The *Tam-o'-Shanter* landed the explorers - thirteen men in all, with 28 horses, 100 sheep, 3 kangaroo-dogs, a sheep-dog, a heavy square cart, 2 spring-carts, a ton of flour, 600 pounds of sugar, 90 pounds of tea, 22 pounds of gunpowder, 130 pounds of shot, a quarter-cask of ammunition, 588 feet of tether rope, 40 hobble chains and straps, boxes and paper and material for preserving botanical specimens, firearms, cloaks, blankets, tomahawks, horseshoes, cooking utensils, 4 tents and a canvas sheep-fold, 24 packsaddles, and harness for 9 draught-horses, etc. The equipment of a particularly well equipped exploring expedition of those days of not so many years ago may be of interest in this dawn of the Atomic Age, when we hear talk of exploration of the moon and tourist trips by space-ship.

They drowned one precious horse in the surf when landing on the beach at Tam-o-Shanter Point, the first casualty, the frantic thing never knowing how lucky it was. Kennedy pitched his first camp just up from the beach by the beautiful trees of a freshwater creek. All hands were in great spirits, laughing and joking, working with gusto to pitch the tents in the form of a square, the sheep-fold in the centre. A brave show.

The *Bramble* sailed north, bound for the wilds of Princess Charlotte Bay. There she would meet the overland party when they should come forcing their way through the bush, and be waiting there to give help, and succour if needed.

There would be dire need, but that rendezvous would never be kept.

If only they could have seen ahead! Hundreds of miles of wild bush, of rocky ranges and bewildering foothills, of razorbacks and precipitous spurs intersected by rivers and creeks, gullies and ravines, here and there gloomy, far-spread swamps choked with tall water-grasses and reedy plants, untrod areas of forest lands and savannah, patches of entangling vine scrub so exhausting to weary horses and men, an occasional belt of dense jungle, and at the far north that deadening, suffocating tangle of turkey-bush scrub, of which no man among them nor any on those ships, no matter what his experience, could have had the faintest knowledge.

It was far worse even than this. For, from the very start, the lie of the land was against them. Foothills, rivers, and creeks fell east, whereas their course was direct north. So that those innumerable foothills, ridges, and spurs would all have to be climbed up and over, and every river, gully, creek and ravine would have to be crossed. Hundreds of miles of it!

And they had brought lumbering carts to do it with - through untrodden bush. Soon they would be riding footsore, weakening horses. And so slowly, with such difficulty, they would be driving sheep over rocky hills, through untamed bush, trying to drive them through jungle! Little wonder that only two living skeletons of white men would survive to tell part of the tale, that only the black boy Jacky Jacky, exhausted, wounded, and in despair, would struggle through to the final objective.

It hardly seemed to matter' that several thousand or more hostile men would dog their tragic march.

Many a time, while plodding along with the knowing old pack-horses over that very same country, seeking the gold it hides so well, I've marvelled how Kennedy dragged himself all that distance. We speak of "indomitable will", but words cannot capture the spirit that drives such men as Kennedy, that drove him as he struggled on and on and on until he fell under the spears of the blacks - almost within sight of the relief ship. For he could have seen her lying in Newcastle Bay, had he been able to see over that last scrubby ridge across on the northern side of the Escape River.

Aborigines have pointed out to me the very spot where Kennedy fell. A dismal place to die alone, among the gaunt mangroves by that weird river mouth enclosed by those scrubby little hills, by those strange pitcher-plant swamps.

After landing Kennedy, the *Rattlesnake, Bramble,* and busy little *Asp* dawdled north along the coast on survey duty, seeking every chance of contact with the natives to gain their confidence and friendship, explaining to them that white men would presently come travelling through their country, promising the natives that any help they gave those white men would be richly rewarded. As a guarantee they gave them presents there and then.

As word spread amongst the wild men more and more canoes came out to the ships for the eagerly accepted presents. Well-armed landing parties also went ashore with the same object, though occasionally these parties were welcomed by a shower of spears. Thus, for a considerable distance along that wild coast, the tribesmen suddenly became more familiar with white men than ever before. Unfortunately, this treatment of the natives was to prove of no help to Kennedy, but it certainly was to help future relations between the *beche-de-mer* fishers and the mainland "savages". That is a point usually overlooked in our history, the manner in which the disastrous Kennedy Overland Expedition helped in the exploration and development of farthest northern coastal waters.

Towards the top end of the Peninsula Captain Owen Stanley did especially good work, slowly cruising back and forth between Peak Point and Newcastle Bay on survey work, anchoring from 'time to time. For it was here that Kennedy was expected to complete his journey. Soon canoes in increasing numbers began to cluster round the *Rattlesnake* when she anchored. And presently those aboard noticed a different class of man - men who came in larger canoes and were noticeably lighter in colour, while a few carried bows and arrows. These were from Albany Island, which lies a mile or so from the mainland. Their canoes plied backwards and forwards between island and mainland; evidently they were friends with at least several tribes amongst the craggy-browed aborigines. One day a large canoe came from the direction of Mount Adolphus Island, manned by well-built, much better armed, befeathered islanders, who scowled at and held aloof from the mainland "savages", and were very distrustful of the whites. Then one day three large outrigger canoes under big coconut matting sails, with foam at the bows, came bearing down upon them from the north, and the *Rattlesnake* crew saw that the men in these were quite a different race. A defiant crowd, they treated the aborigines with disdain. Proud of bearing, with athletic bodies, lighter skinned, all were armed with bow and arrow, pineapple-shaped stone club-heads, spears that were beautifully polished, and carved lances. These were Moans from Moa, visiting the Kowraregas from Murralug, called by Captain Cook Prince of Wales Island; farther north in Torres Strait.

Captain Stanley eventually made friends, more or less, with these distrustful people. While biding the opportunity, he quietly gave them object lessons in the great superiority of the white man's weapons; for wherever he anchored and opportunity occurred he had marksmen shooting at targets. And the distance a musket ball could carry as against a spear, and its penetrative power into a log of wood, were quickly grasped by the awed onlookers.

And when news of these doings drifted to the lonely *beche-de-mer* boats, cautiously fishing by reef or islet, it was received with grim relief, as a man hunted by criminals would feel relief at the sound of a policeman's footsteps somewhere in the night.

Meanwhile the *Bramble* sailed north to the Prince of Wales Group of islands, then dawdled west to survey Endeavour Strait. Where opportunity occurred she also sought to make friends with, and yet to teach a lesson of power to, the very distrustful islanders, in whose waters within fast-coming years fleets of little vessels would eagerly be hunting for wealth of the sea.

16

TIME BRINGS CHANGE TO ALL

ON the arrival of the relief schooner *Ariel,*[30] the *Rattlesnake* and *Bramble* sailed north to survey Torres Strait, while the *Ariel* slowly cruised by Newcastle Bay, waiting for Kennedy to emerge from the bush. As the long wait dragged on and on those trepang fishers in the vicinity grew certain Kennedy would never be heard of again, through questioning their aboriginal helpers, now much easier to come by through the "friendly relations" work of these government ships.

But at long last Kennedy was heard of, when Jacky Jacky came staggering from the bush.

The *Bramble* sailed south, hugging the coast in the hope of picking up survivors. The *Rattlesnake* sailed to her old cruising grounds between Albany Island and the mainland, yet more urgently spreading the news among coastal natives of rich rewards for news of any white men lost in the bush.

Only two living skeletons survived, eventually rescued by the *Ariel.*

The bodies of Wall and Niblett were buried upon the hilltop of Albany Island, a landing party from the Rattlesnake erecting a tombstone there. These ceremonies were watched in silence by the curious tribesmen.

The *beche-de-mer* fishers had never dreamt in their loneliness of such a scene as this. Soon other news startled them. A white woman had been rescued from the Kowraregas. She had come running to a landing party from the *Rattlesnake,* screaming unintelligible words as she fell upon her knees and cried. Her naked body was burnt black from the sun, pitifully scarred from knife and firestick, covered with ochre and ashes. The seamen thought her a native and were inclined at first to give her back to the savage angry men who pursued and demanded her. She was Barbara Thompson.[31] the one survivor from the wreck of the cutter *America.* Boroto, the chief, had rescued and claimed her as his wife, and in helpless despair she had lived with the natives these five years past. There was heart-burning among the trepang fishers as they realized that occasionally at least she must have gazed upon their distant sail.

Time came when the *Rattlesnake* and *Bramble* sailed from Torres Strait for good, blissfully ignorant of being scowled down upon from the highest point on Albany Island, the very spot where but yesterday, with armed ceremony, Captain Owen Stanley had paid the ships' last respects to the remains of Wall and Niblett. And the barbaric figure towering there was one they had wished so very much to meet - to swing him from the yard-arm. For to them he was a murderer, a brutal jail-breaker, an escaped convict, a very dangerous man, particularly so now that he possessed a hold of life and death over some of the most war-like islanders in the Strait.

Thus he was, in the eyes of White Authority. In tum, Authority to him was a horror of oppression, the chain-gang, the lash, the musket, and the gallows.[32] His big chest heaved with mingled fear and hatred as he gazed down and across Albany Pass to the activity on those little men-o-war that woke in him such bitter memories of hatred and despair.

But to his befeathered warriors awaiting him, he was a god, he was Wongai the beloved of Sida, the God of the Crops, friend of Kwoiam, God of War, conqueror of Moa, Mamoose of Badu, War Chief of all Badu and Maubiag. Such he was to them - a Spirit Chief, invincible, reincarnated, come to them from the skies. And he had taught them many things, and made them great.

In hatred, in near despair, under cover of black night the great War Chief Wongai sailed back to Badu. His awed warriors could not understand what had come over their mighty chief, could not know that to Wongai the coming of such ships, above all their long cruising in these waters, could mean the end of his world.

For years he had planned, worked, and trained warriors with the enchanting idea of uniting all the Torres Strait Islands into an Island Kingdom, under the one great chief - Wongai. All that had stood between him and final success was that arrogant swine Kebisu on his miserable Warrior Island - Kebisu, who with his sea-going islanders had enjoyed many a hearty laugh at the fury of the Lamar chief hemmed in on his big islands, denied access to the sea.

But craftily Wongai had built up his resources until he was all ready for a surprise attack. He delayed only that he might first seize his island queen - Barbara Thompson, the white girl captured by the Kowraregas of Murralug.

And now this! Of all things in the world, a man-o-war had rescued her!

The Big Chief's blood ran cold. For he knew that such vessels, cruising along his very own shores, would seek him - to swing him at the yard-arm!

His intuition was correct. Captain Stanley of the *Rattlesnake* had ordered the *Bramble, Asp,* and *Rattlesnake's* pinnace on a month's survey of the western entrance to Torres Strait, and to seize the renegade white man Wongai if possible. They had failed.

That was how Wongai came to be watching from the hill on Albany Island the farewell sailing of the *Rattlesnake* from the waters of Cape York

Peninsula and the Coral Sea. And so Wongai, renegade convict, Spirit Chief of all Badu and Mabuiag, lieutenant of Sida, God of the Crops, friend of Kwoiam, God of War, fled back to Badu and his wrecked dreams, dazed that in this water-waste of loneliness that had seemed as if it could never, never know civilization, ships had now *come - were coming,* after all these years, bringing fear and hatred and turmoil to shatter his freedom and his dreams.

The Big Chief glanced up at the now brilliant stars and ground his teeth in curses. Then his eye brightened as he saw how he could use the belief of his islanders that white men were Lamars, spirits come from the skies to revisit the earth, that wherever their foot trod there followed disease and death and, far worse, the poisoning of the spirit within living humans. Therefore these beings from another world should be instantly set upon and killed. He had managed to persuade them that he was different from other white men, but the general belief was unshaken.

Ah, yes! He would fan the flames of this deeply rooted superstition. Let them beware, these nomads creeping up from hated civilization in their cursed boats, lest their skulls adorn the Zogo Houses. He, Wongai, would *never*, never swing at the yard-arm.

Strange indeed at times is the destiny which has affected the footsteps of Man through the ages. The venturesome trepang fishers who had crept past Farthest North even when the continent was practically unknown had survived many perils, but had never dreamt of this. Nor has history recorded it, for the "Lamars" themselves never realized that some among them were killed, not because they were white invaders encroaching upon the brown man's Coral Sea, but because they were spirits come back to earth from the Land of the Dead.

Yet such is the truth. Strange, too, is it not, that in far-away South America the ancient Aztec civilization had a firm belief that some day white spirit men would come to them from the skies, and that those white-skinned men would be invincible, it would be useless to fight against them. Which helps to explain why Cortes and his few hundred Spaniards conquered millions and enslaved them, eventually wiping out their fascinating civilization.[33] A similar fate befell the Mayas.

Wongai knew nothing about Montezuma and Cortes, Pizarro and Peru, but he, too, was involved in a changing pattern in which superstitions and dreams of conquest had their part.

Time passed. As he crouched alone in his hut on his own island of Badu, in the dreamy silence of the tropic night, his perpetual scowl slowly faded, a shadow seemed to soften that harsh, deep-lined face, almost as if the devil within were slipping back to long-forgotten boyhood.

The spirit within was whispering that the body was growing old.

Yes, to this little Coral Sea change was coming, and also to Wongai, War Chief of all Badu and Mabuiag.

Snoring lustily on his tiny isle, sixty miles away nor'-east, the Sea Chief Kebisu flung out a mighty arm that had wielded a cruel club in many a foray. His son Maino has told me that his father often smiled in his sleep. He may have been dreaming of his fleet of huge war-canoes, black shadows drawn up all along the coral beach, some right to the scraggy pandanus-trees round which his hundreds of sea warriors slept peacefully under the beautiful tropic stars. Thus the mighty Kebisu, another actor in this grim little drama being played so tensely in a tiny world presently to be overwhelmed. Their Supermen and Gods of the Air, Abob and Kos, Kwoiam and Kulka, Sida and the revered others, must have smiled down with amusement tinged with sadness at this tiny drama played with such bitter importance by the little folk below-the cocksure, fighting brown islander, the head-scratching, happy-go-lucky Australian aboriginal, the busy little white men in their busy little ships increasingly poking their noses where such intruders had never poked nose before.

Change was coming to them all.

17

THE GOLD AND SHIPS AND KILLINGS OF ORDINARY MEN

FAR south in Sydney, it was months before the fate of Kennedy's men was known. There was shocked sympathy, then recrimination and fixing of blame by those who didn't know and those who thought they knew. The *Rattlesnake*, sailing into Sydney Cove on 5th February 1850, was given a rousing reception. Incidentally, Barbara Thompson, "the Scotch girl who had lived with the cannibals", shrank timidly from the intense public curiosity. From dark life on Murralug Island to this white human ant-bed proved an almost frightening change.

Captain Stanley, taking advantage of this public outcry and interest, strongly recommended to the authorities the suggestion of J. Beete Jukes, the now famed naturalist of H.M.S. *Fly*, on the advisability of establishing a military post on the Cape York Peninsula, as a haven for castaways and a mercantile coaling station for the future, with the object of ultimately forming a "second Singapore" in the farthest north of this wild, empty land.

But to the quarrelsome little port Cape York Peninsula was as unimportant as shadowy Cathay, and seemed as far away. The tragic Kennedy Expedition was forgotten in a startling discovery - gold!

"Hargraves finds rich gold at Lewis Ponds and Summer Hill Creek, out in the bush in the Colony of New South Wales!"

"Port Phillip separated from New South Wales and becomes the Colony of Victoria, 1st July 1851!"

"Gold found at Ballarat, out in the bush from the town of Melbourne in the new Colony of Victoria!"

"Man conquers time and distance-the breath-taking new invention of telegraph used for the first time in the Colony of New South Wales!"

What amazing events that year of 1851 saw! What swift-moving results to all the continent of Australia!

They gave Authority the excuse to forget all about a haven of refuge in that dim, far-away north - which was to mean a watery grave for many another sailorman.

Little wonder, then, that the trepang fishers, each season beating out through the Heads towards the distant north, never dreamt that from these events would come the impetus that would eventually lead to the charting of their lonely sea. The early gold strikes now hastening development, pushing Australia onward into nationhood, overnight so rapidly swelled an eager, virile population that in the bushlands the struggling overlanders were urged even farther westward, ever farther inland, ever farther north. And when people go swarming over the land, ships appear sailing along the coast. Not only so, but they come from across the oceans also, bringing progress. For England, fed by Australian wool and now suddenly swamped with Australian gold, thought she had better do something about it before others did. So on 3rd August 1852 Sydney greeted with thunderous acclaim the P. & O. Liner *Chusan*. This passenger cargo vessel made the first regular steamship connection with Great Britain and the Colony of New South Wales, reducing sailing time by half. In these days of flying ships and radio it is difficult indeed to realize what regular (more or less) steamship communication meant to our great-grandfathers and their increasing families.

Even through the gold-fever madness in southern Australia, a few little vessels still sailed unheralded into the north, seeking the humble slug of the Coral Sea.

It was on 26th June 1854 that a ship from England reached Sydney with momentous and frightening news. The long expected war with Russia was in full swing, the Crimean slaughter was already raging. Such world-shaking news had taken months to reach the anxious colonies. Now news of immeasurably less importance takes four minutes. When the *beche-de-mer* boats came sailing back at the season's end they found a Sydney grimly preparing for invasion and bombardment by a foreign fleet - and crazily hungry for news. As never before the rival papers were really on their mettle. Far away the senseless slaughter dragged on, and in Sydney the rival boat-crews strained every wit and sinew to be "first with the news", outwitting their rivals by waiting away down the coast for those infrequent sails, hiding by some advantageous point in the bush on the shore of a cove called by the blacks Coogee, or farther out still where the big blacks' camps were by Botany Bay, in all weathers gazing to sea for a sail by day, a mast-head light by night. Then into the boat, and they were racing seaward to intercept that bringer of news. At times of heavy weather hair-raising risks were taken, with miraculous escapes by reporter and boat-crew alike. As those fateful words - "Balaclava!" "Sebastopol!" "Charge of the Light Brigade!"- thundered round the world, the riders who galloped through the night in breakneck haste to bring the news from Ghent to Aix were out-paced by those news-hounds bringing the news to Sydney Town.

Crowds surged towards whichever newspaper office was rumoured to be "out with the news", throwing coins at the frantic paper-sellers struggling under a sea of snatching hands. Time and again the selling of an edition with big news led almost to riots. Doubtless human nature would be the same today if we had to wait three and four months for news of such vital importance.

Throughout this welter of gold and war Sydney never heard of the wreck of the *Grimeneza* in the far loneliness of our Coral Sea. A Peruvian ship bound from China to Peru, heavy-loaded with six hundred and fifty Chinese coolies, she crashed upon the Bampton Reef in Torres Strait, barely a week after anxious Sydney heard of the outbreak of the Crimean War. The thunder her panic-stricken passengers heard was not the thunder of guns on the Charge of the Six Hundred, but the breakers upon the reef, the rending crash of masts, the rolling thunder from wind-filled sails surging down in tangled masses of cordage. It must have been a frightful scene, that death struggle of ship and men, as the coolies went down in those strange waters far from their lands of old Cathay. Their passing left scarcely a ripple upon the waters of memory, so little even now was known of the Coral Sea. The master and three of the crew escaped by boat and were eventually picked up at sea by the whaler *Australian*; otherwise nothing would have been known of the fate of the six hundred and fifty others. During that same season the end of a fortnight's breathless, dead calm weather brought the crew of the *beche-de-mer* cutter *Hazel* flotsam of the sea. This was a large raft of casks heavily lashed to spars, barely moving in the preliminary break-up of the calm, that first tremulous movement of the bosom of the sea so slowly awakening from deepest slumber. Three dead bodies were aboard that raft, nothing else but a nesting sea-bird. Yet earlier there must have been others, for the raft was large and a goodly crew must have lent a hand in the building. What story lay there was never known; there was no sign to tell, just a voiceless relic from some vanished ship.

Soon afterwards these same trepang fishers sighted a ship that was luckier, the *A. L. Johnstone,* a fine barque cautiously sailing through the Strait near where the *Bourneuf* had struck a reef but a year before and gone down to Davy Jones's locker, a greedy locker here, that now welcomed the *Annie* foundering on the Mecca Reefs, now reached up greedy arms to the *Fatima,* so pathetically sinking down. No ship knew when her turn would come next. The following year, 1856, the *Phoenix* crashed upon the Mellish Reefs, never to rise from the locker that opened its maws even for the sturdy French man-e-war *Duree,* which sailed into the same death-trap, sinking slowly down to keep the *Phoenix* company.

The *Lightning* foundered near Albany Island. Two boatloads of survivors sought sanctuary on the island, but the leading boat was rushed by screaming warriors. In that fight to the death twelve lost their heads within sight of the helpless survivors in the second boat, who later told how their mates on the beach fought on with clawing fingers and snapping teeth while being cut to pieces. Little wonder that the lonely trepang fishers of those days dreaded the islanders in particular, and at sight of them or their canoes thought only of snatching up a musket.

Queensland's turn for excitement came in 1858, with Chapple finding gold at Canoona. The rush there was ill-fated, but it led to the foundation of Rockhampton and eventually the development of the great Mount Morgan gold-mine, three hundred and fifty miles north of Brisbane. About this time the little Aleya went down, smashed on a reef in a white squall.

That Canoona rush brought civilization by land three hundred and fifty miles closer to a renegade convict farther north, who one bright morning was fleeing for his life, his canoe chased by a swift trepang cutter thundering with musket fire. Fearful that this heaven-sent chance would never come again, the men in the cutter blazed away as fast as they could reload at that tall figure under its fantastic head-dress of cassowary and bird-of-paradise plumes. Their very haste in trying to kill this most hated of their enemies defeated their object; a cool shooter could have picked off every man in the canoe.

In a howling rage, Wongai heard the vicious whizz of the balls smacking the water to ricochet on ahead of the fleeing canoe, for all the world like the skipping splash of the flying fish, but for their deadly hiss. The indignity of it-the great chief Wongai of Badu chased by other Lamars, fleeing as if he were but a despised savage of the mainland! His warriors, straining at the paddles, could not understand why their invincible War Chief did not turn and slay the aggressors with one blast from his friend the Thunder God.

Wongai would have had those spiteful marksmen torn limb from limb, could he have captured them. A musket ball hummed past his ear as another splintered the bow. He almost leapt overboard in his diabolical fury. His straining oarsmen shot the canoe over a shoal, at which peril the cutter only just came about in time, her crew white-faced at their escape. Another moment and she would have been hopelessly grounded, and then canoes would have swarmed out from Badu and every head aboard that cutter would have adorned the Zogo House.

Far worse would have happened first, as they well knew.

By the skill of his paddle-men and by cunning knowledge of his home waters Wongai escaped that day, glancing in a helpless fury at three of his warriors huddled gasping their lives out in the bloodstained canoe.

Only a month later a longboat filled with despairing castaways sought succour at Badu Island, and lost their heads to a man.[34] But Fate, or time, was catching up with Wongai. Change was fast coming to the Coral Sea. The stage was set, the actors were moving onto it. Ever northward the white men pressed and this change would write finis to the life of the aborigines, who for untold centuries had known no change but the recurring seasons.

The increasing population of the continent was a magnet drawing oversea trade to the southern shore. This again reminded ship-owners and seamen that two thousand miles farther north, if only a passage through that vast coral network could be safely and confidently negotiated, there was a short cut across the Coral Sea, then through Torres Strait into the Arafura, leading to rich trade with the Indies, China, and India, and thence "Home". The successive, thorough work of the survey vessels after Cook - the *Investigator, Mermaid, Beagle, Fly,* and *Bramble,* and now the *Rattlesnake* - had resulted in the charting of an Inner Passage more or less hugging the coast, and also of passage-ways through the Great Barrier Reef allowing entrance from the Pacific into the Coral Sea. Ships could then proceed through still perilous waters westward to join the Inner Passage, or round the Cape as the case might be. When the surveys of the *Rattlesnake,* added to the work of these ships, were made known to the world's shipping increasing numbers of ships made use of this Inner Passage.

Islanders who yet more often watched the white sails of a big ship come gliding uneasily through their dangerous waters frowned in perplexity at this increased coming and vanishing of the Lamars in their giant ghost canoes. Their fathers' fathers had first seen, on rare occasions, such a spirit ship in the great days of the Dutch, Portuguese, and Spaniards. But now they had grown larger and were coming much oftener.

However, the few thousand Torres Strait Islanders, serene in their little world, were not greatly worried, for these big ships did not seek to land but crept as swiftly as possible through the dangerous waters and vanished. When one happily struck a reef within sight of a populated island tumultuous was the joy, the rush for the canoes lest she sink too fast. For experience had shown them that mostly the Lamars would jump into boats and frantically sail away, leaving to them a treasure house of untold loot. These occasional sails appeared from out of the edge of the world with the sun, vanishing with the sun down over the rim of the earth. Islanders firmly believed these spirit ships sailed down from the skies with the rising sun and, so soon as their voyage was completed, would sail back into the skies with the setting sun, back to their Land of the Dead.

Impossible for these islanders to dream of the change coming, that this increasing shipping must inevitably demand "protection", surveys and charting, bringing-conquest! So they carried on with their seasonal life of land and sea, their picturesque ceremonies, ceaseless feuds and raids and little wars, their loves and hates and jealousies, enlivened by that glorious chasing of castaway Lamars in the little boats whenever they thought there was a chance of heads - and wailed with dismay and outraged ferocity when increasingly now some began to fall victim to musket balls.

18

AHOY, *BLUEBELL!*

AT long last the cry of shipwrecked people from the Coral Sea reached distant Authority. Then the suggestion of Lieutenant Jukes of H.M.S. *Fly,* so recently supported by Captain Owen Stanley of H.M.S. *Rattlesnake,* on the advisability of establishing a military post and haven for castaways upon the wilds of Cape York Peninsula, was remembered.[35]

But the Home Authorities were discouraged by their two disastrous attempts to settle Port Essington. They pointed out also that that richly expected trade with the East had not eventuated at all. They had had enough of the crews of their ships getting their throats cut by Malay pirates, their soldiers being marooned in wild bush to languish and die from fever-with never a sign of trade to compensate for it. The proposal of a new settlement in that harsh north was frowned upon. But energetic sons of this coming race clung to the idea, certain of the necessity, though they could not act until the northern portion of New South Wales became the Colony of Queensland,[36] after long years of agitation.

In a fever of gratification the settlers in the new colony began the development of this enormous area with their own energy and resources, their own Brisbane as capital. Sir George Bowen, the first Governor, was a good man, and he needed to be. For a start, he found that this gigantic new colony possessed the huge sum of sixpence in the Treasury. The Government of the Colony of New South Wales had closed all its bank accounts and withdrawn, with the straight-out hint to the ambitious new colony to sink or swim, just as it damned well liked! It is generally believed that the new Governor battled through his first few days' finances with the aid of the sale of postage stamps.

The Governor had no constitutional advisers, no Legislative Council, no machinery at all with which to start a colony. For a camp for himself he had to hire a house as best he could. However, Queensland laughed at such paltry difficulties and strode out to grow into a lusty youngster - today a young giant.

In 1861 Bowen was formed north of Rockhampton, only eight hundred miles south from an uncomprehending Wild White Man of Badu. The unknown coast of the earliest *beche-de-mer* fishers was now rapidly being tamed, but, stretching into farthest north for three hundred miles and more, there was still that huge bulk of Cape York Peninsula, untrodden by the foot of white man.

The taming of this and its Torres Strait waters to New Guinea shores would take hectic years, yet the men for the job were already moving. The Governor himself, sailing north in the little H.M.S. *Pioneer* on coastal investigation work, was an amazing symbol of progress to the scattered *beche-de-mer* fishers, for they never dreamt of "the south" taking any interest at all in their "Sea at the End of the World". But here came this important little *Pioneer,* sailing round Mount Adolphus Island to cruise through the Strait and round the Peninsula, actually seeking a strategic landing for a government settlement.

On his return to Brisbane, Governor Bowen recommended to the Colonial Office the establishment of a settlement, to be called Somerset after the Duke, on Albany Island, near the tip of Cape York Peninsula. It was to be a haven for shipwrecked castaways and, more politically, the foundation of an Australian Singapore, a free port and commercial depot, as well as an important strategical position for British power on the maritime gateway between the Pacific and Indian oceans. It would also serve as a sanatorium for the people who just then were rushing to the Gulf country to take up land.

An adventurously ambitious programme for the little handful of Queenslanders to attempt in that extreme north in unknown wilds, but, like the early South Australians with their northern territory, they meant it. Three more seasons came and went, and in 1862 there came sailing past, parallel with the still unknown coast north of Rockhampton, the white sails of a schooner.

Captain Edwards of the schooner *Bluebell* was bound for the *beche-de-mer* fisheries, the yearly product of which was now being taken notice of in busy little Sydney. He would try his luck with this schooner, which, with its much larger capacity and crew, could stay at sea longer than the smaller cutters and brigs. He chose the northern end of Albany Island as a land station - a wise choice, for the islanders there had learnt from the Rattlesnake that if the Lamars came in strength their weapons were invincible, and also that for services rendered they could pay in wonderful goods. So that the Bluebell could be assured of native labour – "if the lazy devils will work!" growled the mate. True, these grim-faced savages, quietly watching their every moment, had but recently swarmed down to the shore and massacred the castaways of the *Lightning*. But that could happen any day, anywhere, in this sea, An armed schooner was a very different proposition, and looked it, as did the crew, obviously spoiling for a fight.

But a fight was something Captain Edwards wished to avoid, for he was bent on establishing himself in this strategic position. Here he would have native labour and rich fishing grounds to north, east, and south, and, only one turbulent mile across the Pass, the mainland with its abundance of fresh water and the red mangrove wood that was the best for the smoke-house.

So the *Bluebell* crew, with weapons handy, stood by while a boat's crew ashore built the first *beche-de-mer* station in the Coral Sea, within a few miles of Peak Point, often now called "the Fingerpoint", on Cape York Peninsula, Australia's farthermost northern point. At Frederick Point on Albany Island the store and curing house were built strongly of rough stone, the walls loopholed for musket fire. The men toiled from dawn to dark in the warm sunlight, at every opportunity consolidating friendship with the watchful islanders, but never for a moment relaxing vigilance or a show of strength. Then the sparsely grassed land around was cleared of shrubbery, and any boulders that could afford cover to lurking enemies were rolled away. Thus was cleared a field of fire round the rapidly building camp. The Bluebell unloaded supplies, then ferried across from the mainland shore a cargo of red mangrove wood that was quickly stacked in neat protective heaps by the smoke-house. Meanwhile, in his stronghold aboard the schooner, Captain Edwards displayed to groups of islanders, concentrating on the chief and headmen, tomahawks, knives, scrap-iron, looking-glasses, coloured beads, and cheap trade goods that were wealth untold to the envious onlookers.

"I've got them in the palm of my hand!" declared the skipper when the shore buildings were completed.

"Maybe," grunted the mate, "but I'd feel surer if I had them over the sights of my rifle."

"I'm no damn' fool!" snapped the skipper. "I've got them that way too, only they don't know it - yet!"

And when all was snug ashore proof was given that the skipper really did have them in the palm of his hand. Now there were eager volunteers to work at the station ashore, and others to help man the boats as divers. Even better still, they were eager to guide the *Bluebell* to fishing grounds where this worthless sea-slug could be picked up in basketfuls at low tide, before these mad white men should change their minds and sail away with their marvellous prizes.

To a rollicking sea-chanty the anchor was hauled up, while Captain Edwards stood on the poop with the chief and headmen. He pointed to the shore where a little group of now lonely men stood watching by the newly built smoke-house.

"Those are my men ashore!" he said impressively. 'Their lives are now in your hands. See that they are still safely here to welcome me when my ship comes sailing back."

Earnestly the chief assured him the *Bluebell's* men would be as safe as his own children, solemnly adding, "I will guard them with my life!"

"You had better!" said Captain Edwards meaningly, and nodded towards his crew. "You see," he explained slowly, "I have many of your men under my care now. And - I want to bring them all safely back!"

Over the faces of chief and headmen dawned a grim comprehension. The mate chuckled, seeing now that the shrewd old skipper really did have these savages between the sights of his rifle! That mate, who had seen men beheaded with the bamboo knives, dearly would have loved to pull the trigger.

Thoughtfully the headmen climbed overboard to their canoes, silently they watched the *Bluebell* gather way - and sail, quietly they paddled ashore. An uneasy frown was on the face of the chief as he watched the schooner now lazily lifting to the swell. For the first time in his life he was trying to grasp a new conception - one that we "civilized" people express by the word "hostage".

The chief's own son was aboard the *Bluebell*!

So were the sons of other islanders, who now would be responsible for the lives of those hated Lamars left ashore at their mercy.

And thus was established the first solid *beche-de-mer* shore station in the Coral Sea, upon the very island from which, a few years before, Wongai, Chief of Chiefs of all Badu, had gazed down upon H.M.S. *Rattlesnake* sailing away with the castaway girl Barbara Thompson.

Thus did the white man first set permanent foot in the Strait, within this Coral Sea, establishing an industry upon a shore footing. The Lamars had come to stay - the very thing the islanders dreaded most, though they did not realize it when it came.

And barely had the *Bluebell* sailed away than from the south bore up the sails of the *Kate Kearney*, a schooner of many adventures this, the hard-bitten crew determined on securing their share of wealth from these unexploited fishing grounds. And the *Melanie* would soon follow, and the *Woodlark*. She could be a hell-ship, this one, come from waters where men lived hard, toiled, fought, and on occasion died hard, as many did those days in the Solomons, the New Hebrides, the "Fee Gees". As a matter of fact, several of her late crew members had seasoned the cooking pots of the Big Nambas, those sharp-toothed connoisseurs of "long pig", while some of her crew, as on other vessels, had dined at a cannibal feast, and sucked their thick lips at the memory of it. They were a tough crowd aboard, South Sea Islanders, Rotumah men, Malays, Erromangan savages, fighting brutes from the Solomons, always ready for a brawl. The schooner was heavily armed; the skipper and mates were fighting men, as they needed to be, no holds barred. It was going to take a lot more than a few canoe-loads of headhunters to stop this vessel and others like her in anything the skipper wished to do. In time coming she was to play merry hell now and then. I have often wondered at what would have been the result if Fate had brought the *Woodlark* and Kebisu's sea warriors into an all-in fight. Skin and hair would have been flying with a vengeance.

Cheekily now the smaller vessels pushed still farther north among the islands, learning the tricks of this strange little sea - their sea, they boasted - venturing on past the Cape north to New Guinea, east to the Great Reef, west through Torres Strait to the Arafura. But as yet they still kept well away from tiny Warrior Island and Kebisu's savage warriors, and clear, too, of dreaded Badu and Mabuiag, haunt of that hated renegade, Wongai. The Eastern Group-Mer, Eroob, and Ugar - distantly east by Flinders Entrance, near the northern end of the Great Barrier Reef, were also given a wide berth. The catch that season when the *Bluebell* came was particularly good, and the adventurers were light-hearted when, with the first threatening squalls of the coming nor'-west, all vessels sailed the long way back to Sydney market.

When they came sailing back with the coming of the new sou'-east yet two more schooners would sail with them.

True, not all who sailed in high hopes from Sydney Cove returned by any means. Tragedy stained many a page in the now practically forgotten book of those tough and thoroughly brave sea wanderers. And their iron tubs boiled, their curing sheds smoked, more or less in peace, on lonely islets as gradually their numbers increased.

Then one season, when a schooner lost all heads from a too venturesome dinghy cut off by the islanders, two schooners joined forces. And on one of those days that dream as a blessing on the Coral Sea these vengeful devils bore down upon a sleepy isle. Grim-faced men poured down into the boats, which raced for the shore. As they splashed out upon the golden beach muskets were whipped up and a thunderous terror poured into the village.

Startled howls of men, screams of women and children stampeding for the bush. Flame leapt up from thatched huts, vengeful laughter as torches were thrust into the Zogo House. Within moments it was roaring flame and smoke, the avengers with hairy arms shielding heat-scorched faces, as along the blazing rafters grinning skulls shivered in the smoke and toppled over into the inferno. A howl of scorn then as the Great Au-Gud, a squatting giant of polished tortoiseshell caught alight with a "swoosh" and blazed in melting hideousness.

Yes, revenge and death swept swiftly upon that coral-girt isle that day, but far worse to the islanders was the destruction of their invincible god, bringing the gradual awakening that their beliefs, their thousand years of culture, were but a myth.

Yes, change was coming to the Coral Sea.

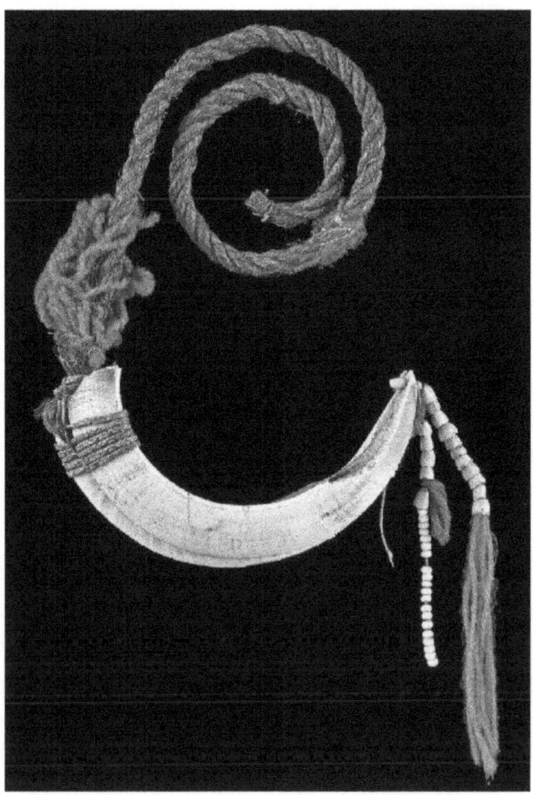

A pig's tusk amulet owned by King Kebisu, removed from Tudu in 1888.

19

JEMMY THE HOOK

IN those days the tomahawk was a necessity aboard the small vessels of the trepang fishers, an essential tool for rough carpentering and general shipboard work. In emergency it was ready for instant use to hack away cordage; a few swift blows and an entangling spar would be cut free in a squall, a fallen mast chopped free in disaster when every moment counts. One blow, and a tough rope would be severed to right a labouring vessel. One blow at a dinghy's anchor rope, and her bow would be up and she would be in action in some sudden emergency.

The sheath-knife at the belt was always a handy tool and weapon, too, but the tomahawk was essential. On the fishing grounds the bark of the mangrove was stripped with it, the trees were chopped down and cut into the lengths necessary for firewood and for the smoke-house. And for trade purposes it could buy "near anything".

Yes, a handy tool indeed, a deadly weapon also, but with two sides to it. For in a flash it could be used by, or against, the owner.

Which explains why, increasingly with the years "Stumpies" appeared among the trepang crews. A man with his hand chopped off at the wrist, another and yet another with fingers chopped off, some rugged face with an ugly hole where an ear had been. Quite neatly, a glancing blow from a sharp tomahawk can slice off an ear. Ever and anon a new "Nosy Bob" appeared, too - an embarrassing disfigurement, this, where the nose has been sliced off. Even the ugliest man does not think he is handsome then. Here and there, too, aboard ship worked a "Kinky", with lopsided grin carrying his head towards port or starboard, because a warded-off blow from a tomahawk had severed a sinew in his neck.

"A poor splicing job, that!" his mates would say with a grin. Others carried scars on face or body, none of them pretty. All were due to tomahawk wounds. The native crew at a prearranged signal would seize tomahawks and attack the few whites aboard. A startled shout, and a man was overboard, else he would be chopped to pieces. Surfacing with a gasp, he would immediately strike out to rejoin the bedlam now raging aboard ship or boat. He would clutch up at the gunwale and-a lightning blow, and fingers or hand would be gone. To that exultant yell he would fall back, floundering, moaning there, bleeding to death in the crimsoning water. If his mates won, then the natives would be leaping overboard around him to swim for their lives from the musket balls and he would be dragged on board for rough-and-ready first aid. Otherwise he would see a row of dark maniacal faces leering down at him; some of his enemies would hold out blood-stained tomahawks towards him, yelling, "Shark's meat" All would jeer, with shrieking laughter, "Shark he come!"

Frightful moments for the man in the water now, knowing how incredibly far away sharks scent blood, how swiftly they come; often there they cruise in schools. And here was his own blood trail oozing away with the tide, to guide the sharks to him.

"Shark's meat!" How often that grim expression was used during those years, and for many years later-even as late as my day.

The man in the water, if his hand had been chopped off, might just stare hopelessly a moment, faintly sigh, and sink. Almost certainly, though, he would "die living", as they expressed it. Usually he would turn his back to the vessel and strike out for the shore, followed by the jeering yells of the crew.

"Shark he come now! Shark he catchem you soon feller now!"

"Ah! Ha! Ha! Shark 'e come! Quick feller you swim!"

Even if the terror of the sea had not yet made its appearance they would speed the wounded swimmer on.

"Die living" - but, even with a hand chopped off, there were some men who would never give up. Nicholas the Greek was one, and Jemmy the Hook, others also.

Such a man, caught thus, would by some superhuman effort of will and love of life fight against the shock. Treading water, he would glare up at the leering crew, probably calling them all the black bastards he could lay tongue to, as Jemmy the Hook did. Undoing his belt buckle, kicking his trousers or lava-lava free but up beside him, still gently treading water, he would take the sheath-knife from the belt and with teeth and good hand cut off a trouser-leg,[37] wrap it in tight folds round the stump, then use the belt as a tourniquet to try to stop the bleeding, watched now in silence by the so interested crew. He knew he need fear nothing from them now, they were eagerly awaiting the sharks so that they could watch him being torn to pieces, preferably just as he was about to set foot upon land. The tourniquet fixed as best he could, he would then strike out for land, though he might exchange a final pleasantry with the crew, advising them to wait until next season, when he would return with plenty of guns and cut their so-and-so's out and make them eat them, each dog his own in turn.

To which the grinning crew would reply, "You come back, eh?

Which way you come? Which way you thinkem first time you come out? Longa shark guts? Longa mouth? Or longa arse?" and as he struck out for land they would yell the further advice that when he did, and if he did come out of the shark's guts, no matter by which passage, then he could go his hardest and chase them!

When it came to be Nicholas the Greek's turn to be thrown overboard and have his hand chopped off he wasted not one word. His turn - he lived through more than one such experience - came in the night. He, in his secretive way, shammed drowned, which enabled him, months later, to catch up with his astonished crew. And his revenge was pretty awful.

After such a fight aboard ship, or out in the boats, if the ever wary whites won, which they generally did, men often survived terrible tomahawk wounds, with the only treatment such rough surgery as their mates could give. But then, history has taught us how grimly the human being clings to life, and what terrible wounds he can survive.

In the early days of *beche-de-mer* fishing most of the little vessels, except an occasional brig, were manned by from four to six white men depending upon bartering for the services of native helpers when they reached the Peninsula coast or islets peopled by small sub-tribes, less warlike than their stronger neighbours. At season's end, preparatory to sailing back to Sydney, the native helpers would be taken back to their island home or coastal tribe, as the case might be. This gave the natives confidence, for the fishing was done in their home waters. Familiarity breeds a measure of contempt. It was when such natives had worked two or three seasons aboard a vessel that the more cunning among them began to hatch plans of a sudden massacre. To kill the white men and sail this vessel back to their home tribe would make them heroes all their lives. The exultant tribe would loot, then burn the vessel, and all trace was gone. They almost always forgot, though, that an avenging, or quite unsuspecting party could easily find the loot in their camp, or upon their person.

Thus, once that first superstitious dread of the Lamar had diminished and they found him to be "near human" after all, many a treacherous act was staged. But they were crafty. Out-numbering the whites, they still remained in deadly fear of the ever ready firearms. For ringleaders to clinch an attack plan with the wavering ones, there must always remain one fair chance of escape should that surprise rush fail.

The favoured method was to wait until the vessel was anchored for wood, close by some mangrove islet that in turn was in sight of the coast or home island, or, for that matter, within twenty or thirty miles of it. Thus, should the attack fail, they could instantly leap overboard and swim under water, rising only for a gasp for breath, then under again, thus dodging the musket balls. The last risk, if they were within range, would be the race through the shallows into the mangroves. And even this hazard they could often dodge by lying on the mud with only nostrils above water until nightfall. Should a searching dinghy come pulling out from the lugger they must jump up and run for it; that was all in the game. Once within those dense mangroves they were safe. Under cover of night they would swim for their mainland home or island as the case might be.

Distance, except for the danger of sharks, or to a wounded man, meant little. Swimmers among them have been known in heavy storms to last three days and nights in the water, swimming, floating, treading water, conserving strength and endurance to the last ounce while making waves, wind, tide, and currents help them. To such a swimmer, ten to twenty miles is child's play when life is the prize.

This method of attack near land could work both ways, for it also helped a wounded white man who leapt or was thrown overboard. In the open sea he would bleed to death or inevitably be torn to pieces by sharks. But if close by an islet he had a chance of reaching it and, if very lucky, of eventual rescue.

And this happened not once, but twice, to "Jemmy the Hook".

Some men are born under a lucky star. If Jemmy the Hook had been born in these times I'm sure he would have won the Lottery twice.

After Jemmy had had his right hand neatly chopped off at the wrist he coaxed a sympathetic blacksmith in Sydney to make him a hook to his design. Jemmy had had the time to give deep thought to that design. He was determined to return to the sea, the life he knew and loved.

"Them black swine will never beat me!" he swore.

A sharp-pointed, neat little steel hook, it was fastened snugly into a light plug of wood, comfortably padded to fit over the stump and connected with oiled straps, laced like the trappings of a Roman gladiator, that fitted round the short, muscular forearm to the elbow. Jemmy was a short, nuggety man, a powerful little brute, with only his labour to sell. But what counted far more was a native shrewdness, an iron determination, an almost unbelievable endurance, which was proved by his survival. A happy-go-lucky nature must have helped him a great deal, too, though he could fly into an almost ungovernable rage if deeply disturbed.

His mates, of course, took Jemmy aboard ship again, agreeing among themselves that he would come in handy as cook, and for "mindin' ship". Long before they came sailing back to Sydney they were pleasantly surprised by what Jemmy already had taught himself to do with his hook.

In Sydney, Jemmy went to his blacksmith again. The following season he sailed with a new hook. It had been lengthened a little and given a slightly new shape. Long ago, the fish-hook was developed from a piece of bone, until, after much time and thought, it came to have that simple, yet so efficient twist, and the deadly barb. Jemmy had improved his hook in far less time.

The wooden plug was also shrewdly improved, and made several inches longer, with short ridges protruding along it, and cunning little grooves cut into it. Jemmy believed these would give his "wrist" more power, and enable the hook to do more jobs. He was right. As he kept improving upon it, he grew very proud of his hook.

When Jemmy lost his left hand his two surviving mates thought he was surely done this time. Not Jemmy. His blacksmith made him another hook, and a still further improved hook for the right arm.

Jemmy the Hook sailed again.

20

THE THIRD TIME

JEMMY THE HOOK amazed his shipmates, until they grew quite used to him and his hooks. If there was anything they could do that he couldn't, they were unaware of it. Automatically he took over "minding ship", which lifted a lot of drudgery off their shoulders. With time, they cheerfully acknowledged the fact that "Jemmy with his hooks does more work than any man aboard", which pleased the independent Jemmy immensely.

It was miraculous the way in which he taught himself to use those hooks, with the cunning ridges cut upon the wooden sockets giving grip and leverage; to develop those movements of arms and body and jaws, and of those strong teeth, to accomplish the work that hands and fingers used to do. The simple cooking for his crew mates and for the natives, too, was child's play. So was looking after the lugger while the boats were absent fishing. He could lift and stack and handle bags of trepang, cases and casks of shipboard stuffs, armfuls of wood for the smoke-house, or do any such rough work with the best of them. And he was tireless. He did a lot of boatwork for the ship, too. He was not much of an oarsman, but he quickly developed into easily the best sculler in all the Coral Sea. To see Jemmy the Hook sculling a dinghy was a picture. Standing in the stern, short legs braced, leaning slightly forward with the oar handle clasped to his chest by hooks and forearms, his shoulders swaying a little from side to side, he made the dinghy simply fly over the water. He could scull all day, covering miles and miles with seldom a glance back or forward, for he possessed a natural sense of direction.

"Jemmy must have a compass back o' his head!" declared his shipmates enviously.

It was a treat, so his mates told with pride, to watch Jemmy loading his musket, quick and smart with the best man aboard. The musket gripped between tight-closed knees, butt firm upon the deck, he'd reach for the powder-flask with his teeth, hold it to his chest with his wooden paw, pull off the thimble-like measuring lid with his teeth, and lay it, open end up, upon his right forearm, clasped across his belly. With left forearm and hook he would deftly tilt the flask and fill the lid with the exact measure of gunpowder, not one grain overflowing. Then with his knees he would tilt the muzzle to the lid, gently up-end the lid with his arm and that cunning ridge cut into the socket of the right hook, and down would flow the powder into

into the barrel. Lift the lid with his lips, squeeze it over the neck of the flask, then press it down tight with that stem-built chin. Lift the flask with his teeth and lay it upon handy box or deck, rip off a wad with his teeth-though he generally had a boxful of them cut handy to size and shape in his spare time - chin-push wad to muzzle and poke in with hook end. Then, teeth to ramrod end, he would jerk up his head, while standing on his toes, and thus lift the ramrod completely out of its barrel groove. Stretching out the musket, using those grooved sockets, he would place the ramrod end fair and square on the wad, hold it straight, lean downward, and with teeth and bull-neck push wad and ramrod straight down the barrel to the charge. Then, gripping the musket with his knees, left hook round the muzzle, with his right hook he would easily lift up the ramrod, then ram her home deft and true, quick and smart, ram charge and wad snug and light. Reaching to the pouch at his belt, his teeth would grip a ball, lift it to the muzzle, and drop it down. Teeth or lips would seize another wad, then down he'd ram the wad snug and tight against the ball, the ball rammed tight upon the wad "mothering" the charge. With hooks and forearms tilting the musket, he would reach down and with his lips "nose out" and delicately lift the little brass percussion cap from his tin. He would upend cap on box, and delicately blow that last dangerous grain or two of sawdust that always seems to cling to the mercury fulminate deep within. Turning the cap over with his tongue, he'd have the end in his lips, then lift it to nipple, fit it, and push it gently home.

To cock the hammer with his hook, to lift musket to shoulder and hold it with left arm and socket and hook, to aim, to pull the trigger with his right hook, was just natural. Jemmy had always been a good shot. He was just as good now. But any stranger seeing this man, with two hooks for hands, so swiftly, easily, and expertly going through all the movements of loading a musket, was amazed.

In part only his shipmates guessed of the determination of the man, of the hard hours of secret thought; of frowning trial and error, of the heart-warming moments of success, of the deep struggle within to make himself "as good as the next man". Cruise after cruise, they took him for granted. Occasionally, though, as they lay smoking on deck under the stars, dead beat after the long day's toil, the gruff joke would come: "Ah well, Jemmy's the lucky one! If ever the niggers do tackle us again he's only got his hooks to lose!" And Jemmy would join in the grim laugh.

Another remark was bound to be blurted out some time, doubly distasteful to superstitious seamen aboard a very lonely little ship:

"I seen an albatross today! The next time the niggers tackle us Jemmy'll lose his head!"

An albatross, and - the third time!

In the ensuing silence, while the speaker could have bitten his tongue off, came Jemmy's low chuckle. Another thing they did not know about their shipmate was that the grey-eyed little devil was almost praying for that "third time". In training his hooks into claws more cruel than the leopard's, how many, many times he had whispered within himself, "The third time! I'll get even with those black swine the third time!"

None aboard on any cruise ever noticed or imagined that the energetic, cheerful Jemmy was waiting for, ever watching for that third time. The natives they employed with each cruise certainly never suspected him. He fed them well, and never bullied them. His manner towards them was always hearty, though he knew they thought him but half a man, sensing it by the tone of "the lingo" when from up for'ard came some sneering joke at his hooks. They coveted those hooks, too - for shark-hooks!

He must have developed some deep, intuitive instinct, for when the attack did come it was so well planned that nothing else could have saved him, or the ship.

A perfect day of warm sunlight, as the days are when the turtle are mating. Calm water all a-sparkle, kissed by the faintest breeze, the air so clear that the chattering of birds away across on Cairncross Island sounded like an aviary nearby, the dark line of mainland towards Orford Ness standing up sharp and clear; through the glass they could even see the peculiar shape of Pudding Pan Hill where Costigan, Dunn, and Luff of Kennedy's Expedition perished, or were speared.[38] The lugger was anchored off Douglas Islet, her reflection lovely in the still, crystal-clear water. The boats were away fishing towards Aplin Islet; they would not return until sunset, loaded with fat *beche-de-mer*, for their obliging native crew had put them on to a goodly patch there. From the islet close by the echo of tomahawk blows seemed to bounce off the water. Tom was ashore with six of the native crew, stacking wood for the smoke-house and stripping mangrove bark. Jemmy the Hook was minding ship, clad only in the comfortable lava-lava, cheerily whistling by the galley cooking pots. Their three white mates were away with the boats and native swimmers.

It had been a pleasant and profitable cruise, the blackboys working with a will, ever ready with a joke, eager to load the ship and be paid off with their presents. Barely a month more at this rate, and as a loaded ship she would sail early back to Sydney with ten tons of the dried sea-slug aboard - £140 a ton! Yes, there was money in the slug if weather held and you could get a good native crew.

Jemmy straightened his back, his bellow went rolling across to the islet: "Ahoy there! Kai-kai!"

A rollicking shout came answering; the chopping ceased as all hands made for the dinghy, stepped aboard, and pushed off. Jemmy had three buckets on the boil, one of turtle soup and one of turtle meat and fish; the other was the tea billy. Those big-mouthed boys possessed the ravenous appetites of sharks. Deftly Jemmy lifted off the buckets, smiling as each hook slid over a handle and two buckets at once were lifted clear of the galley fire. Ha-ha! He could do two at once, while a whole man had to think of his fingers before gingerly lifting off one hot-handled bucket. Grinning broadly, he lifted off the tea bucket. Yes, his hooks were more use to him than men dreamt of.

Laughing voices as the dinghy drew near, click of rowlocks to powerful strokes. Tom, sitting astern at the tiller, was cutting a wad for his pipe, musket beside him, one easy eye on those tomahawks piled at his feet. Idly Jemmy noticed that Tom's body was burnt almost as black as the six crew boys, for he, too, worked only in the short calico lava-lava as the natives did, as they all did. Before the dinghy bow could bump the side a boy fended her off, leapt up, painter in hand, and tied her to the rail as his joking mates jumped up beside him. Jemmy turned to his cooking pots as Tom stood up in the dinghy and grasped the rail. A boy whipped round, snatched under his lava-lava, and the tomahawk swept up to flash straight down upon Tom's head. Another sprang at Jemmy, but Jemmy had wheeled round with both hooks up, striking well under those blazing eyes, that savage face that was convulsed in a frightful grimace as the right hook pierced the body. The tomahawk dropped, and even the man's clutching hands seemed to scream as Jemmy leapt backwards, and the hook ripped out, dragging a steaming mess of entrails. As Jemmy danced aside his other hook was warding off tomahawks from the tigerish others, frenzied by the sight of their screaming comrade writhing on the deck, vainly clutching his entrails. Jemmy's left hook pierced another belly; there was another dreadful scream as two agonized hands clutched his forearm in a death-grip. With a howling cry Jemmy jumped at the others, his right hook flailing at them while his victim, in bent agony as the hook pushed and jerked within him, clung to his left forearm. Against that awful right hook and the terrible things so swiftly done, the four natives leapt straight overboard. Jemmy glared into his victim's face - one face screwed up in maniacal triumph, the other in a beseeching agony. Thus a moment one crouched, straining to hold immovable that arm, the other panting, gloating now, neither man's bare, straining feet feeling the stickiness of the warm mess welling over the deck. Meanwhile the other wretch, lying all screwed up there upon the deck, was still alive, with glazing eyes, as Jemmy's big toe caught in a rope of his intestines.

Jemmy's face broke into a wolfish grin, neither human nor animal. Almost gently he pushed with his forearm, feeling upon it that grip that would only break in death. Slowly he brought up his bloody right hook, the sick face swayed agonizedly from side to side as the hook threatened to gouge the eyes - but the victim did not let go. How could he, with that fiery left hook deep in his belly, twisted round his entrails?

Overside, his four black mates were treading water, in awe-struck silence gazing up at this dreadful thing, this so terribly unexpected thing, that had happened - that was happening!

Steadily pressing forward, waving that threatening right hook before his victim's face. Jemmy grinned to feel the convulsive resistance.

The man knew that the Hook sought to push him to the rail.

Then, when he fell overside, his weight would drag out his intestine's; as he fell he would see his entrails running out up there above, held by the Hook!

Gurgling strange sounds, he crouched immovably forward, his sick face now unresponsive to the sharp hook almost lingeringly pecking at his cheeks. But the hook inside slowly screwed round. Against that agony he began to give way, his feet sliding backward, though he could feel nothing but the Hook. Inch by inch he was fainting back, but when he should feel the firm rail behind him he would prop and never give way!

And the face leering into his, it knew his every feeling - he could feel it.

Jemmy, breathing more easily now, took his time. When he had his victim jammed hard against the rail he smiled at him, an awful smile, suddenly twisting into tigerish hate as his right hook whipped down and behind and up under the lava-lava. As the man felt the sharp hook ripping into his back, he screamed convulsively and threw himself back over the rail. And there were all his intestines streaming out as he splashed into the water, caught on that bloody left hook of the Face laughing over the rail.

He sank in a welter of blood that spread like a cloud.

He rose up, thrashing feebly about - so the old-timers told the story - then sank, his mates staring aghast. Never in their fierce, primitive lives had they witnessed anything that shocked them like this.

Jemmy the Hook leant over the rail, grinning down at them while they gaped, treading water instinctively, just gaping up at him. Then Jemmy vanished, to reappear quickly, carrying in those arms an awful thing. Carelessly he dumped it across the rail, then toppled it over. And there splashed down among them the red, raw, bloody body of their other mate.

They watched it slowly sink, then gaped up again at Jemmy the Hook, leaning over the rail, grinning down at them.

Only then does it seem to have occurred to them-! With an urgent yell they struck out for the islet. Sharks!

All that blood and guts in the water with them, flowing away with the tide!

Jemmy could have shot them, man after man; their haste was so extreme they dared not swim under water. But Jemmy just leant over the rail, grinning.

They were but half-way to the shore when the first black fin appeared, travelling like a torpedo. Others came swiftly. Jemmy watched as three of the swimmers were torn to pieces. One man escaped.

As the old-timers told the yarn, Jemmy quietly climbed down into the dinghy, wrapped a blanket round his dead mate Tom, climbed back aboard, then began methodically to clean up ship. He easily guessed what the plan had been. He and Tom were to be killed by the woodcutters, then, when the boats returned at sunset the three whites would be attacked as they were about to board ship, both from ship and boats. Then the triumphant natives would sail loot and vessel back to their mainland tribe.

Jemmy, who could have signalled the boats back by two quick shots of a musket, decided to "let the black swine work the day out". Then, when they returned, he would be aboard - waiting with muskets ready. The boat boys would not dare attempt anything against his mates, sensing that something must have gone wrong.

And it worked out that way.

21

SOMERSET IS BORN

THE authorities in Brisbane in 1863 appointed John Jardine, then Police Magistrate and Gold Commissioner at Rockhampton, Government Resident to establish the new settlement in the north. Jardine sailed for the Peninsula, brimming over with hopes and ambition. He was amazed to find on Albany Island a *beche-de-mer* station firmly established. He climbed to the top of the little hill, paid his respects to Wall and Niblett, then gazed across the turbulent Pass at his domain - a vista of broken coastline, scrubby ridges and unknown bush stretching far as the eye could reach. The only sign of life was a distant smoke-signal of wild aborigines.

Undaunted, Jardine decided to form "Baby Singapore", not on Albany island, but on the mainland directly opposite, a few miles south of Peak Point. By establishing the settlement on the mainland, Jardine would have all Queensland behind him. Many thousands of square miles of it were as yet untrodden by the foot of white man, of course, but this energetic man was confident he would soon alter all that. Accustomed to a position of authority, proud of his "connections" with the Old Land, sure of his own and his family's destiny, he jumped at this chance to build a second Singapore and thus lift his name high in the nation's roll of fame. Poor Jardine! He was to learn, as many a man had learnt already and would learn in the future, that this new land was a very different proposition to the old. Caring not whether a man was the son of a king or a cobbler, it could give great rewards, but such must be earned by a hard, often bitter way. So often, too, that way was long, and seldom was it spiced with fame.

To support Jardine, Dr T. J. Haran, Medical Officer, and Lieutenant Pascoe with twenty-five marines, stores complete, landed at the new Somerset on 25th March 1863. The second Singapore of Lieutenant Jukes's dream was born.

John Jardine, with military precision, supervised the landing of his tiny army and supplies under the pandanus-trees upon a little beach lapped by the softly gurgling tide, the sailormen's rude feet trampling underfoot the sweet-scented flowers and creepers clinging to the grassy spur that leads up to the low cliffs above. Brown and grey, these cliff-faces reflected sunlight from the bluest of skies. Dreamily a breeze sighed over the dense jungle, whispering on over virgin forest and savannah stretching for unknown distances. Above the landing party and on the ridge-crest to right and left, dark faces of wild men peered down. At a military command listened to by the wondering bush an advance guard of three marines, muskets at the ready, warily climbed up the steep spur to make sure all was clear upon the cliff above. The guard posted, Jardine gave orders, and marines and sailors grasped box, bag, or bundle and commenced climbing to carry the stores and goods up to the first camp in some open space amidst the future Singapore. The flag was the first imperative duty, of course - the meticulous selection of an upstanding sapling as flagpole, the stepping of the pole, the bugle call, the hoisting of the flag. The little squad, drawn up under impressive military ceremonial, was observed by hundreds of primitives with the liveliest curiosity.

From that day for many years to come the hoisting of the flag at Somerset was attended by stiff ceremonial at dawn and evening. Even when the time should come when gentlemen would file into the residency dining-room in immaculate evening dress, but sometimes of necessity In bare feet, dignity would be upheld.

The little ship carried cut timber from Brisbane for the immediate erection of a few huts, but to build the Residency Jardine soon had the axes ringing, while warily attempting friendly contact with the local tribesmen, for imperialistic grandeur has never been averse to cheap labour. The local tribe Jardine found to be the Gudangs, a timid people, fearful of the aggressive Cockyrugga tribe encroaching upon their northern tribal land and of the Indooyamoos pressing in upon their west, and in deadly terror of the numerous and warlike Yardaigains only twenty-five miles south down the coast, in whose tribal lands, the Escape River country, Kennedy had been speared. As Jardine was to learn, these Yardaigains comprised four hundred aggressive spearmen, a large number for an aboriginal tribe. But for that fatal tribal distrust of the Australian aboriginal, the Yardaigains alone could have wiped out Jardine's men in one rush. To the timid Gudangs, this White Chief with his overtures for friendship, with his dreaded "thunder-sticks", was a saviour indeed. They would cling to him and later to his son with labour, and be the bringers of news who would hurry many a timely warning to Somerset.

Had it not been for the Kennedy Expedition, the restraining influences of the *Freak* and *Rattlesnake* and *Bramble,* then finally Captain Edwards of the schooner *Bluebell,* the baby settlement would have been completely surrounded. The hostile aborigines would have been on three sides by land, and the Albany Island tribesmen only a mile across the water. But these, now partly tamed by the *Bluebell,* looked curiously from their island hill at the bare patches appearing in the scrub on the toast opposite. Warriors of the Yardaigains canoed across and harangued the Albany Island men, urging them to cross the water by night and creep up from the beach upon the white men's sleeping camps, while the Yardaigains encircled the settlement from the landward side. With the dawn war-cry all would rush the settlement.

But Captain Edwards of the *Bluebell* had firmly established his station. His payments were welcomed, the schooner's weapons overpoweringly deadly. The Albany Island tribesmen decided to just wait and see - a characteristic of the Australian aboriginal.

The site of Somerset House, which would be the Residency, was carefully chosen. Perched on top of the red hill that rises sheer from the beach, it would overlook Albany Pass and much of the island, while its enclosing verandas would command the abrupt, scrubby little hilltops to north and south, and, by telescope, a view of the sea and coastline far to southward. Strategically placed, too, were the sites of the Imperial Buildings, with store, barracks, and hospital, even to a customs house. It was to be a brave little show. On 21st August 1864 Somerset was officially founded, after the important arrival of H.M.S. *Salamander* from Sydney with stores and a few more men. Henceforth the *Salamander,* and later H.M.S. *Freak* would arrive, God and weather permitting, every four months at Somerset with supplies and official correspondence.

On top of a tiny hill a quarter of a mile north of the Residency Jardine built the barracks, the hospital, the doctor's house, and the married men's quarters. He began building the "Colonial Buildings" and the "Parade Square", while over a surprising acreage, the scrubby little hilltops were cleared of timber with the aid of the Gudangs, thus making the Black Man carry a little of the White Man's Burden in the founding of this military and naval outpost of Empire. All was done under strict military discipline, on guard night and day against attack by these threatening Yardaigains, who now boasted they would fill this white invader Jardine as full of spears as a porcupine is of quills.

It was just as well for the baby settlement that Jardine took the Gudang's warnings seriously and insisted upon his tiny garrison being ever ready, day and night. For one morning, just before the first chill of dawn, a Gudang runner came leaping on the Residency veranda, yelling, "Yardaigain he come! Yardaigain he come!" Jardine was out of his bunk, snatching a carbine as he shouted for the bugler, and seconds later the alarm blared out over the startled bush, across the starlit Pass, to echo against the black cliffs of Albany Island. As the marines sprang to arms a sentry challenged, a shot thundered out, then with a thunderous yell painted figures sprang out of the night and howled down upon the buildings. An orderly volley from the barracks echoed across the waterway, bringing Captain Edwards's men at the *beche-de-mer* camp leaping from their bunks. Musket shots from the Residency, ribbons of flame stabbing out from the quarters, and all the time that howling roar of voices. Then almost as suddenly as it started the yelling ceased, though agitated muskets still blazed out into the night. Not until ten minutes later did the bugle blare, "Cease fire!"

A brave little show. I remember smiling when, so many years later, in the peace of a tropic night, I read it all in Jardine's clear handwriting in one of his musty old journals - huge, leatherbound books of five hundred pages - in the old house at Somerset. Reading it thus, with only a handful of survivors of the broken tribes hanging around the place, the trappings of old-time warfare seemed a bit theatrical. But circumstances were very different at the time, and that first concerted raid, had Jardine's lonely men not been uneasy and prepared, could have meant disaster to the new-born settlement. As it was, the overwhelming numbers of the attackers were only defeated by the superstitious terror inspired by those fire-spitting, thunderous weapons.

During the affray several marines were wounded. The damage to the attackers was not stated. From this time began a guerrilla warfare, with an occasional wary attack at broken intervals, but mostly the aboriginal fighting of hit and run, a shower of spears from ambush, or dogged pursuit where not a foe is seen until a spear is hurled at the back.

And this would be the rule for years to come.

22

THE GREAT TREK

CAPTAIN EDWARDS, cruising back to the mainland with the *Bluebell* loaded with *beche-de-mer* from off the Melanie Shoals, was amazed at his luck in having chosen Albany Island as a shore station, with now that military outpost just across the water.

"Who'd ha' thought it!" he chuckled to the gloomy mate. "I'd sooner have believed it would rain cats and dogs. Death-or-glory boys perched away out here in this God-forsaken wilderness! Why, they must be expecting the Frenchies and the Russians to come all at once!"

"Huh!" grunted the mate. "Whatever they're here, for, they're here for no good!" He detested authority in any form.

"I'm not so sure," replied the skipper thoughtfully. "A spot of civilization in this heathen waste might swing things to our good. The powers that be must be expecting overseas shipping through the Strait, which would help chart these waters, and save many a good ship. Then again, a post like that must arrange for regular communication with the south-and that could mean a big help to us if only they would play ball. But who'd ha' thought it! All the pretty military, too - with flags and bugles and bang-bang guns! We needn't fear the niggers now - not around our base, anyhow."

"There might come worse!" growled the mate. "Much worse!"

"How come?"

"Well, all this military-marine business might mean a frigate by and by - to patrol our waters."

"What the hell for?"

"Well, some of the boys are beginning to play up. Each season sees a couple more schooners arriving. We're even pushing right out towards that New Guinea coast as more ships come. We run this little show - so long as we keep clear of that blasted Kebisu and that bloody cut-throat Wongai. And their day will come! This sea is ours. It'd be a pity to see the place spoilt."

"You mean the girls?" The captain frowned. "Some of the boys have taken a fancy to those lively little island she-cats."

"They've taken more than a fancy!" replied the mate grimly. "Well, half a dozen have paid for it with their heads already, but that goes on everywhere. Most of us are here to fill our holds with the sea-slug and sail back to market as we can. A frigate isn't going to come nosing around here just because of a few grass-skirted girls and musket-happy boys!"

"Those cutlass-swinging hounds would poke their nose into any kennel" growled the mate. "I don't like it, anyway - civilization spoils everything!" and he stepped morosely below.

The captain shrugged, remembering the mate carried a "love kiss" upon his chest. The knife had been driven into him by a girl of Ugar.

"Some men are never satisfied," the skipper thought. "They'll cut his liver out and stake him to a sandbank next time!"

"Shark-bait!" was the opinion of the kanaka crew. Indifferently, Captain Edwards's eyes swept the clear horizon to come to rest upon Albany Island, now looming up clearly above the bows. He felt happy at the gleam of sunshine reflecting from the bare, grassy pate of the rounded hill so weirdly crowned with monoliths like those of ancient Druids, spikes upon the skyline that were gigantic white-ants' nests. Presently, up rose the signal smoke to tell for many miles the schooner was coming. Under a stiff breeze the island swiftly grew until the bays and baby beaches down below the hillsides showed plain, all lapped by a lazy blue sea.

The captain's enterprise had succeeded very well. No trouble to speak of with the tribesmen, and his shore station now comprised a house at Frederick Point, comfortable huts, a stone-built curing house, and a supply store. This organized base meant that the schooner, loaded with fish from her small boats, could leave them working, return with the fish to the base, unload, stock up with water and stores, then sail straight out to the fishing grounds again. Meanwhile the shore men would clean, boil, smoke-dry and bag the fish ready for season's end and the sailing back to Sydney market. Thus the season's catch would be much larger and less expensive to procure, for no valuable time would be wasted.

Ah, yes, there was money in this game - given a schooner and organization. The skipper felt well content.

While founding the mainland settlement, John Jardine grew intensely aware of that vastness of unknown bush between him and the nearest civilization, completely isolating Somerset by land. For communication, help, stores, and everything this young Singapore would need, he was entirely dependent on a visit by some small government ship once every four months or so. The vagaries of this sea, particularly with the wild cyclone season, would cut the settlement off from the outside world for longer, perhaps disastrously longer, periods of time. As if it were just an ordinary workaday job instead of a great undertaking fraught with peril, he determined to open up a trail that would bring cattle overland from the nearest civilization right up through this wild peninsula to Somerset. That, just across the Pass, within sight of his own veranda, the graves of Wall and Niblett bore silent testimony to the wreck of that very same idea, that Kennedy had recently been speared to death only a few miles south of where Somerset now was did not seem to enter Jardine's head at all. He believed a road could be made and all that unknown country opened up for settlers, with the express object that this coming Singapore would no longer be dependent for very existence upon sea, weather, and a little ship. An object dearer yet to his heart was that it would give him the power to wield authority also. For he visioned with time a little army marching up along that overland track[39] to garrison his Singapore. Toiling horses with that army would haul the little guns, and in time big guns, which he would set in commanding positions upon the cliffs to overlook Albany Pass, and farther north upon Peak Point to command all shipping entering or passing through Endeavour and Torres straits. Thus this second Singapore would command the sea route from the east to the Australian south.

Such were Jardine's visions of empire as, in the autocratic fashion of the day, he planned and supervised the work in that increasingly cleared area in the farthest northern bush, dreaming in the quiet of the tropical night, or in warm sunlight as tree-tops rustled to laughter of the wind. But how to curb that mad, mad tidal race between here and Albany Island and thus make the Pass a safe harbour for shipping caused him much anxious thought. His idea was a huge breakwater of stone from the southern end of Albany Island right across the Pass to the mainland outpost just south of the Residency.

Yes, Jardine was in earnest over this second Singapore. But then, so was the Government of the day, little understanding the distances of untamed bush, of that sea of a thousand reefs under the howl of a cyclone.

That dream of a second Singapore in later years brought forth a cynical comment from a schooner captain who had good reason to hope the baby settlement would die a natural death. He declared that the reason the Queensland kookaburra does not laugh as its southern brother does was because it had "laughed its throat out" on hearing of this second Singapore.

There was another sort of sailorman, though, who had far more reason to fear the establishment of a naval-military post, let alone a second Singapore, upon that wild land in that wild sea. And that was the blackbirder, only just now making his appearance upon the stage. Though not playing merry hell in earnest here, as generally supposed, he began to sail through the southern area of this sea, and was to appear ever more frequently, too often with his cargo of human misery. His goal was the increasing sugar plantations away down south along the Queensland coast. For these had just begun to import labour. The blackbirders were now hiring, buying, or seizing their cargo mainly from the Solomon Islands and New Hebrides, the Gilberts and Fiji and Tonga, well north and east of the Strait, more easy of access and much more heavily populated than its island groups.

With hatches battened down on their crammed human freight, the majority then sailed south-west, just outside the Great Barrier Reef in the open Pacific, to enter the Coral Sea through one of the entrances as near as possible opposite their mainland port. Some, however, skirted south-eastern New Guinea into the north-east Channel, across the Coral Sea, and down the Cape York Peninsula coast. These thumbed their noses towards Jardine and his second Singapore, though they were uneasily aware of what the presence of a man-o-war stationed in those narrow, treacherous waters could mean to them. But such a danger seemed far distant indeed as, almost daily, the more inhuman among them slung overboard to the sharks such of their overcrowded cargo as had died in suffocating misery during the night.

The short life of Somerset abounds in many historical romances, swift-fading as comets vanishing into the depths of time. One epic which has lasted is no story of the seas, but of the overland - the epic of the two young Jardine boys, Frank and Alick, with the toughened bushmen Charlie Scrutton, Roy Binney, and Alf Cowderoy, and the laughing, recklessly brave, ever cheerful aboriginal youth Eulah, with

Tracker Peter and Sambo, bringing their mob of cattle overland right to Somerset. For hundreds of miles, through bush never before trodden by white men, they were compelled to fight their way through tribe after tribe of hostile aborigines. They succeeded in this almost impossible feat by battling their way up along the west coast.[40] Kennedy had tried to do the same thing along the east coast.

Greatly relieved by the safe arrival of his sons Jardine, after twelve months' secret anxiety, turned his whole attention to happenings of the sea. His boys' and their men could now start opening up that back country and press back the hostile tribesmen who ringed the settlement, while from distant civilization settlers would come plodding up along the track his sons had made.

Poor Jardine! His great ambitions, his dreams of empire, to be so completely overpowered by the wild Australian bush!

Certainly the flag fluttered bravely at the settlement, but with only the wild sea breezes to caress it, that ocean of tree-tops to see it. Jardine could not even' tell the marines, at least for some time to come, that Somerset was not only the seat of authority over this sea and land but was also a special sanctuary for shipwrecked castaways. For a letter to the Colonial Secretary asking the news to be spread among shipping in Brisbane, Sydney, and London could take six months from the day of writing to reach Brisbane, let alone "the world". And as for actually policing these seaways, he realized now he was practically helpless.

Thus many a time this "Autocrat of the Strait" muttered darkly as he stood on the Residency veranda, frowning at the turbulent waters of Albany Pass. For news had come drifting in of dark happenings upon the Barrier waters south, and particularly among the isles of the Strait northward. For some among these free and easy schooners had already made a terror of themselves amongst the islanders, while the ribald gestures of the schooner's crews whenever Jardine or the second Singapore was mentioned made the Resident's blood fairly boil. Yet what could he do, anchored here on land with a force of twenty-five marines and no ship? Fiercely he swore that come what might he would build up this settlement until he had a man-o-war under command, then swiftly clean up this sea and develop a second Singapore in earnest. In dead of lonely night, the little breeze that so often rustles over the hilly tree-tops there would sigh with his uneasy dreams.

Frank Jardine and brother Alick, full of zest for life, found the baby settlement virtually in a state of siege. Naturally so, for inexperienced men on foot dared not walk into the bush out of musket-shot of the settlement unless in company, and even then only with a mob of the friendly Gudangs as scouts.

In the enthusiasm of youth, the boys vowed to alter all this as soon as the remnant of their horses recovered strength. They had long since proved that, mounted, they could break through any mob of natives at the gallop, wheel round, and blaze back into them until the enemy ran.

They had had to fight their way thus for hundreds of desperate miles. How much easier this would be, they laughed, with a settlement, a "Great Resident", and a company of marines as a base! Let alone that mighty man-o-war H.M.S. *Salamander* looming up over the sea every four months or so. A mighty atom she, symbol of Her Majesty's power.

Jardine chuckled at their boyish banter, thankfully relieved.

Such reinforcements at present were worth a hundred marines to him. Only quick-moving, experienced horsemen could open up that back country. The boys were obviously bushmen now, and fighters, with Scrutton, Richardson, Cowderoy and Binney all proved men. Of great value, too, were their aboriginal boys Barney, Peter, Sambo, and Eulah, whom they enthusiastically declared was as good a man as any of them. The boys seemed almost to worship this agile, cheerful Eulah. Yes, with these tough mounted men, with cattle that he felt confident would soon be increasing inland from the settlement; Jardine was sure Somerset must now rapidly develop.

In renewed enthusiasm he prevailed upon yet more Gudangs to work for him and commenced clearing a large area upon the cliffs and ridge tops preparatory to the building of the fortress-town. Here Richardson, the surveyor, was of great help. And when the *Salamander,* after calling again with supplies, sailed back south she carried plans of the new Singapore, with the streets all laid out (on paper) and suitably named, of course. The plans were addressed to the Colonial Secretary of the day, for shipment to the authorities in London. The building blocks were to be auctioned, then would come the builders, the trade and commerce developing into the city to be.

The night the tiny man-o-war sailed Jardine pored over the new, expertly prepared, genuinely official map in the Residency by aid of a ship's lantern, with loaded revolver on the table and cutlasses and oiled and loaded muskets neatly stacked ready in the arms rack.

Welling up over the grassy headlands came the sea-born murmur from the uneasy Pass. Through blue night the lovely stars of the tropics shone serene above. Over all was the faint tang, the dreamy sigh of the great, wild bush, awakened suddenly by the startled challenge of some trigger-happy sentry alarmed by the thud of a wallaby hopping through the night. False alarms were caused thus, particularly when the Yardaigains were on the prowl. Jardine listened. But there settled down again that breathing silence of the bush. He bent over the plan again, dreaming of fame and empire.

23

THE ATTACK

THE Jardine lads with their men were soon riding out from the settlement north and west, locating grazing areas at localities they named Bertie Haugh, Lockerbie, and Galloway. These names would become famous as cattle stations, they declared enthusiastically. With the energy of the born bushman they started felling timber for the first huts which would develop into big station homesteads with the growth of the second Singapore. All this was to be built up from the survivors of their leg-weary horses, the remnant of their pathetic mob of cattle. These dreams they fashioned as they toiled, or by the campfire when, healthily tired out, they smoked the last pipe before they rolled into the blanket and slept - except for the alert watch, of course - like father Jardine back in the Residency, with his dreams of development by sea. Somerset was now very busy, very much alive, crowded with the boatloads of survivors of two shipwrecks. Jardine, as usual, had set the seamen to work while acting the autocratic host to the officers, gentlemen passengers, and a few lady survivors. The crews would be looked after by the marines and water police. But all must help, more or less, with the development work of the settlement until such time as H.M.S. *Salamander,* or *Freak* would arrive and could take them on the long voyage back to Brisbane or Sydney. It naturally would be some months before the vessel would arrive.

All were happy to toil, blessing this unexpected sanctuary in the wilds which had saved them from the perils of a thousand-mile open-boat voyage.

The Jardine brothers had matters all their own way for a time with their "outside" bush work, making good use of the friendly Gudangs, now doubly detested by their enemies to the south; north, and west. They were wedged in so tightly to the settlement, they had so definitely thrown in their lot with the white intruders, that the fate of Somerset was their fate. Thus day by day, week following week, the brothers built their stockyards while hostile natives were conspicuous by their absence.

It did seem they had the natives bluffed. Within a few miles of them from any direction they had Somerset at their back, a settlement laid out in "military formation", all authority and bugle-calls and flag and armed marines. Such power and force must have seemed a veritable Gibraltar, let alone a Singapore, to these primitive tribesmen. Forming stations under such conditions was very different to fighting their way utterly alone and isolated over hundreds of miles of wild bush, peopled only by numerous hostile tribes. Then, every moment of the day and night, they had had to be alert for their very lives, but under these conditions surely they could at last relax.

Charlie Scrutton, a bit grizzled now, hardened by the most experience, frowned. "Never trust a native-otherwise you'll stop a spear in the back. Remember that every time we ride out from the settlement we take a chance. Better watch out, or someone among us will be losing the number of his mess."

To which the Jardine brothers, doubly anxious now through the responsibility of the precious horses and cattle, heartily agreed.

So, by his very silence, did Peter the tracker. Binney and Cowderoy shrugged, Sambo turned his big face away and grinned broadly, while Eulah, delighting in his close friendship with the two brothers, laughed at the sombre tracker with witty jokes that brought grins to all. The laughter of Eulah against the grim silence of Tracker Peter was a joke in itself.

But Scrutton's warning proved prophetic, while Tracker Peter had been reading the signs of the bush in his own silent way. Poor Eulah should not have laughed.

The Yardaigains and the Gomokudin were only biding their time, taking care the despised Gudangs did not notice. They were watching every move of these new strangers who could move about so swiftly and so far and wide on those terrifying animals, horses, observing the other strange animals, cattle, too, to learn in what way they might be dreaded, to learn what weapons they might possess, how these huge beasts might use those ugly-looking horns if attacked. They watched, too, the slaving of these strange beings out in the bush, so senselessly chopping down trees, though every ring of the axe woke their envy, axes so marvellously better than stone axes. They could not understand guns, or the utterly unfamiliar horses and cattle, but they could understand axes. In their own primitive but very efficient way they were absorbing the habits and strength and capabilities of these threatening strangers whose obvious knowledge of the bush and power of swift movement made them far more to be feared than those timid footmen bogged down in huts in their stronghold by the sea.

Thus time dreamed on with activity by sea, and land. H.M.S. *Salamander* arrived and, after naval and military ceremonies punctiliously carried out in this wild bush setting, sailed back to Sydney loaded with castaways. Several *beche-de-mer* schooners lay at anchor in the quiet water just below the Residency cliffs. Immediately after the sailing of the mighty atom the suspicious skippers rowed ashore and were presently "in confab" with the Resident, a definitely "official" Resident prepared to throw his weight about, despite the fact that the only real force he could wield at sea was fast dipping her sail into the south and he would not see her again for four months. Meanwhile, down on the little bay, the tough crews of the schooners, sprawled on the decks, puzzled as to whether this second Singapore augured well for their future, or not.

For Jardine had threatened to police the seas, with a threat seemingly directed against the roving schooners rather than those dreaded headhunters.

"He doesn't own these seas," growled the skippers as they lumbered down the little hillside to their waiting dinghies. "And neither does any other country, either!"

The aggrieved *beche-de-mer* fishers sailed on their lawful occasions with the pious hope that the bloodthirsty natives would rush that "tin-can Singapore" and "teach those Empire swabs a lesson".

Yet again came a day when two whaleboats heavy-laden with castaways pulled wearily towards Somerset. To these at least the little house showing boldy upon the cliff with the flag waving beside it was a haven of hope indeed, a heaven-sent sanctuary to shipwrecked mariners in this wilderness of hostile sea and wild, unknown lands. Those people, too, were allowed to rest a few days, then put to work until the supply ship should come sailing north again.

There came one of those beautiful days when sunshine floods the whole great Peninsula, alive for thousands of square miles with the song of birds, the gleam of silvered streams, the lonesome sighing of the vast bush. The boys were now working at Vallock Point, only a few miles north of Somerset. Here they had formed a meat depot to serve the now growing settlement. As the cattle increased so killers would be driven from the bush grazing areas to this convenient point, killed, and dressed, then the beef would be sent by packhorse to the settlement.

A big team here, all hands busy, with foreheads, bared chests, and arms glistening with sweat - Charlie Scrutton, with half a dozen Gudangs, carting freshly cut timber; Frank Jardine, with brother Alick and half a dozen castaway seamen, busy at enlarging the killing yards; Cowderoy, with Sambo, Barney, and Peter, building a salting shed; Binney, with Eulah and team of Gudangs, working the pack animals and doing odd jobs. All were toiling with a will, immersed in their different jobs, when a shower of spears came whizzing upon them and a castaway sailor leapt erect with an agonized scream and swayed a moment, clawing at air, a long barbed spear-head protruding hideously from his chest. He clutched it as he swayed, then reeled over sideways to the war-yell of the Yardaigains and Gomokudin, as another shower of spears came hissing. It was Scrutton who whipped out his revolver, and the report sent the brothers leaping for their rifles. Scrutton fired again, then staggered back with a spear through his shoulder. He grasped the spear to steady himself, then fired rapidly as the brothers fired to a roar of war-cries. Binney and Cowderoy had snatched rifles as Eulah raced to the brothers, only to plunge writhing at their feet with a spear through his body. Three of the Gudangs were clawing the grass, the others in terror rushed to throw themselves behind the trees and posts from which all the whites were now firing.

The attack was beaten off, but it had been a very close go indeed. The castaway sailor lay gasping his life out; Eulah was dying horribly, too, his eyes trying to speak to Alick, who was kneeling beside him with his arms round the stricken black boy. Frank stood shouting for horses, but at the bloodcurdling roar of war-cries the horses had bolted. Sailor mates knelt round another castaway whose ashen-green pallor showed that he would be lucky to last out the night. Four Gudangs lay dying, yet another would not last long. Scrutton sat immovable upon a log as Cowderoy cut through the long spear half hanging eight feet out behind his shoulder. It was quite a time before the more daring of the birds began to sing again. Yes, it had been a very close go indeed. Alick Jardine knelt there, sickened, stroking Eulah's forehead, his eyes blinded with tears as he gazed down into Eulah's glazing eyes. Eulah had been through so much with them, he had grown into their hearts as a brother. Only in their dreams would they ever hear Eulah's laugh again.

24

QUEENSLAND STRIKES GOLD

WHEN the settlement was more or less shipshape after the attack the Resident carried on with his government and sea-port duties with an unusual quietness, unnoticed by all others in the settle¬ment. Even those closest to him had too much on their own minds and energies to notice the quiet change in John Jardine. As for the shipwrecked people, some of the crew had lost the number of their mess. After the burial parties had completed their unhappy job it began to dawn upon all of them that they had a lucky escape. For in this well-planned attack, they realized now, the whole settlement had come within an ace of being wiped out. To reach haven after the disaster of shipwreck only to fall under the spears of savages when within shelter of a "military post" would be a good bit over the odds. They slaved uncomplainingly at strengthening the settlement; joking when one of their number was caught guiltily gazing over the sparkling, empty sea to southward.

"What cheer, maty? Sail-ho?"

"Mebbe it's the Frenchies he sees a-comin'!"

But most of them secretly yearned for the appearance of one of those mighty atoms, the supply "man-o-war" *Pioneer* or *Salamander*. Either would have a crowd of rescued passengers for the south this time -

That a weather-worn brig sailed up the Pass one day to anchor below the Residency, that her tough-looking crew climbed up the steps seeking "the noos", that they seemed more inclined to grin than sympathize when they heard of the attack on the settlement, puzzled the shipwrecked people. These rough fellows from that stinking trepang ship did not appear to like the settlement at all.

The Resident toiled quietly on. Maybe hard facts had gradually exploded his dream of this second Singapore. In Sydney, two thousand miles away, and in far-away London the "sites" of this future city had been eagerly bid for at auction, street after street had been bought, after which the investors sat back comfortably and waited for the wealth to pour into their laps. Not one thought that he might bestir himself by crossing the seas and giving a hand in building this city that he believed was to bring him in untold wealth.

Meanwhile Jardine had become tired of keeping those "streets" clear of the ever encroaching bush. When the wet-season rains poured steadily throughout the night, when the nor'-west howled in fury, he lay in his bunk grimly thinking what a shock the investors would get if now they had to look for their city out in that wind-tossed bush.

John Jardine had been disappointed with affairs of the sea, too. He lived - existed, he called it - completely out of touch with affairs of the world. Communication by land was impossible; he now realized that none would follow, or not for many years, the tracks of his sons. He had been promised supplies and mail by sea every four months; he had soon found he was lucky if he received them once every six months. Then again, here he was representing Colonial and Imperial Authority in its glory, and yet those low-down scum of schooner captains simply thumbed their noses at him. And he could do nothing whatever about it. That the authorities could not or would not see that he must have a man-o'-war at his command to enforce his authority he bitterly resented.

The news that came to the settlement in these years gave many hints of the great development that lay ahead for Queensland. There was talk of gold and copper being found, and, from those dense jungle lands north of the main settled areas drifted the startling news of the first sugar produced from Queensland-grown sugar-cane. It was breath-taking to think what this might eventually lead to. And then came the news that those two insignificant coastal hamlets called Mackay and Townsville had been "opened" as real shipping ports!

In the dreamy quietness of a tropic night the Resident gazed down from the Residency veranda upon the still waters of the Pass. The settlement, too, seemed deathly quiet; all but the sentries were asleep. Right down near the steps, just out from the beach, the upright mast, the perfect outline of a little cutter showed as if carved from immovable ebony.

"Nicholas the Greek!" the Resident frowned. "That scoundrel never sleeps!"

In this he did Nick some slight injustice, for he really was asleep, but, as always, with one eye and ear open.

The Resident turned his gaze southward, over a starlit sea now quiet as the bush. It was born into John Jardine's mind that he was being wasted in this outlandish place. Soon afterwards he applied for and received leave of absence to attend to personal affairs south in Rockhampton. He never returned.

Captain Henry G. Simpson, R.N., took over the Residency from John Jardine in early 1866 and Somerset carried on according to naval routine and etiquette.

Again it proved itself to be a sanctuary, a port of Refuge, a heaven-sent haven for shipwrecked sailors and castaway voyagers, for the barque *Adelaide* crashed upon the Great Barrier Reef, then the barque *Cathay* waswrecked on Bramble Cay, Eastern Fields, followed by the ship *Conqueror,* wrecked while attempting to sail through the North-east Channel. The three wrecks happened in good weather, fortunately, so that most of those aboard had time to tumble into the boats and survived. Two men from the *Adelaide* landed upon a dreamy, peaceful-looking little bay on the coast. Utterly ignorant of what lay before them, they started out into the bush with the intention of "walking overland". Of course, they were never heard of again. A few others were lost.

The survivors of these three ships were fortunate that several of the officers had heard of "Somerset Marine Outpost", said to be being built up towards the northern end of that Cape York Peninsula. For nearly ten years would go by before world shipping became fully aware of "the Haven", a fact difficult to realize in these days when, if a ship is merely in distress, the whole world knows it almost at once through wireless, and aeroplanes and shipping speed to her rescue if necessary.

Those of the crews who so thankfully reached the harbour of refuge were allowed scant time to settle down. The Resident addressed them from the Residency veranda: "Men, on behalf of the Queensland Government I welcome you all here. I only wish that all of your shipmates had reached shelter with you. Here you will receive protection, shelter and food and clothes, such as our scanty stock can supply, until we can signal some passing ship, and arrange for your passage south. By good fortune that could be within weeks, though much more likely in months. Meanwhile, I put it to you that every man should do a job of work, each as he is willing and capable of doing. For, as you can see, we are entrusted with a very big job here, and our supply of European labour is not only scanty, we simply can not get any in this complete isolation. Even worse is the matter of protection. For the settlement is surrounded by thousands of hostile natives who may attack at any moment. We have beaten off such attacks as occurred. But now I have received word that the strength in marines for the settlement is to be reduced. Probably native police under European officers will be substituted. Whichever way it goes, the effective strength of the settlement against attack will very unfortunately be reduced. So that I put it to you that while awaiting a relief ship each man lend a helping hand in the development work of the settlement, also to help all of you pass the time away and for the protection of the settlement and of yourselves. Now, what do you say?"[41]

Immediately then all hands cheerfully agreed to do their best, calling out for foremen and tools and instructions to start straight away.

So that in his next letter to the Honourable the Colonial Secretary, the Resident wrote:

The arrival of the shipwrecked sailors from the wreck of the barques *Adelaide* and *Cathay,* and the ship *Conqueror* is proving a very welcome addition to the Force of the Settlement in the event of conflict with the blacks. I explained to these men that in return for shelter for their issues of food, twill shirts and moleskin trousers, they would be required to assist in the work of the Settlement, to which they cheerfully assented.

For the Jardine boys and their stockmen, who must work out in the bush from the settlement, guerrilla warfare, such as the aboriginal wages, had again broken out and would last for years. This led to the withdrawal of the marines and the substitution of native police under a white officer and men. After all, the marines were "anchored" to the settlement and could not penetrate in reprisal more than a very few miles into the surrounding bush, also, since even yet Somerset possessed no vessel, they were useless to police the seas; whereas native police could penetrate the bush and live out in it and play the native warriors at their own game.

Sceptical of further use for his abilities in this frontier post, Richardson returned south on the supply ship to carry on his profession as Government Surveyor, to the regret of Alick Jardine, who had been deeply affected by the death of his friend Eulah. Brooding over the lad's fate, he took a dislike to the place and the life. In earlier boyhood he had dreamt of becoming a great engineer. Encouraged by Richardson, those dreams had returned, and grew stronger, with a longing that would not be denied. He determined to return south and study, as soon as brother Frank "got on his feet with the stations". Finally he did sail for the south, eventually to attain the position of Engineer in Chief for Harbours and Rivers in Queensland.

Cowderoy and Binney, as time dreamed on, felt the call of the growing herds; they would return to the great cattle stations developing in Central Queensland. Then at last Charlie Scrutton would seek new adventure far west in the Gulf Country, the untamed Northern Territory. It was there, when he was an old man, we yarned about those early days of Somerset. What a book this quiet and secretive bushman could have written had he only felt inclined! Charlie went over the Great Divide only a few years ago. Of that handful of originals, only Frank Jardine would hold grimly on to Somerset. But all this lay in the unknown.

There were stirring years ahead for the battling young colony.

It was a passing brigantine that brought great news to Somerset. Three months ago a prospector called James Nash had found rich gold out in the bush somewhere along the Mary River. They called the place "Nashville". There was a big rush on now. "Down south" people were very excited.

With very good reason. For, slowly recovering from dire poverty and the miseries of an awful depression, Queensland was transformed overnight by discovery of the rich gold of Gympie,[42] and was never to look back again. But Somerset was far away from this great relief and feverish excitement.

To his chagrin, Captain Simpson, R.N., the Resident, developed malaria. There was no one to help except Frank Jardine, who thus learnt of a "Great Official Secret". A proposal had been made for a private company to colonize New Guinea, that great, mysterious island lying only a hundred miles across the Strait, for the safer future of the Empire and of Australia, and "because of increasing maritime traffic to the Indian Isles by way of Torres Strait" - a proposal that in later years the colonial Governments were to follow up by urging the British Government to annex New Guinea.

At long last would come the reply that the Colonial Office was just not interested. Thus would Frank Jardine get his first bewildering taste of the vagaries of "diplomacy" and of "international politics", which amazed this straightforward bushman. In coming years he would add many a rueful experience to this.

Simpson was forced to apply for sick leave. He, too, never returned. In 1868 Frank Jardine, still in his twenties, was appointed Government Resident at Somerset, the still-coming Singapore, with naval and military honours, with bugle calls and parade, with a man-o-war just down below the Residency cliff, a Solomon Islands schooner, three *beche-de-mer* brigs, a handsome island brigantine and half a dozen cutters there, too, a score of big island war-canoes and, it seemed, a whole fleet of aboriginal dug-outs. It was a big occasion on the Coral Sea. On that day, Frank Jardine was dedicated to Somerset - for life!

25

THE SECOND SINGAPORE

BRIMFUL of youthful energy and fired by the ambition to really build Somerset into this second Singapore, young Frank, always short of white labour, except when sheltering shipwrecked people, neglected his cattle work for the ever pressing needs of the young settlement. Driving his men from dawn to sunset, he had more "streets" cleared through the bush according to "the Plan", new and stronger stockyards built, and all the buildings enlarged and strengthened, particularly the wide enclosing veranda of the Residency, so well adapted for observation and defence. The Residency grew into practically one "Great Room", which was court-room, sitting-room, dining-room, and official room all combined, solidly built of good Australian cedar. There were skillion and kitchen rooms behind the back veranda, and three or four bedrooms. With hammocks round the verandas, sleeping room could be found for nearly a hundred people if necessary. At the back was a large detached kitchen, a bedroom for the married constable in charge of native troopers, and a store for the Government stores. The stockyard for the Residency mounted work was strongly built; so was the plain, solid furniture indoors. Racks round the Great Room held well-oiled double-barrelled muzzle-loading carbines, always loaded, and there were pistols, cutlasses, axes, knives, ammunition kegs, flasks, lead and bullet moulds close at hand. Ships' lanterns for light at night, strong doors, heavily shuttered window recesses, and of course, on the front veranda by the broad timbered steps, the huge bronze bell from some unknown shipwreck.

Across on the opposite hill, stood the neat, sturdily built barracks.

The hospital, and store, and the customs house were widely spaced, each building in a commanding position, with the timber cleared well away from it. Those well-planned, well-spaced, carefully marked "streets" stood out clearly where the timber had been felled. And all were enclosed by that dull-green semicircle of brooding bush, which to a nervy man could seem sullenly intent on gradually pushing the settlement back over the coastline into Albany Pass.

Jardine's men - how the Gudangs loved using those biting axes! - now cut back deeper, making a wider and larger semicircle, thus not only giving a greater field of fire against possible attack but ensuring that an enemy would be compelled to charge or worm his way twice the distance when once he had emerged from the covering bush.

"We'll make sure they're pretty breathless before they get near enough to use their spears!" Frank said grimly to Scrutton. Although not yet master of the sea, he was determined at least to be master of the settlement on land.

So appeared the settlement of Somerset in those brave days, when Frank Jardine, Police Magistrate and Government Resident, could pause long enough to draw breath and have a look at the result of his labours. He was boyishly delighted when at last he was able to obtain paint and the Residency stood out white on top of the little red hill, with the flag lazily flying beside it-the perfect picture of an outpost of Empire. Viewed from ship-deck upon the turbulent waters of the Pass below the scene was both impressive and attractive - the snouts of the two tiny guns poking out over the cliff-top to command the Pass and the long, bare line of Albany Island opposite, the scrubby headlands and low brown cliffs bright from water-reflected sunlight, the little beach where a brave new landing-place had been built, the palm-like leaves of pandanus-trees, the green tangle of tropical shrub and creeper fringing steps cut in the rock to lead up a steep slope commanded by the mouths of those two little guns.

And a red-letter day came once every four months or so, bringing cheery activity in Residency, barracks, police quarters, and down on the tiny jetty where, just out in the bay, the little H.M.S. *Virago* lay unloading stores and precious mail, bringing eagerly awaited news of the far-away outside world. For the *Virago* had taken over from H.M.S. *Salamander*, and was the one faint vestige of sea authority that Jardine could cling to. For he impressed on the skipper of each roving vessel that called at Somerset for "news", or out of sheer curiosity, the information - which was sheer bluff - that the man-o-war was soon to be permanently stationed at Somerset, and then he, the Government Resident, would police these seas.

With this by no means veiled threat churning in his ears, each skipper would sail away to grumble about it to fellow adventurers, who received the news with varying degrees of contempt, disbelief, or open defiance. By keeping ever alert and ruthless when need be, Frank Jardine was authority by land; by sea, he had long since found it was a different matter altogether. You cannot go chasing naughty ships across the sea on horseback with a carbine in your hand.

Rarely indeed, by some "gathering from the waters" Somerset would find itself a crowded port. On one such occasion the *beche-de-mer* schooner *Melanie* was at anchor close inshore; she had just brought news of the wreck of the brig *Reliance* at Raine Islet. At anchor, too, was the *Woodlark,* on which the water police working on the tiny wharf were keeping a close watch, spied upon in turn by the grinning black and brown faces of the *Woodlark's* daredevil crew of South Sea men. Plenty aboard there had tomahawked their men; it was common knowledge that a number of them had feasted on "long pork"; these were the "big men". The fat-fisted skipper was even now up in the Residency, facing Jardine across the huge cedar table, thumping his greasy fist on the table as in hoarse-voiced, domineering manner he half roared some point of complaint home to this "whipper-snapper damned Government Resident". And Jardine, watching him from cold grey eyes, his mouth tight shut, was wondering what this hulking pirate was trying to put across, and in imagination fitting a coarse hempen rope round that thick neck. Such was his heartfelt wish, as he frankly admitted in years to come. For the high-handed deeds of the *Woodlark's* crew riled him into fury again and again. From down on the calm waterway came a roar of laughter from the *Woodlark,* and the very tone of it caused one of the water police, a man of too amply rounded proportions, to growl to his mate, "I'll bet those cannibal swine ate licking their chops thinking how tasty I'd be, simmering in the cooking pot!" He was right, for the crew of the *Woodlark* were gossiping with the crew of the *Melanie,* who in turn told the tasty joke to Captain Edwards of the *Bluebell,* who in turn repeated it to Jardine, who grimly retold it to his water police to sharpen their dislike of that hard-case schooner crew. They had not only expressed the wish to cook and eat the fat water policeman, but had described how expertly they would slit his throat, bleed him, and cut him up into long pig, and with gusto had enlarged on just how they would instruct the women to cook and season him, their thick lips slavering as in imagination they sank their teeth into his tenderest morsels.

That water policeman slept uneasily for many a night after the *Woodlark* had sailed away. However, while the kanakas were "eating" him, another craft again lay in the bay, a sleek little cutter anchored just off the beach, and the smiling, dark-visaged, sinewy little devil idly smoking beside his lazing crew had already lived through more adventures than the *Woodlark* would ever know. Nicholas the Greek again - the "cat with nine and one lives"! Nicholas with the disarming smile, the cat-like tread and sharp ears that had enabled him to overhear many a whispered scheme, Nicholas with the devilish cunning that matched his ruthless courage, Nicholas the silent when silence was truly golden, he who could strike with the swiftness of a viper and yet, if need be, nurse his revenge until time brought about the reckoning. Well known among many an island group in the South Pacific, he was to appear every now and again at Somerset, almost as a shadow comes and goes. Thus he had appeared that very dawn, when the *Melanie's* crew rubbed their eyes to see the stealthy craft gliding to anchor. Just for a finishing touch, Nicholas's crew were even now conspiring to murder him when they should sail away. They would tomahawk him, seize the craft, and, with the cutter's firearms, sail to some pleasant isle where they could take food and girls to their hearts content, where they would be the boss; where every man, woman and child would fear them.

Poor fools, as if that devil-master would not guess - he who could smell treachery! Chuckling inwardly, he despised these clumsy swine for their stupidity. Presently, in his own good time, maybe today, tomorrow, or the day after, he would quietly walk up the steps cut in the little red hill to the Residency. There, as Captain Nicholas, quietly, courteously, he would lay "the trouble" before the Resident. Then by and by the water police would come rowing to the cutter, and the crew would find themselves being marched ashore. Nicholas would pick a new crew from these fine-looking islanders he was watching in their big canoes, and would pleasantly sail away and leave his rebellious crew to stew in their own juice.

The canoes that had taken Nicholas's eye were large outriggers, manned by muscular Kowraregas, whose broad chests and big shoulder muscles showed them to be born divers. These men are as yet untamed, distrustful, too, but the lure of *toorook* has brought them in the hope of trade to this Lamar settlement. They will barter yams, their strength at work, or, above all, their skill as boatmen and divers, for any trifle of rusty old iron, will barter themselves for anything that is magic iron.

Nicholas will give them iron, and will treat them well for so long as they work well for him. Should greed and familiarity breed in their minds the idea of how easily they could kill him and take all, then he will give them short shrift. Meanwhile he is amused at the expressive contempt they show for the despised "savages" in their rude dug-out canoes lazily coming and going, these Gudang aborigines who seem so familiar with the settlement. How quaint it was, mused Nicholas, that each of the many island tribes he knew feared, hated, or despised the others. Just like the white races! He grinned, then glanced up to the ringing call of a bugle as the tiny garrison came to attention by the barracks above.

So the days passed in the life of Somerset, "outpost of Empire", in the wilds of Cape York Peninsula, commanding the Coral Sea.

Maino, son of Kebisu.

26

FOR THE CORAL SEA, THE MOVING FINGER

RAIN-BATTERED Somerset saw out that nor-west season of 1868, its squalls and storms, its periods of brilliant sunlight swamped again by rains and howling winds, till out of the south appeared a sail upon the lazy blue sea under the warm sky of the steady south-east trades.

Away up on the Residency veranda upon the red hill Jardine first spied the far-away sail. All hands were eager to greet this first sail of the new season. If only she would call in at Somerset!

Jardine could not have known that this growing sail was really a "sail of destiny". Not in his wildest imaginings could he have dreamt that these lonely waters would be developed by a "rush", exactly as a rush of gold-seekers suddenly, miraculously opens up an area of wildest bush.

Thus appeared the singing sails of the stout brig *Julia Percy*, bearing Captain Banner, several white officers, and a hefty South Sea crew. She had been adventuring in the South Seas, and now was coming to try her luck at the *beche-de-mer* in the Coral Sea that was so much spoken about on the Sydney waterfront.

Captain Banner was a jovial, upstanding sea rover with a broad, keen face above a luxurious black beard. Though if need be he was as tough as they make them, his understanding eyes suggested that he preferred to use his head instead of fist or gun. This certainly was the reason he had survived so many years through that stormiest period of the South Seas, dealing with the fighting men of Erromanga, Tanna, Rotumah, the Solomons. He had known at first hand of a dozen schooners overwhelmed, their crews killed and eaten. But always the black-bearded captain, in his steady, methodical fashion, had obtained his objectives and sailed away unscathed, careful to leave friendly memories behind him, in case through some unforeseen circumstance he might wish to return and call again.

And now he was cruising in strange waters, dangerous indeed, yet much was lovely. Sky and sea azure blue, little islands bathed in sunshine, sandbanks gleaming cloth of gold, the snake-like head of a turtle peering inquisitively from an oncoming wave, a cloud of Torres Strait pigeons speeding overhead to feed on the mainland peppermint-trees.

Sailing to seaward past Albany Island, Banner was speculating with the mate about this settlement Somerset, which he had heard lay somewhere on the mainland over opposite that bare-crowned island. A very good job it was there, too, as a haven for shipwrecked seamen. But they needed no glance at this empty sea to doubt whether it would ever be anything more.

Sailing well out from Mount Adolphus Island where the shaggy bowmen prowled, skirting the Dutfield Rock and Melanie Shoals, they spied the Three Sisters Islands, and in a golden sunset anchored off Coconut Island. A moon of liquid silver rose up and its searchlight reached out, bathing a schooner and isle in silver, touching beehive grass huts to silver under silvered palms. The sheltered lagoon speckled in gold-dust from the kisses of the stars, dreamy throb of a drum; haunting melody of some reed instrument as moon-bathed girls in rustling grass skirts began dancing on the lagoon edge, chorus of brown men's voices, happy and carefree, chanting an island love-song across the halcyon water... To the silent listeners leaning over the brig's bulwark that song sounded sweet indeed. Thus have I, too, drunk in the beauty of Coconut Isle, though half a lifetime after Banner's crew first saw it.

Next morning the brig was sailing warily parallel with the huge Dungeness Reef, past Dove Island, Arden Island, then the scraggy pandanus-trees of Warrior Island came in sight and the islands and chain of the great Warrior Reefs, which Banner was to find, stretch for eighty miles, almost to the shore of New Guinea.

Warrior Island!

"Finish!" to Kebisu, Sea Chief of all the Torres Strait Islands of the Coral Sea.

"Finish!" to Wongai, Wild White Man of Badu.

"Finish!" to the islanders of every peaceful and warring tribe, to their beliefs, organizations, culture, life, that so far had stood the test of a thousand years.

"Finish!"

The Lamars were coming in earnest.

"Finish!" to the aborigines in the Great South Land.

This was just a year after James Nash, far to the south, had found the Gympie goldfield which started Queensland on its broad road to prosperity.

And this day Wongai, Wild White Man of Badu stood scowl¬ing upon the Peak of Moa.

What stories that sombre Peak could tell! But it is doubtful if in all its lurid history it had ever seen a stranger figure upon it than this white savage, this Lamar chief, reincarnated spirit man from Spirit Land, scowling far out over the islet-studded sea at a distant sail, a little brig sailing towards Warrior Island.

The *Julia Percy,* Captain Banner. The end had come.

Of course, neither the renegade chieftain, nor Kebisu, nor the islanders, nor the aborigines, could realize this fully.

To all of us life is but a mist, through which ships pass and vanish.

Through his spyglass, Captain Banner could see miles and miles of reefs fading into hazy distance northward. This great line of reefs, though only a midget compared to the Great Barrier Reef, interested the black-bearded skipper immensely. He was seeking *beche-de-mer*. It seemed to him that the surroundings of these huge reefs, containing many hundreds of .square miles of sea foods of almost unlimited description, might easily hold undiscovered beds of the valuable sea-slug he sought.

With look-outs at masthead and bow anxious-eyed for the pale green that would betray shallow water, the brig bore cautiously down towards Warrior Island, constantly swinging the lead in these treacherous waters of sandbank, shoal and reef, powerful tides and unpredictable currents.

In a wondering silence now they bore down upon that growing blur of dull grey and sombre green, all eyes bar the look-out's upon that isle of fearsome repute. Such an insignificant isle, flat upon the water, merely a bank of coral sand that long since would have been engulfed in the sea but for the mighty coral ramparts protecting it. The only relief it offered to the eye was the dull green of its tall pandanus-trees. And now. there were wondering growls from the tense crew at big white things stretching out from the bases of the trees, about half a dozen to each, like snow-white troughs arranged in star shape on the sand.

And troughs they were, natural tubs, huge shells of the giant clam, set to catch the precious rain-water when it rolled down the trunks. Weird they looked below the long, umbrella-shaped roots - which grow above ground of those rustling, droopy-leaved, stunted trees. But for the rain-water these giant shells caught there was not a drop of water upon the islet.

The strangers on the slowly oncoming brig stared at the one big village, from which rose the smoke of numerous cooking fires. Bending forms of brown-skinned women digging out the kop-maori cooking ovens, busy children lending a helpful hand - every sign here of a big, important feast in preparation. And some among the brig's crew licked thick, moist lips in hungry longing, though instinctively knowing they would be even less welcome now than at any other time. They were certain they were gazing upon preparations of a feast of "long pig". For there were also a few cannibals - for the time being ex-cannibals - among this crew. It mattered little in those days, providing all hands were good seamen and fighters if needs be. The few whites among the island vessels of those days took scant notice of a few "cannibals on holiday" among the crew, so long as they were "good men". The whites themselves were long used to living with weapons ever ready night and day. It was all in the life, all in the hazards of both sea and land. To survive one must expect anything, and be wide awake when it came.

Such a mixed crew, when once at sea away from their own islands, were very efficient, if capably handled, as certainly they were on this brig. They would stick to the whites like glue. They had to. For these were very strange waters, unfamiliar people, hence very dangerous to any disgruntled crew foolish enough not to stick together.

But the crew were mistaken about that coming feast ashore.

These kop-maori ovens were not to roast human flesh, but great hunks of dugong and turtle, amazing quantities of fish and crabs and shellfish.

And - something else! Something that was going to make Captain Banner gasp in amazement, something that was going to make him disbelieve his very eyes. Though few have heard of it, this feast was to prove historic in Australian pioneering development.

As the brig glided yet closer in, the crew, in deep-voiced wonderment, admired the huge war-canoes drawn up on the beach; even the largest canoes of their own islands did not carry the bridge-like, broad fighting platforms they saw on these.

With an occasional quiet order, Banner was surveying the scene ashore from calculating eyes. He had never sailed here before, but the reputation of this tiny island was known throughout the Coral Sea. As he noted those canoes, those groups of hefty brown warriors regarding the brig almost upon them, he realized that a false move would buy serious trouble, even for a well-armed schooner and a crew who were fighting fiends if cornered. To lose a fight at close quarters here would qualify all hands for the kop-maori ovens. He grinned to himself as his men's expressive gestures, their faces, told him their thoughts. But the last thing he wanted was a fight. Coolly he weighed the chances, strong in confidence of himself.

He did not want even to interfere in the life of these people in any way. He would have sailed on and kept well clear of this hornet's nest, but that through the days, as he had cruised slowly on beside those great reefs, there had been born in him a certainty that here, somewhere along these miles and miles of so richly "fooded" waters, there must be the particular wealth of the sea he sought. These last two nights he had even dreamt of vast beds of unexploited *beche-de-mer*.

And who was to save golden time and wasted labour by swiftly finding this wealth for him? These very people, those sulky warriors squatting on their hams sourly regarding the brig as she came now drifting to the very edge of the Warrior Reef, barely two bow-shots away now. He felt a certain admiration, too, for these seamen warriors so arrogantly holding their tiny, utterly barren, even utterly waterless islet right in the centre of this great line of reefs, this little handful in their fleet of sea-going canoes commanding all the Strait. He had been told that the fathers of these people had bossed this little area of sea for centuries past. Those brown-skinned seamen ashore would know every inch of these waters. If *beche-de-mer* lay anywhere they could immediately take him to it. The brig was well stocked with better quality trade goods, fabulous riches to those children of the sun ashore. He would buy their services if he could.

And what labour! Every man, woman, and child of them born to the murmur of the sea, almost born within it. The very toddlers gazing up at the brig could already dive, he felt sure, could swim like fishes! Yes, he must make friends with these people.

His eye was running along the numerous canoes, not the war-canoes now but the light, handy fishing canoes. Well manned by swimmers, these could load up with trepang and unload onto the brig or paddle back to the island itself, where a smoke-house could be built. Meanwhile the brig would be kept busy by sailing to and fro from some adjoining island, loaded with wood and water. The ship would have only to keep things going, then load up with the bagged trepang, then heave-ho for Sydney, in less time than it takes to tell. And he would sail back early next season aboard a bigger ship!

Certainly the skipper was cooking his fish before it was caught. But with each passing moment he grew yet more certain those precious fish were here - somewhere.

Captain Banner gave a quiet order to the helmsman, slowly the bows turned inshore towards the very end of the island.

It had been so slow in coming - but then, what is half a century and more? So slow, yet so steady - but swifter now. For the Coral Sea the Moving Finger had written.

27

THE LESSON BEGINS

COOLLY, Banner took a big chance, sailing into the blue of deep water betraying a narrow passage between the ends of Dungeness and Warrior Reefs, the only anchorage visible to the redoubtable Captain Bligh in years gone by. Bligh, in H.M.S. *Providence* and *Assistant,* had been forced to fight his way out of this same tight corner with cannon and musketry.[43] Banner saw the trap - the brig hemmed in by those two reefs and island, those warriors watching so quietly from the shore,' those canoes that could be manned in a moment and come speeding out. But he must anchor or sail on. Coolly, he gave the order to drop the hook. Then he turned his glass on that chief ashore.

"Kebisu!

A savage giant in towering headdress, his bearing sheer untamed arrogance. Banner, big and powerful himself, felt admiration tinged with envy at this perfect physical brute, bedecked now in barbaric ceremonial dress for the feast dances soon to come, polished sharks' teeth gleaming in his jet-black beard and long black ringlets falling down over the massive shoulders. Banner was staring at the grim jaw, full nose, broad forehead and cheeks - a bold face this, now alive with pleased thought. There was much more than animal power in that motionless figure. Banner was trying to read behind those big brown eyes staring into the focus of his glass. And what he saw told him he was up against the test of his life.

Kebisu, breathing deeply, smiled. He was boyishly excited over this unbelievable luck. A Lamar ship to come quietly sailing right into the very trap, all of her own accord! Anchored now, she was a hooked fish; his canoes at signal could dart out, cut her off fore and aft, then race down and board her. His warriors would swarm upon her from all sides before she could even up anchor. She was his.

Thoughtfully he frowned. Don't be too hasty - lose as few men as possible!

Should she show signs of departure he would attack immediately, attack at night, when her crew could not see to use those dangerous thunder-sticks. Time was on his side now. The Lamars had anchored; they must intend to come ashore. Let them - the more the better. Then some of his men could fall upon these suddenly while the canoes raced out to the ship.

Seriously he scanned her. How many thunder-sticks might she carry? She was heavily manned. Plainly he could see a few white Lamars, but many brown, many black.

Kebisu frowned. For a long time now, ever since these small Lamar ships had been creeping in increasing numbers into the Strait to fish for sea-slugs, the islanders had been wondering about those brown and black Lamars among them. They, and their fathers before them, had previously believed all Lamars to be white, but these brown and black men sailing in a spirit ship must be reincarnated spirits, too! The islanders had come to believe the brown Lamars must be the fighting men of the white Lamars, while the black Lamars were the slaves of the brown Lamars. Kebisu did not care how many Lamars were aboard, nor what colour they were. But he must plan to surprise them so that they would have little chance to use their fearsome weapons.

Ah! Now a boat was being lowered. Yes, it was coming away from the ship.

Only three men manned the dinghy, the bo's'n and two kanaka seamen with a wide knowledge of native languages. The bo's'n carried a small but choice present for the chief, with an invitation for him and a dozen of his headmen to come aboard.

As the dinghy steadily pulled to the shore the three men knew their lives might well depend upon a whim of fate. Encouragingly, behind them soon followed a longboat manned by sharp-shooters. As the dinghy grounded on the coral beach the longboat came to a stop, about one hundred and fifty yards out from the beach. Closely the crew watched the bo's'n and the two kanakas walking casually up the beach to the motionless figure of the chief. If the three men were killed the men. in the covering boat could do nothing except fire in swift revenge, then row for their lives back to the brig, the crew of which were standing by ready to cover *them.* These were the usual safeguards taken in those wild days.

From the brig all hands watched the bo's'n deliver his present.

A few moments' conversation, then casually the three men walked back to the dinghy, quietly launched it, and came steadily rowing back to the brig. As they passed the longboat she came rowing back, too.

Captain Banner put down his glasses with a smile. He had seen Kebisu accept the present and condescendingly nod acceptance of the invitation as clearly as if he had been standing beside him.

"He's game," said Banner to the mate. "It's his turn now to put his head into the lion's den-and he's not going to flinch!"

"I feel a bit bothered about your tum," replied the mate uneasily.

"You know just what to do if they knock me on the head," said Banner with a shrug, "and you'd better be quick about it." And he turned his full attention to the shore.

A little later Kebisu and a dozen warriors pushed off in an ordinary fishing canoe. As they came swiftly alongside there was no sign of any arms aboard, but Banner knew that under the strip of coconut matting covering the bottom of the canoe were weapons to hand.

The big chief climbed agilely aboard with a grin, like an athletic schoolboy on holiday. He had climbed more than one ship-when looting wrecks.

He bounded over the rail to the deck and stood gazing into Banner's smiling eyes. For a moment they stood thus. Then Banner reached out his hand, took the chief's huge paw, and shook it in firm grip. After a momentary puzzlement Kebisu smiled broadly and reached out his heavy left arm for a firm grip upon Banner's shoulder. Thus in mutual salutation they gazed yet again into one another's eyes, deeply this time. With a quaintly puzzled expression Kebisu dropped his arm and gazed swiftly round the deck.

Long afterwards Kebisu used to talk, still in puzzled wonderment, of gazing thus into Banner's face and eyes. .

"I never felt like to man like that way before," the big chief would muse. "I wanted to kill him - I often wanted to kill him - I should have killed him but always something me stop! Yes, I should have killed him, him and all his men," he would mutter, and sadly muse on the very different fate of his people had he but killed Banner and thus prevented the big discovery.

Unfortunate Kebisu, unfortunate islanders! It was all written in the stars. Had Kebisu killed Banner, the discovery would only have been delayed for the time being. There was no more hope of preventing what was to be than there had been of Wongai of Badu becoming the island king of his now fast-fading dreams.

Kebisu again glanced swiftly along and around the deck, then carefully, a smile of admiration dawning on his big brown face.

Strategically placed were the few white officers; every man of the crew was silently alert at his post. With a growing admiration Kebisu glanced down along the rail at the black faces, the brown faces all so ready for a fight, the strong black bodies, strong brown bodies bare except for lava-lava and cartridge belt, mops of frizzy hair over big black hooked noses, mops of curly hair over piercing brown eyes, sneering challenge in many a black and brown face. Kebisu favoured them all with one contemptuous curl of the lip as he took in the dreaded thunder-sticks, the loaded muskets to the hand of every man, the cutlasses, the tomahawks. The tomahawks - favourite close-quarters weapon of the South Sea Islanders. How Kebisu's own islanders would love those tomahawks! But - not in the head.

Yes, Kebisu saw at a glance, this ship would be a tough nut to crack, very tough. He glanced at Banner, their eyes met, and both men laughed. Again they had read one another's thoughts.

In high good humour Kebisu strode to the rail and shouted down. In an instant a dozen of his men had sprung grinning to the deck.

"Phew!" whistled the mate, in imagination seeing two hundred in blood-lust madness thus leaping up the sides.

Swiftly the warriors glanced at the crew, exactly as Kebisu had done, then, grinning broadly, cast hungry eyes at the tomahawks and cutlasses.

Through the interpreters Banner yarned quietly to Kebisu while. two hefty Solomons boys spread food upon the deck. No second invitation was needed. The warriors squatted down and fell to with many a "Wah! Wah!" of big-eyed curiosity at this unusual but tasty Lamar food. It was not altogether unfamiliar to them, for they had tasted similar food in the loot of Lamar ships, but not cooked as this was. And such exploits were now recalled with gusto, with sly wink and laugh, for they anticipated that soon they would be looting this ship, too.

The mate, keeping his weather eye ashore, noted that gradually a few more warriors were appearing in the village, and others were now lazing on the beach. Several canoes had pushed out, too, the canoemen quietly fishing. But the mate noted that the tide was very slowly drawing these canoes down towards the brig. When several more canoes were unobtrusively launched he warned Banner.

Banner nodded, and smiled. "Here's where we do our stuff." He nodded to seamen and a tin was thrown overboard. When it had drifted two bow-shots away a marksman sank it with one shot.

Banner smiled at Kebisu. Kebisu laughed broadly with an enthusiastic "Wah!" and slap of hand upon thigh.

The warriors had watched motionless; the loud report startled the sea-birds, and those on shore froze into statues at the dreaded report of the thunder-stick.

But Kebisu again laughed admiringly and asked that the display should be repeated. Banner obliged, his marksman aiming farther and yet farther across the water, to the admiring "Wah! Wah!" of the warriors as bullet after bullet splashed the water.

Kebisu knew perfectly well that these thunder-sticks could kill a man much farther away than his strongest bowman could shoot an arrow. He understood, too, the lesson Banner was trying to impress upon him. He looked at Banner and laughed knowingly. Banner smiled back, then felt a chill of puzzlement. What was this big chief thinking up now?

Kebisu was picturing the dark of night and his men, heavily oiled and armed, hundreds of them, slowly, noiselessly, Boating out towards the brig, swimming under water now and then, until the brig should be completely encircled. Then, at an underwater signal, which would be heard only by those in the water, all would vanish, to come up, hundreds of hands groping, clutching the bottom, the sides, the bow, the stern of the brig. Then, hundreds of unseen noses just above water, quietly breathing. Then - the last under-water signal, and on the instant hundreds of blood-maddened warriors would be swarming up the sides of the vessel. Of what avail then the thunder-sticks of the Lamars?

Kebisu chuckled agreeably. And Banner thought, "What devilry is this cunning brute planning?"

The mate was on his job. He had noted another dozen canoes launched; there was quite a little fleet of innocent fishing canoes now on the water, drifting slowly down. And there definitely were more men lazing in the village. Uneasily the mate again trained his glasses on those big war-canoes drawn up on the beach. But he could see no men near them.

There were men there. The entire crew of each canoe was buried in the sand beside it, only their eyes and noses above the sand. All were waiting for a signal from Kebisu.

The mate quietly called Banner's attention to the canoes drifting down.

Banner spoke to the interpreters, chuckling at Kebisu. The suggestion was that, just for a joke - only a joke, mind! - Banner's men should fire just in front of that near-by fishing canoe out there. Not to hurt the men in it, of course, but just to surprise them, just to see if they would jump.

Kebisu and his headmen laughed uproariously and crowded to the rail to see the fun. Yes, they could appreciate a joke like this.

Ten of Banner's marksmen took steady aim over the rail, aiming a few feet before the bow of the leading canoe. At the mate's sharp "Fire!" the volley rang out; viciously the balls smacked the water before the canoe and ricocheted away back among the canoes behind.

On the instant every man aboard the canoe leapt overboard, as did the crews of several others. Kebisu's men roared with laughter, pointing at the overturned canoes. Yes, it had been a great joke, a very great joke.

Some of the canoes were hurriedly paddling back for shore.

The others came no farther.

Kebisu's hearty laugh was rollicking out over the water. It ceased, as with a puzzled grimace he scratched his head. He had not seen it because of the great joke. But now - !

Clearly he visualized what would have happened had it not been a joke, had those ten musket balls struck men or canoe, instead of water!

He turned round slowly, to gaze into Banner's smiling, understanding eyes.

28

SOMETHING NEW COMES TO KEBISU

BANNER then played his trump card. The brig carried two small guns, one for'ard loaded with slugs, any old chunks of broken iron, one astern loaded with a small iron ball.

A flash and thunderous report, a belch of smoke as the for'ard gun fired, a wide swathe of water thrashed into spouting foam from the scattering chunks.

The warriors stared open-mouthed, those ashore trembled fearfully as the smoke drifted away with the thunder. This was the thing that woke their dread, the "Big Thunder-stick", this super-human power of the Lamars to call on the very Thunder God to belch massive death at them in fire and iron.

In the deathly silence that followed Banner nodded to the interpreter, who spoke to Kebisu.

"The Captain orders me tell the Big Chief he is glad one of the Big Chief's canoes was not lying out there!"

Instantly Kebisu's men visualized what would have happened.

Without warning those slugs would have raked a canoe fore and aft, splintered her and her crew into a foam-lashed death.

Banner let the lesson sink in. Quietly then he beckoned Kebisu's men to follow him astern, while behind them right smartly the bow gun was reloaded.

The stern gun was elevated, fired and the ball sailed away out over the water, to strike with a splash and ricochet and splash and ricochet again farther and farther away into a furry pencil of foam.

That ball had first struck the water ever so much farther away than the island was from the ship.

The islanders were not to know that the bow gun, loaded with slugs, would not shoot nearly so far as the stern gun with one solid ball.

It was all very light-hearted, of course. Grins on all sides, especially on those big-mouthed faces of the crew, to Kebisu's inward anger. As the intepreters explained to him, "Of course, it could never have happened, but what would have happened had the thunder-sticks been trained upon the village?"

Kebisu had no doubts. But he knew the villagers would not have been there, and, after all, it was quite simple to build a new village! He grinned.

But - Kebisu frowned deeply. This Lamar ship could lie off his island and blaze away at any part of it. It was so very small and flat, there were no hills to which the people could flee and shelter from the Lamar's wrath until the ship sailed away. A man could walk all around the islet in an hour. Kebisu had never realized before how fatally small his beloved island was. Should these Lamars attack before he attacked them the only hope for his people would be to run and bury themselves in the sand.[44] Kebisu did not know enough about firearms to realize that burial in the sand is very efficient protection against musketry. He frowned more deeply. He must quickly now, but much more carefully, plan to overwhelm this accursed ship with his war canoes.

He grinned genially at the interpreter. At a word from Banner, the interpreter, with a broad smile, pointed his arm at the island beach, and asked what would have happened had the stern gun been fired at anyone of those huge, priceless war-canoes?

And Kebisu in a panic realized what would have happened.

His heart missed a beat as instinctively he glanced out towards the greatest canoe of all, the most feared canoe in all Torres Strait from the waters of the Great South Land right to New Guinea, his own beloved canoe, the Skull Chief.

Each great canoe, acquired by their fathers' fathers and themselves from the canoe-makers[45] of New Guinea only after much time and at the cost of many lives, much trade, effort, and risk, was of greater value to them than a battleship is to us. Not only so, but those ocean-going canoes meant their life. Without them, their island power would be gone as in a flash. They would perish, marooned on this barren little islet, at the vicious mercy of far more numerous neighbours - neighbours lusting for long overdue revenge, who, though they might still be too afraid of their fighting powers to meet them hand to hand, could simply ring the islet with canoes and in delight let

let them perish of thirst. For in the long dry season they often had to take the canoes to the chief's Yam Island, to load up with fresh water, and if the war fleet were smashed they could never fight their way through from puny fishing canoes.

With a cheery, almost boyish smile at Banner, the big chief intimated that he had business ashore. The women must almost have prepared the feasts by now. The ceremonies, the dances would start at sunset; he must away.

Banner signalled to the bo's'n to bring along the presents for the chief and each of his men. And those presents were good. While they were being eagerly admired the interpreters inquired about trepang, and produced a handful of the dried fish. Kebisu and his men, with loud guffaws, pointed away out over the reef where, here and there between gleaming sandbanks, every few miles the despised sea-slug lay in abundance.

This was great news for Banner, the whites, and all the crew.

And, yes, after the ceremonies were over, in only a few days, certainly the Sea Chief's men would show the Lamars the feeding grounds of the sea-slug. And, yes, they would even dive for them from their canoes-for suitable presents such as these. Indeed, they would very soon fill up the ship-especially if there were more presents for the women! The women, explained the Sea Chief in dignified fashion, were much better divers than the men. For his warriors, of course, had much more important duties to attend to.

Banner assured him that he certainly would not neglect the ladies.

The Big Chief and his men stood erect, clutching their presents, their sparkling eyes betraying how eager they were to be ashore and display these treasures. In dignified fashion then, Kebisu invited Banner ashore that night as an honoured guest at the opening of the ceremonies. Banner heartily accepted, at which the mate breathed uneasily, though saying no word.

As the canoe was paddled to the beach the smile left Kebisu's face; thoughtfully he gazed at the brig, at the figure of the big, black-bearded captain standing watching by the rail. He understood the power of the Lamars now. Never, of course, had he been given such a detailed lesson. He had absorbed it all. But he still was not afraid of the Lamar ship. It was that big, easy-going, smiling Lamar chief, who directed all that the ship could do, he felt so wary of now.

The canoe grated on the beach. Kebisu stepped ashore and turned round to gaze back at the brig, while his warriors walked away to show the curious people their wonderful presents, to tell all they had seen aboard the Lamar ship. Kebisu did not understand the reloading of guns. Like all the islanders, he believed the Lamars had merely to point their thunder-sticks and they could belch fire and death without stopping.

In an attack, the two little guns might have sunk, at the very most, six canoes-probably only two, for the attack would have been so swift there would not- have been time to reload the muzzle-loaders. But Kebisu, of course, did not know that.

He was up against a difficulty such as he had never experienced before; something quite new, the more fearful because not understood, had come into life. And he knew no man who could help him. He felt he must destroy that dangerous thing out there before it destroyed him and his people and the island, too. But - he must not make one little mistake.

Cleverly he realized there was no immediate danger. Those Lamars had given him a deliberate lesson for a purpose, otherwise they would have sailed on, or attacked the island immediately. For the time being, at least, they wished to be friends. Not for one moment did he believe the reason was because they wished to gather in peace those worthless, despised slugs of the sea. As if bewildered, in queerly helpless fashion he rubbed that big brown paw across his frowning brow. What was their real purpose?

Never mind. They wanted peace for the time being. He must use that time to destroy them!

Still staring out at the brig, he grew more and more certain that night attack without canoes was the only answer. His men floating down with the tide, quietly, noiselessly, invisibly swimming under water, until in maddened hundreds they swarmed up the sides of the brig -"Kill! Kill! Kill!"

Only one tiny, elusive doubt flitted across his mind. The black beard, the friendly face, the understanding eyes of the big sea captain.

With a disturbed grunt he turned and walked slowly towards the village, back to his people and the preparation for the feasts, still thinking deeply.

And his thoughts were those I have written here for you, as they were given me many years later by his favourite son, Maino, Chief of Warrior Island, last Mamoose of Tudu and Yam.

29

THE GREAT DISCOVERY

JUST over the calm waters the Sun God set and evening fell, unusually dark and quiet. Dark, too, was the dull cloud over the bows that was Warrior Island. Then fire after fire sprang up, to the fierce, crackling blaze of dry pandanus leaves, throwing ruddy fingers out across the still water towards the brig. Torches borne by whooping children danced like gigantic fireflies. In a moment the village stood out in fiery illumination among the weird growths of .the crooked pandanus-trees; within the foreshore glow the gigantic war-canoes looked like prehistoric monsters crawling up the beach. Sharp thrum of a wasikor drum, another and another and another joining in rhythmic beat, hoarse blasts of the boo shell, thin wails of reed instruments, shrill rattling of goa-nut rattles. A burst of girlish voices in native song, presently joined by the slow, deep voices of men. A patter, like the rustling of leaves in this stillest of nights, a pattern growing into a murmur, a low stamping, a steady stamping, a heavy stamping swelling into thunder, as with a roar every man, woman, and child was lustily stamping in shouting, rhythmic song. Ah, how such a full-throated, thunder-vibrating song can carry out far over the still waters!

The stars blazed out, those golden stars of the Coral Sea. Now the dancers broke into squads. Warrior's dances, women's dances would go on until with the coming of the full moon the kop-maori ovens would be opened and the first relay of the feast commence, the delicious aroma rising as the women peeled off the banana leaves from the steaming, tenderly roasted meats.

So it would go on-dance, feast, sleep, dance, feast, sleep - for three nights and days. The crew of the brig, leaning over the rail, surmised in murmurous tones on the activities of the squatting, dancing, prowling groups ashore. With dilated nostrils they awaited the whiff they were sure would come to them on the cool night air when those kop-maori ovens ashore were opened. Some were positive those ovens contained "long pig", succulently roasted.

The two unusually lean interpreters, sulkily frightened men, were unconvincingly sure it was not long pig. These "uncultured" Torres Strait savages, they said, killed not to eat, but for the heads. All they ate was the tongue, and such other delectable morsels, that would give cunning, and strength, and courage to the eater.

With this the amply proportioned cook, with a wicked leer, agreed. And he added softly to the boys that it would not matter to their two skinny mates if only their tongues and kidneys, hearts, and livers and other unmentionables were eaten, for the rest would be thrown to the sharks anyway. They were certainly not plump enough to be bundled into the kop-maori ovens.

Other similar jokes were accepted with good or bad grace, according to the feelings of the victim selected. The cook, who had been first to joke at the interpreters' expense, reacted with a snarl when a Rotumah man laughingly commented on how "Cooky's" goodly hindquarters would bubble in the pot! With more than one pair of tigerish eyes turned upon him reflectively, the cook slunk sullenly away to his galley.

Feeling the throb of the song beating in their own hot blood, the crew leant silently over the rail, listening, awaiting the rising of the moon.

And soon, when she rose, the captain would be going ashore with the two interpreters alone - not even with a covering boat's crew!

"If they mean to scupper us," he had explained to his mates, "then they'll only get the three of us. Otherwise they would club all who went ashore and the cover boat crew as well, for the boat would be cut off before it could race back to the brig. If only three of us go ashore then you'll have every man aboard to defend the brig - if need be. But I don't think there'll be trouble."

Leaning over the rail a little apart from the crew, smoking their pipes, the whites eagerly discussed the probability of a rich find. It seemed plain sailing now. Only keep sweet with that hulking big savage ashore, and new trepang grounds would be theirs.

"The crew must never be given the chance to interfere with their women," Banner said emphatically, "or we'll miss out. And have our throats cut into the bargain."

"I'll let them know the first man who grabs a girl stops a bullet," promised the mate grimly. "But I doubt if there'll be trouble. We're in a ticklish position and the crew know it - those tough boys ashore would cut our livers out alive if they could lay hands on us."

And he nodded towards. the massed savagery silhouetted now in roaring action by the fires ashore.

On that night, with the high tides and the water deathly still, the slightest sound carried far. No sign now of the huge Warrior Reefs; all were under water. So, too, was the Great Barrier Reef stretching a thousand miles north and south, under water still as the quietest river. Brilliant phosphorus ripped past the brig as some giant fish chased its prey, then the water boiled astern in a fascinating blaze of blues and reds and orange as a fish shoal leapt in frenzy from the jaws of destroyers. Sharp and rhythmic from the shore came the growing tempo of the dance, waves of sound hitting and bouncing off the polished glass of the water.

"They'll keep the war-dances until the last night," said Banner, puffing at a million stars, "but I'll stay aboard that night!"

Presently she came, the eagerly awaited, the feared, the honoured guest, gliding up out of the Great Barrier Reef in a radiant disc of light. She seemed to pause a moment, floating on top of the Barrier, a flush of rose in the gold of her kiss on the waters. Then they fell away from her in shimmering silver as she climbed, and silver, too, were brig and islet and palm-fronds. And night was bright as daylight, but with an unutterable loveliness, the loveliness of a full moon smiling in a quiet night over Australia's tropic sea.

The mate had seen many a lovely night in the tropics, but even he was impressed

"She looks like a beautiful new pearl tonight," he said, nodding admiringly at the moon, "a new pearl fresh born from the sea", and paused abashed at his words.

"Yes," said Banner, "a good omen. But there'll be light in plenty for the feasts now - it's time for me to go ashore."

"Good luck," murmured the mates, and fervently meant it, for they liked and admired the "Old Man".

Banner and the interpreters climbed overside down into the old dinghy, and casually rowed to the shore. Banner's appearance was the signal for the first feast to begin, he was the guest of honour who sat beside the Chief Kebisu and was treated right royally. For the islanders on such occasions had a deeply ingrained courtesy. They might be calculating on the guest's skull as a prized trophy, but if they had invited him to a feast they would first entertain him.

While the women were busy opening the ovens Banner presented his own contribution to the feast, which was gracefully accepted. And the feast began.

"Must be five hundred or so here," thought Banner, "but there could be more, away out past the fires among those farther trees."

Squatting groups of hungry warriors were being served huge helpings of dugong, fish, and turtle by laughing women and children. And it was a starry-eyed, laughing youngster who set himself as Banner's personal attendant. The big sea captain with the genial smile took an immediate liking to this hefty little lad with the friendly disposition, so unafraid of, so boyishly curious of, the dreaded Lamar.

Banner made much of him, not then realizing that his friendly interest in the boy was the very best thing he could have done, that it was to bring him reward far beyond his wildest dreams, that in the long run it was almost certainly the deciding factor that saved his life and ship. For this lad was Maino, the Sea Chief Kebisu's favourite son. Maino, destined to be the last Mamoose of Tudu and Yam, and staunch friend of the white men, the once dreaded Lamars. He would save the life of Sir William MacGregor in the "big" New Guinea days to come. In his own way, in his own sphere, he would become known far and wide in the future development of the Strait.

Kebisu's day was really finished tonight, as was that of all the mature islanders. From now on was to begin the complete disintegration of their race, of all their beliefs, until a new generation would shamefacedly disown them, except for the last few stalwarts such as Maino and old Passi of Mer. Today their descendants[46] laugh to scorn even the memory of a culture that lasted a thousand years and more. Thus the earth rolls on, and only the stars look down on vanished dreams, vanished cultures, vanished people, vanished civilizations - stepping-stones, it may be, to some wonderful future.

Banner had become so engrossed in the little boy who, to the manner born, kept ordering his friends to entertain and wait on the Lamar, that for a while he did not notice a new dish being prepared - a mere nothing, merely an *hors-d'oeuvre* in between mightier dishes. The hot stones from the ovens everywhere had been spread out and women were laying upon them greyish, massive objects about the size of a small dinner-plate. Banner idly watched the chattering women at the nearest fire. Puzzled, he stared more intently. Then he leant forward with a quick intake of breath. Presently he sat back, gazed unbelievingly at the stars, then slowly stared at that fire again. Surely not! Surely not! Young Maino strode across to one of the women, took one of the objects from her hands, and brought it smilingly to Banner.

He reached out unbelievingly and turned it over and over, his face transformed. This thing must weigh all of seven or eight pounds! Just a flattish, thick shell of dull grey, with roasted coral weed still adhering to the two rough valves. But heat had opened the shell, a glint of starlight kissed the translucence there. In an unbelieving, helpless sort of way Banner turned his face to the sky, and smiled. He was breathing in that strange, hurt way in which a toiling prospector breathes when his pick sinks into a nugget of gold. Pearlshell! Mother-of-pearl! The largest by far he had ever seen, such as he had never expected to see in his wildest dreams.

They were roasting pearlshell, roasting them just for the sake of the fish inside! Thousands of wonderful shells, a ransom for a king, being destroyed upon the cooking fires of savages!

He held the shell with big hands which, for the life of him, he could not prevent from trembling. He was smiling at little Maino, standing there in bright-eyed curiosity. Kebisu, mistaking Banner's agitation, shouted to a woman to bring the Lamar the first big fish cooked. They thought he disdained the pearl oyster, thought he was only hungry for fish!

The shells now were popping open in the heat, the thick-muscled fish inside stewing in their own juice. In anguished amazement Banner watched as fish after fish was wolfed and the beautiful, fire-destroyed shells tossed aside. A fortune destroyed before his eyes! There must be an enormously rich pearlshell bed where these mighty shells had come from. He wanted to jump up and shout at them to stop, to offer them all in the brig for these shells. Hold fast, or they would fall upon him in a frenzy for interrupting the feast. But he felt he could not sit and smile like an ape at this frightful waste. He was in a fever, too, to hurry to the brig and spread the wonderful news. Hold fast! He must sit right here and see it out and smile, smile!

The sea-slug was utterly forgotten. What was the humble *beche-de-mer* beside these majestic mother-of-pearl?

Half an hour later a warrior beside him bulged his cheeks, then: spat out something as he wolfed an oyster. That "something", a small marble, plopped on the sand. Little Maino, watching Banner's staring eyes, rather undecidedly picked up the marble, half held out his hand with a smile. Banner reached out a paw like a ham - there was no hesitation on his part - and examined the marble.

Kebisu, the nearest warriors, and little Maino and his friends watched Banner in surprised curiosity. He could not hide his agitation, his excitement, his regret at this beautiful thing destroyed; his eyes shone from almost a fevered face at this fantastic discovery.

The savages wondered what it could be all about. Little Maino decided to find out. An order to his childish bodyguard, and they were rooting about in the sand, searching for relics of other feasts. Presently they found two burnt pearls. Yes, it was what the strange Lamar sought. And yet how disappointed he seemed. Puzzled again, silently they watched.

Banner had a brain-wave. Smiling, he gestured towards a heap of uncooked shells. One was brought him, and swiftly he opened this with his sheath-knife, gasping in excitement at the fresh, lovely gleam of mother-of-pearl as the moonlight bathed the opened shell. Smiling at Maino, he groped about in the shellfish, then held up his fingers as if he held a pearl. He grimaced questioningly at Maino.

The boy thought a moment, then with his toes picked up a burnt pearl. Banner smiled and shook his head. He picked up a cooked pearlshell, put the burnt pearl in it, then shook his head and frowned as he threw both away.

Then he picked up the raw shell and again groped about in the fish. His face broke into a delighted smile as he triumphantly held up an imaginary pearl.

Maino's faintly puzzled expression was followed by a smile of understanding, and again he gave an order to his bodyguard. They scurried away like monkeys, but soon were back. And one held out to Banner five dull, sheeny pearls in the palm of his little brown hand.

Here is the explanation. At times the islanders sun-dried the pearlshell oysters, preparatory to taking them as food on a voyage, instead of roasting them. And the younger children sometimes took any pearls that were found and kept them as playthings. It was from a child's little hoard that these pearls had come.[47]

Banner stared at the "live" pearls in his palm, while a thousand brown eyes amusedly, contemptuously watched this big white Lamar gaping at a child's plaything. And the moonlight smiled down upon the Coral Sea and bathed her children and the pearls, too, with her silvery light; and the polished masts, the cordage of the quiet ship just out from the firelit shores, was silver.

Banner sat and gazed entranced, living in a world of dreams come true, a world such as comes to very, very few men. But even his dreams could not tell him that he had found the richest pearlshell beds in the world's history.

30

TREASURE OF THE SEA

CAPTAIN BANNER'S crew went nearly crazy with glee when aboard the brig he called all hands for'ard and spread the news. Urgently he warned them to go carefully lest they lose all, including their heads. Friendship and confidence with those fighting men ashore must be developed by every means possible. Above all, no "hanky-panky" with the women, for that certainly would ruin all. He warned them again that they were completely isolated, with hundreds of savages at their very anchor chain, proved fighting men who could draw a bow powerful enough to shoot an arrow through a plank. "And don't think just because you've got a musket and cutlass we are going to run this island as we like. For I've just watched the dance showing how their fathers were game enough to tackle two men-o'-war and came within an ace of boarding and overpowering one of them, so that both ships cleared out while they could! That's a fact!. Now get that into your gizzards and digest it!" He glared grimly round. "If we work cautiously," he resumed, "and control ourselves, we have a fortune-for the owners and for every man aboard. Within a few seasons, a very few, every man aboard this ship can be landed upon his own island with money enough to buy all the land he wants, his own house, his own pigs and wife. Think of all the pigs you'll be able to buy when we fill the brig with pearlshell! And if you want wives, then every man jack of you will be able to take your pick of all the girls on your island. Every man jack of you will return richer than your chief even, you'll be able to buy and sell him if you want to! Now just chew that over - every man aboard here has his chance to return home and buy his own chief-and all the chief's pigs, too. So see that every man keeps a tight hold on himself for the time being, works with a will, obeys orders quick-smart for the good of himself, for the good of all!"

To which, with a medley of exultant voices, all agreed. And they kept the compact, too.

Several days after the feasts Banner, nobly aided by little Maino, prevailed upon Kebisu to set his braves to work collecting the shell. He had no difficulty, for the rewards offered were stupendous in the eyes of the islanders; they were dazed by such gifts for these so common shells of the sea. That the Lamars did not even want to eat the fish within the shell was utterly beyond their comprehension. And that a special reward of a priceless tomahawk was offered for every worthless "stone" found within a shell sent them nearly crazy with exultant wonder. To them, a pearl was only a nuisance that grated on the teeth and had to be spat out when they ate the oyster. Probably not a man among them but had swallowed some in the course of his life.

So men and boys, swiftly outdone by the women, paddled their canoes to the reef near by and at low water picked up the shell and threw it into the canoes. For the beds were so rich in patches here and there that the pearlshell oysters were almost at the surface at low water. Over many, many miles of these great Warrior Reefs there was abundance of shell only a fathom or two deep, mere play to these deep-chested swimmers. And the women were quickly to prove the best of them all. Not for several years after the first rush would the islanders have to dive more than a couple of fathoms for shell.

As the canoes were filled the boys paddled them to the island shore, where old women and children took over to open the shell, extract the fish, and wash the shell. The warriors, of course, would never do such plebeian work as this. The women soon became the experts not only in the diving, but in running their fingers under and around the fish in search of pearls. And a laughing scream whenever a pearl was found would be echoed by shouts from the men out in the canoes until it was known whose woman had found the pearl. For of course it was to the warrior that the great reward must be given. But Banner saw to it that each woman who found a pearl was quietly rewarded, too.

Banner quickly found, as the trepang adventurers had discovered elsewhere before him, that the women were the most willing divers. Such continuous work was beneath the lazy dignity of the men, the elder warriors of whom soon resumed the pleasant task of lording it ashore. So quietly the women took over the work, and Banner saw that they were fully rewarded, while craftily promising yet richer gifts in the future to the Sea Chief Kebisu and his chief men for the women's services.

Especially would these riches come to the Sea Chief when the captain returned with a bigger ship! This brought a pleased smile to Kebisu's broad face, followed by a thoughtful frown. For the brain of the savage was busy with that age-old puzzle about killing the goose that lays the golden eggs!

Only a pearl in about every thousandth shell - but soon the handful of white men aboard the brig, at night under the ship's lantern, were gloating over a little pile of gems. To their intense disappointment, and astonishment, they would find on arrival in Sydney that this fortune of beautiful pearls could be sold only at prices far below their worth.

The reason is easy to understand - now. With Australia's then so tiny population there was no market for such magnificent pearls in quantity, and the distant world knew nothing about Australian pearls. In fact, even at this time[48] comparatively few people in the world knew that Australia existed. It was to take quite a number of years before a Continental market would become interested, and buyers in increasing numbers would sail out here to bid eagerly for these lovely gems.

Precisely the same thing was to happen, thirty years later, with Australian opals.

For some years the pearlshell would be more eagerly sought than the pearls, for there was a ready market for this. But for Banner and his happy men these problems were still in the future; they took life as it came and found it good. Bright sky and blue sea, good sou'-east weather, good diving weather, the islet beside them, the ship under their feet; fishing canoes out along the reef, sunlight kissing golden-brown bodies of young girls diving from canoe and reef, lithe bodies gliding down through transparent water to flash up entrancingly, clutching a big pearlshell, up through the surface to throw the shell into the canoe with a laugh - and, squatting on the beach there under the shadiest palm, that hulking great savage Kebisu, complacent old devil, calmly smoking his zoob and drinking in the admiration of his headmen as they wondered at the presents all around him.

"How'd you like to liven him up with a musket ball?" growled the cook one morning.

"Cut that out!" snarled .the mate, who had overheard. "We're in danger enough without putting that into their minds. Get back to your galley, you greasy cow dugong, before I cut your liver out!"

Yes, though the crew took life with a laugh these days, with wealth untold before their eyes at every sunset in this wonderful take of pearlshell, they were in peril night and day; their lives depended on their "keeping sweet" with those bloodthirsty headhunters. And the Sea Chief Kebisu ate and slept and laughed time away, but scowled and planned, too-and smiled when Banner came casually ashore for a yarn, always with a present. For the first time in his "bull-at-a-gate" life the Big Chief was plagued by that curse of mankind - indecision.

Meanwhile, ninety miles south-west on the mainland, at that settlement of Somerset, the Government Resident was eagerly awaiting the arrival of the schooner *Reconnaissance*. For Jardine was to sail to Brisbane on twelve months' furlough to lay very important recommendations relating to the lack of Her Majesty's Authority upon the high seas, and to the tragic neglect of most necessary man-power in the development of Somerset, before the Colonial Secretary of the day. The schooner would bring him his relief, the Acting Resident and Police Magistrate. Grimly he hoped this officer would be used to roughing it, would be a fighter, but especially would have knowledge of the bush and the aboriginal, the sea and the islander.

He would need all the experience he could muster. And one evening, her lonely sail blotted out in the mists of a grey squall, the *Sperweer* sailed by, to seaward of Albany Island. Alas, she did not call in at Somerset. But then, Captain Gascoigne may not have known of that haven of refuge, perhaps not of its position. Sailing all the way from Melbourne, the little cutter had safely negotiated the thousand-mile dangers of the Great Barrier and was now anchored off Friday Island, but thirty miles north of Somerset. Unhappily, it was also within a few miles of the shore of big Murralug, which the Lamars called Prince of Wales Island, and which was inhabited by the savage Kowraregas.

Captain Will Gascoigne, his wife and twelve-year-old son, with a Malay crew, were aboard. Gascoigne was hoping to make a fortune by discovering a new bed of *beche-de-mer*. His wife was fearful in these strange, so lonely, so wild surroundings. The crew seem not to have understood their danger, but apparently were nervy. Surely Captain Gascoigne could not have thoroughly understood either, otherwise he must have been a recklessly foolhardy man so to endanger the lives of his wife and son.

Separated by only a narrow channel from Murralug is large Horn Island, with Entrance, Hammond, Thursday islands and others of this group but a stone's throwaway. All were inhabited by branches of the Kowrarega tribes, all good canoemen, practically "born in the water", all hating the Lamars with a superstitious fear, and used to handling bow and arrow, heavy spear and club, and the opei knife.

And on a beautiful tropic night here was the tiny *Sperweer*, beyond the reach of any help, peacefully anchored in the very heart of savagery. Many a time I have breathed in the beauty of such a scene, the still water all diamonds from the reflections of the stars. That light from heaven kisses the deck of the cutter, too; surely she is breathing dreamily, or is it a murmur in the tide gliding along her bows? In the clear, faint blue of the night the moveless islands stand up like silhouettes of black velvet. The air is glorious, carrying an elusive tang of both sea and near - by land, while, if you listen, you become aware of the faintest sigh over all.

It was on such a night that the *Sperweer* slept, unaware of Kowrarega warriors from Murralug crowding into canoes and paddling silently across to Friday Island. Here they landed, and with turtle oil greased their brown, muscular bodies. When they become excited I have seen how their eyes glare in the night. Picking up their weapons, these night prowlers walked across the little islet to a tiny beach. There, out in the waterway, the *Sperweer* lay like a toy carved in pearlshell upon a plate of blue velvet. The shadow warriors spread along the shore, then seemed to melt into the still water. When they are on such errands not even a tell-tale flurry of phosphorus marks their way.

It must have been a terrible awakening for those on little *Sperweer*. One moment the dreamy peace of a beautiful tropic night, the next the sea vomiting up dark shapes all over the deck as howling savages smashed down upon them with spear and club.

We can only hope it was all over in a few seconds. Unhappily, they did not complete the massacre, for they took the mother and son captive. They looted the vessel, then fired her - a dreadful pyre that, to the eyes of the frantic mother and boy.

A war head-dress, taken from Tudu in 1888.

31

THE SETTLEMENT'S FIRST MAN-O'-WAR

FROM the Residency veranda one morning through the glass Jardine caught the glint of sunlight on a sail. Delightedly he hurried along the veranda to make doubly sure quarters were prepared for his relieving officer, the new Acting Resident, Lieutenant H. M. Chester, late of the Persian wars and the Indian Navy, and recent employee of the Queensland Government at the Gympie goldfields. With him were his wife and son, the wife a noted beauty of the day used to the admiration, the pomp and ceremony of naval etiquette, to glittering uniforms, to the fanfare of an Indian rajah's court, now coming to Somerset and the bush, the naked blacks, the almost empty sea. What a shock was awaiting the lady! Her son, now adventuring so early in life, was up on the poop with Captain Hannah, as the stiff sou-east trades gaily drove the schooner along. It had been a fast trip indeed, only sixteen days from Brisbane.

Jardine, in an enthusiastic hurry to lay his plans of empire before the authorities in person, gave Chester a week in which to absorb what he could of this problem. settlement. He liked the new man, and believed he would fit in, though he was doubtful over his lack of experience with the Australian aboriginal.

"Don't take him too cheaply," he cautioned. "He may not look so impressive as the native troops you have seen in action, he may be armed only with a wooden spear and nulla-nulla, but in these surroundings he is not to be despised - as you will find out most painfully if you should even leave this veranda without a revolver at your belt. You see how it is here. The settlement, at present without help of shipwrecked people, is actually in a desperate position. There are now only six white police and half a dozen native troopers to hold Somerset, apart from the Gudangs I have trained. No water police until reinforcements arrive from the south. And now three of the white police have their wives with them. With your wife, that is four white women to think of - and your son. I advise you strongly to abandon the house on the southern hill. If the place is attacked the police from the barracks could not come to your assistance, they would be speared from behind trees without ever seeing their assailants. The blacks will probably burn house and stockyard, but you can't help that."

Chester looked worried a moment. "The Government might think I was afraid," he said doubtfully, "if I threw away valuable government property like that. This is the chance of a lifetime for me; I could not get another such appointment in all Australia. Also, jobs of any sort are painfully scarce down south. I would much prefer you to report the seriousness of the position to the authorities when you arrive in Brisbane."

"As you wish." Jardine shrugged.

He was just ready to board the *Reconnaissance* when Gudang spies hesitantly muttered to him a rumour that the men of Murralug had attacked a "white-man canoe". It was a small vessel, and they had massacred all aboard, except a woman and child. The scouts did not know what had happened to the white woman and boy. But they were evasive and frightened, they had only "caught a whisper", they sulked when Jardine sternly questioned them.

"You see," said Jardine to Chester, "just how it is. There may be truth in this rumour, there may not. I should have a swift, well-manned and armed vessel ready here on all occasions to sail immediately and investigate such rumours. I have not. Do the best you can. Become established here, meanwhile bribe the Gudangs to canoe to Murralug, that is, Prince of Wales Island, and return with further news. Then commandeer a whaleboat from the first vessel that sails into port and investigate. And here comes a vessel now - what a stroke of luck!"

She was a small *beche-de-mer* brig, calling at Somerset for news, and bringing a startling rumour also, but only a rumour. The skipper had fallen in with a canoe-load of Aureed Islanders on a turtle-hunting voyage and they had told his men that a "white-man canoe" was fishing for pearlshell somewhere out along the Warrior Reefs. These natives had joked with his coloured seamen about the wonderful presents the Sea Chief Kebisu was squeezing from the white men for the useless pearlshell! Kebisu was taking all he could get from them, was lulling them into a false security while laying his plans. Soon, so these turtle-hunters declared, Kebisu would fall upon the white men and take their heads, loot the vessel, then set her on fire.

"You don't seem to know anything about it," said the skipper disappointedly. "I sailed out of my way on purpose to make sure whether the yarn was correct. I thought that here at the settlement you'd know all about it!"

Jardine shook his head. "This is the very first news I've heard," he replied. "I know nothing about her. She certainly did call in here," he added sourly, "as all vessels should do, but I've heard nothing since. If she is in trouble the captain will have to look after himself. I can do nothing about it."

"I suppose it's only a rumour anyway," replied the disappointed skipper. "A man's crazy to imagine pearlshell in this wilderness, anyway. All the same," he added in puzzled tone, "those natives did describe pearlshell to me pretty well, or so it seemed. Well, I must aboard."

And he sailed south. Had he been a little more enterprising and investigated for himself he could have anchored beside Banner and fortune.

As Jardine boarded the *Reconnaissance* he turned to Chester. It was plain to see he was excited.

"Surely this rumour of a pearlshell find cannot be correct! And yet - why not? In a new sea like this, a sea a maze of coral reefs and gardens, turtle and dugong, and countless shoals of fish and fish things known and unknown! Those would-be pirates have long since found *beche-de-mer*, and valuable tortoiseshell too. Why should not the pearl oyster grow in this strange sea? It seems unbelievable, I know. But should this rumour turn out to be correct," he added impressively, "then you'll have your work cut out with a vengeance! For, added to all these *beche-de-mer* vessels, you'll have a rush of ships and adventurers from all the seas, and they'll play merry hell in these unguarded waters. The Government surely cannot refuse me a man-o-war to police these seas when I bring them this news!"

Exultantly he sailed, straight into the teeth of the south-east trades. Day and night it was "tack, tack, tack", gaining barely a mile of seaway, the schooner helpless almost as a butterfly trying to battle against the wind. It was one of those positions in which irritable man occasionally finds himself and learns how small he really is. Jardine gave it up at last, he was forced to. The schooner turned about and ran before the wind back to Somerset, then carried on right round the northern and western coasts, at last to round Cape Leeuwin. Instead of having a straight run south Jardine was forced to "follow his tail" all round the continent for twelve thousand miles. It was three months before the Reconnaissance hook rattled overboard in Brisbane River.

Meanwhile, at Somerset Chester immediately found his hands full. He had told his wife of Jardine's suggestion of abandoning one of the main buildings for safety reasons. She refused point-blank, to Chester's relief. She had taken a fancy to the furniture, mostly made by shipwrecked ship's carpenters. She liked the place; it was comfortable; she declared she would not budge. As to safety - well, after all, she had been through the Indian Mutiny. And what she saw of these naked savages made her believe she could fight the lot of them herself. And that was that!

So Chester, with a wry smile, arranged with the police sergeant that if an attack did come the police were not to venture to his aid. All hands would fight it out from the houses on the two hills. That settled, Chester turned to master his duties with a feeling of the keenest interest.

Fortunately for him, he was already an experienced campaigner both by land and sea, in India and Persia and the Indian Ocean. He knew nothing about the Australian bush, but a great deal about the sea, and small craft in particular. Naturally it was to the sea that he eagerly turned. Jardine to the bushlands, he to the sea - they would have made a good working pair.

But the lack of a vessel, which Jardine had complained of so bitterly, brought him up with a jerk. Here he was, in at least temporary authority over all of this Coral Sea, and he did not even have a fisher boat to police it with! How he longed for one of the frigates of the Indian Navy, even to the smallest one of all! Like a fish out of water he gazed at the sea.

He was worried, too, at that rumour of the massacre of some vessel's crew near the big island of Murralug, away north some-where, that rumour of a white woman and boy taken captive. He doubted that sulkily. told native rumour; certainly he did not believe that a woman and boy had been spared. And yet Jardine had thought it should be investigated.

A fortnight later a canoe-load of Kowraregas from Murralug, with Chief Tipoti aboard, arrived at Somerset and boldly approached the settlement, offering to barter tortoiseshell for iron.

Chester, forewarned by the Gudangs, seized the chief and his main warrior as hostages for the lives of the white woman and child. The chief, sullenly helpless in the grip of this martial strength, finally admitted the massacre, but swore that the Mount Ernest natives had done the killing. Stubbornly he shook his head as if ignorant of the facts when questioned about the woman and the lad. Chester was a worried man now.

Several days later the schooner *Georgina Godfrey* anchored off Somerset. Captain Godfrey willingly lent the schooner to Chester. He manned it heavily, and sailed for Murralug, to find the remains of the *Sperweer*, burnt to the water's edge. The remains of two white men, were also found, one with five inches of a barbed arrow-head embedded in his thigh bone. The others of the crew had been clubbed and thrown overboard. But there was no trace of the woman or boy. Chester released his hostages.

While Chester was in this state of baffled frustration folk aboard the barque *Tynemouth* would soon be in a far worse plight. Manoeuvring to pass in from the Pacific into the Coral Sea through the Great Barrier Reef at the Raine Island entrance, she struck in all the terror of shipwreck. From that desolate coral speck a boatload of the castaways gloomily set out on the long, long pull to Timor. Several days later, to their inexpressible delight, a sail bore down upon them, a vision from heaven in that lonesome sea. It was the trading schooner *Georgina Godfrey*. She sailed with them east towards the mainland, where at Cape Grenville, not far south of Somerset, natives gathering *beche-de-mer* for the schooner told the skipper that a white man's boat was lying at anchor just along the coast. Immediately curious as to neighbours in such a place, the skipper sailed to the locality and there, right enough, a vessel lay at anchor. A goodly sized ship's longboat of about six tons, cutter rigged, decked over, her bottom coppered, her masts standing and sails bent, she was all shipshape to up anchor and sail away;

But - not a soul aboard!

Her hold empty, her papers missing, they could find no name or mark to identify her. A nameless, empty little vessel lying quietly there at anchor awaiting a crew that had vanished.

In growing apprehension they examined her more carefully. "Ah!" cried the boatswain, pointing to dried bloodstains splashed upon her starboard side. And that was all that was ever known of her. The castaways from the *Tynemouth* gazed upon her apprehensively. Had natives killed the crew of this boat? If so, why had they not burnt her after the looting, as was their custom? Had they left her as a decoy, hoping that some day castaways might come this way and see her and investigate, to find themselves suddenly surrounded by canoes? No one would ever know.

The *Georgina Godfrey* took the vessel in tow and sailed north for Somerset.

"A haven of refuge set up just south of the tip of Cape York York Peninsula by the Queensland Government," explained the skipper of the *Georgina Godfrey* to the castaways. "A durned good idea, too. It's already saved the lives of many a good sailorman, both from the savages and from perishing at sea."

The captain of the late *Tynemouth* was amazed, never imagining a settlement on that wild coast. This caused Chester to write to the Colonial Secretary, suggesting that a notification be sent to the Board of Trade, to Lloyd's, and to the *Mercantile and Shipping Gazette*, with a view to knowledge of the settlement of Somerset being widely disseminated. "Had these men not fallen in with the schooner," he wrote, "it is probable they would have perished, for they were without a compass, had only a little biscuit and water, and having no firearms were afraid to land and look for food."

Chester, as Government Resident, immediately took possession of the mystery longboat - in keen delight, for she would be just the very thing for cruising among the islands, seeing that the Government of the day had pointedly ignored Jardine's requests for a policing vessel. Busily he refitted her, naming her the *Alerta,* for the Resident believed in being ever alert. Almost immediately he had his excuse for a trial cruise in a report of the shooting and kidnapping of natives on Half Way Island, only ninety miles across the Strait. Eagerly he put to sea, but ran fair into heavy seas with a sou-east gale beating up. Making heavy weather of it, the little vessel began to leak badly, despite continuous bailing. Sullenly, her coloured crew declared the "hoodoo" sailed with her. Unknown men had died in this ship. They would die, too, if she did not put back. Chester was forced to beat back and only just made Somerset as the vessel was going to pieces. And that was the end of the *Alerta*.

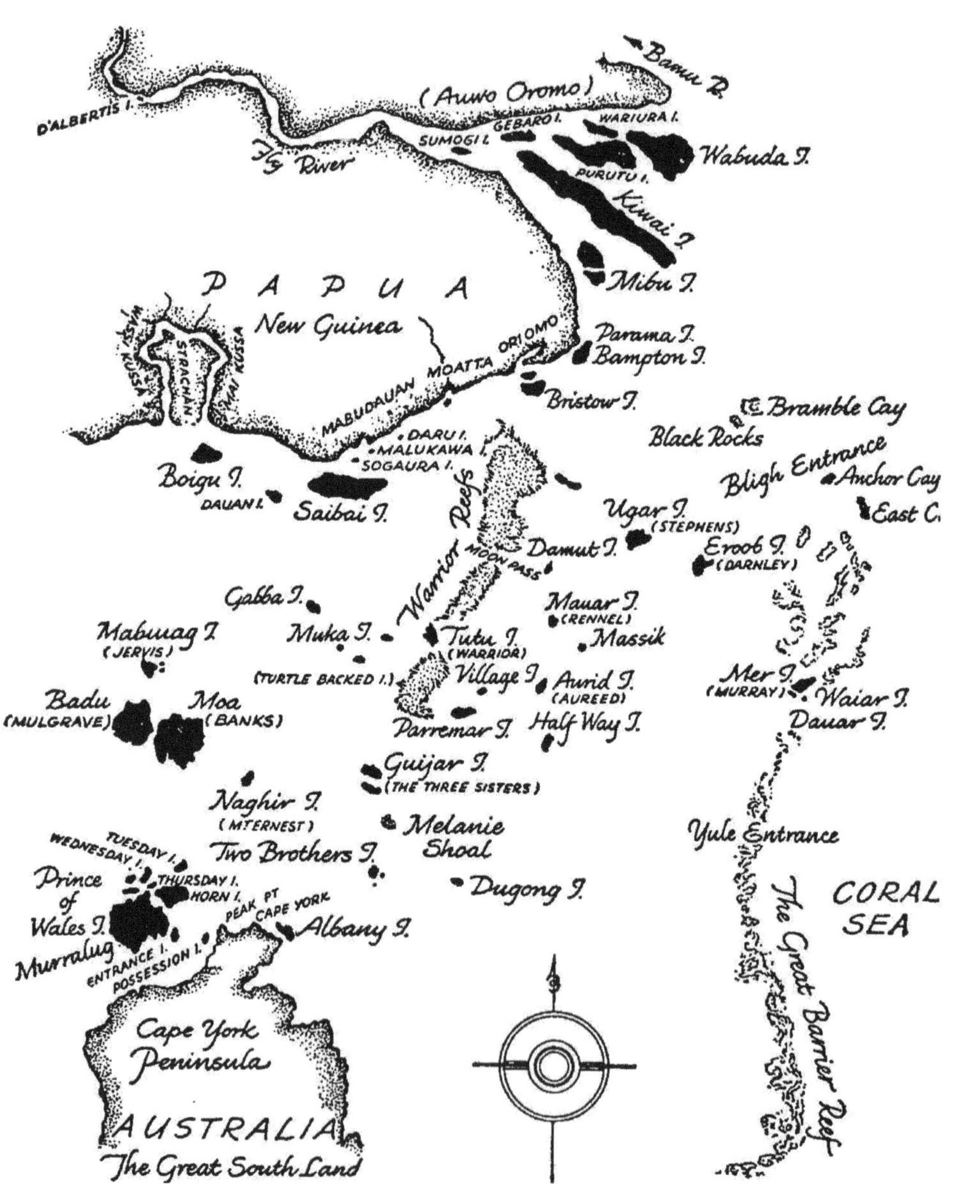

32

THE SEA OF PEARLS

AND during these months Captain Banner and his men cheerfully toiled with Kebisu's people, still on maty terms. The grim-visaged chief had taken a grudging liking to the black-bearded captain, and could not make up his mind to order the massacre. Meanwhile the jovial, wary captain spared no effort to keep this moody warrior in good humour.

And not a sail hove in sight to disturb them, though with this abundance of sea wealth there was room for all. The brig was loaded with pearlshell just nicely in time to avoid two dangers - Kebisu, alternating between moods of goodwill and ominous silence when he shut himself up alone with the persistent Zogo-man whispering that the Lamars should and must be killed; and the threatening nor-west season, with its first thunderstorms rumbling over a brazen sea, ribbons of lightning stretching a curtain of flickering brilliance from horizon to horizon - a human and a natural storm fast brewing. But it would be the storm of nature only that would come to a head.

Banner explained to Kebisu that when the brig was loaded he would sail away with the nor-west winds far down the Great South Land to a great white village called "Syd-nee", But that, after the Wet, he would surely return with the sou-east trades, with a bigger ship. He knew of one, a fine ship, she was called the *Pakeha*. This was a name given the white man by mighty warriors of far-distant islands called New Zealand.

"Brown men like your own strong warriors," explained Banner impressively, "fierce in war as your own men, great seafaring men, too, with fleets of mighty canoes near all as large as your own Skull Chief. Yes, great warriors, great seamen the Maoris, just like your warriors of Warrior Island!"

When Kebisu listened entranced to talk like this Banner knew .he had him-for the time being, anyway. Patiently he had to explain all he knew of the Maori customs, their fighting men and gardens and canoes, their weapons and fishing and stockaded villages, before grudgingly Kebisu would allow him to proceed.

He would return, explained Banner, in this bigger ship the *Pakeha,* heavily loaded with presents, far more than she had before, all for the Sea Chief and his men as reward for the gathering of more pearlshell.

And the two men, fast learning to know one another through and through, smiled into one another's eyes.

"So now it would be foolish of me to kill you and your men and seize the ship," Kebisu said, laughing, "for then you would never return with the presents!"

"The Sea Chief is wise," Banner replied with a smile.

In such an environment it seemed strangely human, the grudging regard of the fierce Chief Kebisu for Captain Banner, who all this time was regarded as a "spirit chief" capable of doing them great harm. Again and again Kebisu had worked himself almost up to the point of attacking Banner, only to refrain at the last moment. And then he would have a fit of the sulks, and fall into a truly dangerous mood, for deep within himself Kebisu felt he should kill Banner and all his men.

"You will never kill him," little Maino said, laughing, and ran for his life. Maino, friend of the white men in the stirring years coming, was right.

When the grey of years gone by was touching Maino's hair and beard, his voice would grow soft, and quite reverently he would speak as he told me of this unbreakable fondness that grew between his tempestuous father and the calm sea-captain. I could see in Maino, the boy, the link between that strange savage culture and the white man's civilization. For in the years now advancing upon them the young folk that survived were quickly to throw in their lot with the whites.

The change had come.

Farewelled by canoes filled with laughing islanders, songs from the shore, and deafening blasts from boo shells, the loaded brig sailed out into the teeth of white horses whipped up by a growing nor-wester. And there seemed a saucy swing to the dip of the vessel, as if she knew her dingy little hold was heavy-loaded with pearlshell, and in the skipper's cabin was a coffee-tin full of pearls, pearls fit to grace the neck of a Cleopatra. There was boisterous horseplay among the crew, for on arrival in Sydney Town their reward was to be great indeed. Smiles and cheery hearts among the whites aboard, for what a discovery they had made-a vast pearlshell bed in this uncharted sea!

Upright in the bows of his father's canoe, little Maino stood straight as an arrow, waving at the tall figure of Banner as the brig gathered way. Little Maino was a warrior, but now he was fighting to keep back tears. Long after the canoes returned to the island Maino still watched the brig, watched until like a vanishing gull she faded into the southern mists.

But fiercely Maino knew she would return, the big, blackbearded captain with the smiling face would surely return with that wonderful present for Maino.

To the islanders, the Lamar ship was sailing back to Spirit Land. To them the world was islands and water, much water stretching far, far away. At the end was built by the gods a vast circular wall, so that the water could not fall away. This wall was the rim of the cup which was the world - the cup filled with sea, with islands and reefs and sandbanks, and all the fish and birds, the dugong and turtle and other things therein. The cup firmly rested upon a mighty pillar; they did not know upon what the pillar rested. When the Lamar ship at last sailed to this rim of the world she would be transformed into a spirit ship, her sails would turn into wings and she would fly up and over the great wall and far away up into the skies, flying into the Spirit World of the Lamars to that great village which they now knew was called Syd-nee. As the spirit ship flew over the wall the Lamars aboard would, of course, turn into spirit form and again become true spirit men. The same thing must happen in turn to every man, woman, and child upon the island, when the hand of Death would touch the brow and the spirit form must fly far away and up to Boigu, Isle of the Blest.

Thus, when the time came for the return, as the Lamar captain had promised, then when the spirit ship flew back over the wall and alighted upon the sea her wings would turn into sails again, she would be changed into the Lamar ship. And the spirit men aboard would be transformed again into Lamars, spirit men in human form, for a short time to revisit the earth.

The *Julia Percy*, sailing south under a stiff nor'-easter, could have by-passed Somerset, but Banner was human, he just could not do it. Mount

Adolphus Island, then the misty mainland, then Albany Island hove in sight. Then, as often happens in such weather, a shaft of brilliant sunlight rippled down from the skies and the toy white house up on the little red hill stood out sharp and clear. With a knowing smile the skipper noted that the bows of the *Julia Percy* had seemed automatically to have nosed towards Albany Pass.

He dropped the hook near the tiny beach, rowed ashore, climbed the steps cut· into the little red hill, and smiled at the cold brown snouts of the two little guns pointing threateningly at Warrior Island. Wondering whether this settlement really would ever come to anything, he strolled on and up the steps to the broad veranda to pay his respects to the Resident. Of course, he was ceremoniously invited to dinner, for the wary but ambitious Acting Resident was always on the look-out for news, and knowledge. And who better to teach him of those strange waters between here and mysterious New Guinea than these adventurous schooner captains who wandered into Somerset just now and then when it suited them?

And it was after a courteous dinner over the huge cedar table, that Banner, warmed by the hospitality, blurted out his great news.

"My brig is loaded with pearlshell," he almost whispered, "great big pearl shell! Huge stuff, and beautiful. The most beautiful pearlshell ever found in the world!"

Chester stared across the table with shining eyes. Remembering Jardine's words, he realized what a breath-taking discovery like this might mean to this sea in a wilderness - could mean to him!

They yarned far into the night, almost in conspiratorial tones as if even the dreamy bush might be listening. Not a few historical romances of the north were to be enacted at Somerset, but nothing so pregnant with big events as the unheralded arrival of the "Pearl Ship".

"I must sail with the tide," said Banner at last.

One final fill of the glasses, the glass in Banner's big fist seemed like a pearl under the ship's lantern as he reached out a long arm across that cedar table. Smiling into each other's excited eyes, the men clinked glasses musically.

"I know you'll keep it dark," said Banner meaningly. "Don't say a word! If it gets out they'll be after me like a pack of wolves."

"You mean," said Chester, "when the news gets out many ships will follow you back into this Coral Sea."

"Whole fleets of them!" The captain laughed. "And then watch out for lively times upon these same high seas! You'll have to build up this baby Singapore of yours quick and lively then, believe me."

"Nothing would please me better," said Chester heartily.

"Your very good health, captain!"

And Banner sailed south for Sydney, with bellying sails as the white horses of a galloping sea whanged upon the bows, spout-ing spray aloft that drove across on the wind. The mate on the poop aft was humming a sailor's love song, the big skipper all a-grin as he sniffed the salt in his whiskers. Who wouldn't be happy, loaded to the hatch with pearlshell? The South Sea crew, too, had one huge grin as they worked the ship, each watch flew like magic with talk of their big reward and what they should buy in Sydney Town.

The first Pearl Ship to sail the Coral Sea. "Keep it dark! Breathe not a word!" "Pearls! Pearlshell in the Coral Sea!"

Why, the very sea-birds would shriek the news far down south to Sydney Town!

On board a pearling lugger in the Coral Sea, about 1910.

33

VENGEANCE

EXCITED with this great secret he held, Chester wrote to the distant authorities of the extreme urgency of the need for at least a light vessel to police this sea, which within a few months now, even before his letter was received, might become the scene of feverish activity, and almost certainly of outrage and all manner of uncurbed lawlessness upon the high seas. Then he had to wait in growing indignation for some passing vessel, at its own pleasure, to carry the letter to Brisbane. The mails were a constant source of irritation to him, as his letters show: "Could not the mails be sent via Sydney? The last mail received was by H.M.S. *Blanche,* after an interval of twelve months. During that time two vessels from Sydney called direct here." Probably one mail in twelve months would lead a lonely, ambitious man to believe he was left somewhat out of the world.

Telescope in hand, he fumed now as he gazed out over this fascinating sea he was now so very anxious to know, must know! But soon his irritation was changed to cold fury, for bloody revolution broke out in his own stronghold.

The black troopers shot a comrade who would not conspire with them to combine with the wild blacks and sack the settlement. That aboriginal trooper was surely a hero, knowing what he was up against. But for his stubborn refusal the settlement must have been wiped out. His enraged comrades, believing that dead men can tell no tales, shot him, but thus alarmed their officers. Hurriedly they deserted with their arms to the Yardaigains, who in yelling delight fell in with the plans of blood, fire, and loot. Thus these fine troopers, leading a yelling mob of Yardaigains, suddenly emerged from the bush and fell upon one of Jardine's stations in a frenzy of yells, flying spears, and bullets. Two of Jardine's tame stockboys leapt bareback on handy horses and, clinging to their manes, managed to gallop through and break away on the twenty-mile race to warn the settlement. The unlucky ones were battered to death. The homestead was looted of everything, then burnt. The cattle were driven away to be speared at leisure.

Not really a big affair, though very much so to Jardine in particular, and to the settlement. The homestead was only a large, sturdily built pioneering hut, the stores and tools of the roughest. But the lives of the aboriginal stockmen of course were irreplaceable, and the loss of those few head of cattle, the valuable stores, and so much work gone up in smoke was a serious blow to the absent Jardine, while the "big victory" boosted the morale of the numerous hostile tribesmen and did no good at all to the prestige of the settlement.

The Acting Resident wrote bitterly to Brisbane:

"Five of the native troopers sent up were only recently released from gaol with considerable portion of their sentences for serious crimes unexpired. It will scarcely be credited but I found that these troopers were released prisoners from St Helena, who had served half of a sentence of ten years for attempted rape and robbery under arms; and yet the Government armed these men and sent them to me as troopers. I wrote privately to the Under-Colonial Secretary that, if the Government chose to make me keeper of a convict prison, they need scarcely enquire what became of the convicts, for as there were only 8 native police and six Europeans to guard the Settlement, some of the convicts would not return to Brisbane should they become mutinous."

Most assuredly the Empire's second Singapore was being hard pressed. However, the worried Acting Resident was enabled to pull the harassed settlement together with the timely arrival of the frigate *Blanche* and Captain Montgomerie with stores, water police, reinforcements, and supplies for the settlement of Somerset. Captain Montgomerie had also to inquire into sundry reported massacres, killings, and any unlawful actions in general allegedly occurring upon this Coral Sea. Chester swore there were plenty and to spare. Up in the big room in the Residency, with the flag flying and marines and water police stiffly standing to attention on the parade ground as befitted the arrival of a captain of Her Majesty's ship of war to pay formal respect to Queensland's representative, the Acting Resident of Somerset, they clinked glasses across the big table.

Then Chester heatedly inquired, "How can I garrison this wild mainland and at the same time keep order upon the most dangerous and troublous sea in the world when I have not even got a naval pinnace to do it with?"

To which Captain Montgomerie of H.M. Frigate *Blanche*, in the naval manner, made cool and diplomatic reply.

Gudang scouts had brought word by canoe that the killers of the *Sperweer's* crew were gathering upon Wednesday Island, but a few miles nor'-west in the Strait.

A punitive expedition was quickly organized. Chester, with eight troopers and twenty Gudangs, sailed in the *Blanche*, which anchored on the lee side of Wednesday Island, landing a force of fifty blue-jackets and Chester's party with Lieutenant Markham in charge. Native scouts returned within an hour, reporting that the Mount Ernest tribe were gathered in force on the weather side of the island.

Lieutenant Markham formed his party in line, then cautiously marched on through open forest until they came to a thin belt of mangroves. Plainly they heard native song and laughter coming from the other side of the mangroves.

Markham led his blue-jackets, Chester took the left flank. At a signal they dashed into the mangroves. Chester's men, used to mangroves, emerged onto the beach much quicker than the blue-jackets. Lazing on the beach, a large number of natives stared amazed at Chester's men, then sprang up and ran to the water's edge. Chester saw in an instant that it was dead low tide and the canoes had been paddled out to deep water by the women and children. But now the warriors wheeled threateningly round, believing they had only to deal with this small party. Shouting threats, they lined up on the beach, hurriedly grasping bows and arrows. Then, stamping in the war-dance, they commenced singing while fitting arrows to tautening bowstrings, taunting their nervous black adversaries with the promise of a warm reception indeed. The Gudangs stood firm, though Chester was anxious while holding his fire awaiting the blue-jackets. They came running out through the mangroves only just in time and, swiftly lining up, had the natives completely outflanked and hemmed in by riflemen on both sides. Motionless, silent now at the gleam of steel, the warriors glanced back towards the sea. But the tide was too far out, the canoes too far away.

To a sharp order from Chester, they sullenly threw their weapons to the sand.

In the chief's gunyah was found ample plunder from the *Sperweer*, even to the ship's log-book, with the last entry made by Captain Gascoigne just before he was speared through the skylight while lying in his bunk.

While they were searching the camp, and each article of plunder was being laid accusingly before the prisoners, one of the chiefs sprung up and, darting between the guards, raced for the beach. They fired, but he had a charmed life. Reaching the water's edge, he rushed in great splashing leaps out over the shallow water. How his heart must have pounded as he cursed that low tide with the musket balls whizzing past him! He was still splashing out there, now fully three hundred yards from the shore, when the *Blanche's* best marksman put a bullet through him. As he fell in his last great splash a howl of hate and sorrow arose from the women in the distant canoes. He was their man. After all, their men had only killed the Lamars, the ghost people.

A drum head court martial was held on the spot. How those silent, uneasy warriors must have wondered at these strange doings of the Lamars! Wondering and wondering, "What are they going to do next?"

Three of the chiefs were pointed out by Chester's natives as being concerned in the massacre. These were sentenced, lined up, and shot.

How the others must have wondered! Warned never to attack a ship again, they were allowed to rejoin their canoes.

H.M.S. *Blanche* sailed to explore Mount Ernest Island itself, and further put the terror of authority into its native inhabitants if this were thought necessary. But a greater judge sent a warning. The vengeful man-o-war struck an uncharted reef - very luckily for her, in calm weather, and with the tides rising. They threw even guns overboard to lighten her. She stayed on the reef three days, and the weather remained halcyon calm, to the inexpressible relief of every soul on board who, on the third day, watched with bated breath the big spring tides coming slowly, the ocean seeming quietly to swell, then they felt, slowly, so slowly, the rising waters lifting her.

She was refloated undamaged. But as to what fate befell Mrs Gascoigne, that remains a mystery of the bush, as with Leichhardt and others who have vanished without trace. Even years later, when the islanders became "civilized", when many of them loved to boast of what happened to the Lamars, the whites who fell into their hands, not one would mention the fate of Mrs Gascoigne, though some said that the boy had been passed on from island to island. When deliberately questioned one and all grew quiet and shook their heads in a frowning ignorance, stubbornly denying knowledge of what happened to her. Even the Gudangs, the aborigines across on the mainland who from the start were the eyes and ears of Somerset, who had even brought Somerset first news of the massacre, persisted in denying that they knew what happened to the white woman. Yet, of course, they knew. A few other white women of whom far less is known vanished amongst the isles of the Coral Sea. Just native rumour, quickly suppressed upon questioning, then an impenetrable silence.

34

CHESTER FINDS HIS GREAT AMBITION

FRANK JARDINE now returned to Somerset to take over the Residency once more, to the bitter disappointment of Chester, who by now was taking an almost violent interest in this fascinating sea and what lay across the Strait and beyond it to New Guinea shores. Jardine, realizing what an invaluable man Chester was and could be by sea, managed somehow or other to have the order recalling him shelved. So Chester stayed on to his destiny.

There occurred now one of those numerous, quickly forgotten incidents that helped keep alert the *beche-de-mer* adventurers, one that was to have big consequences in the years to come. It was just one of those little things from which develop ever accumulating results, the end of which we cannot see. Through it Chester found his real life-work.

The schooner *Active,* mothering her fishing boats among the vast reefs in the Great North-east Channel between the mainland and New Guinea was caught in a sudden white squall. One of the boats broke adrift and vanished into the howling mists, with its crew of good divers aboard. And by nightfall all aboard. the schooner knew that if their comrades were not quickly found their chance of hanging on to their heads would be slim indeed.

At dawn the schooner searched north-east along the reefs; Captain Delargy with thirty heavily armed Tanna men in three whaleboats searched among the islets to leeward. Some days later, in forlorn hope, he made northward towards the forbidding shores of that great, mysterious island, New Guinea. He made the south-east coast close by a large island called Saibai, and there was the boat, hove-to well off shore, with its crew in the dilemma of their lives. Utterly exhausted, perishing for water and starving, they just hung on their oars, staring longingly at the island.

And at the reception committee awaiting them. For on the beach stood several hundred brown-skinned warriors armed with long bows. Behind them beautiful groves of palms sheltered a large village. At the edge of the palms some hundreds of shapely women with frizzy heads of hair stood silently staring. Silent, brown-skinned youngsters were everywhere.

The starving men in the boats could see there was abundance of food ashore. But - would they supply it?

Captain Delargy's boats clustered round the nearly hysterical cast-

castaways and fed them, then some of the brown men ashore, carrying huge bunches of bananas above their heads, came wading out to trade. Delargy, scenting business, his eyes roaming over the little he could see of this apparently large island, taking in the broad chests and powerful shoulder muscles that told of born divers and sea knowledge of these islands, immediately wished to see the chief and try to arrange that his men should collect *beche-de-mer* for him for trade. So, with his well-armed men, he followed these traders ashore.

They immediately rejoined their comrades and picked up their weapons, then, the two hundred of them like a disciplined company of European soldiers, marched up the beach, while at a signal the women and children vanished inland. The men turned about, formed a compact square, set their long bows, and challenged the intruders to fight.

Olive-skinned men of magnificent physique, intelligent faces with eyes fairly shining at the prospect of a fight, great bunches of well-combed, woolly hair dyed a vivid brick-dust colour, arrows fitted to the huge long bows.

This was the picture Delargy's men saw, and in their turn they fingered their double-barrelled guns eagerly, their eyes flashing from black and brown faces, teeth a-gleam in wolfish grins, fairly boiling for a fight. The odds meant nothing to them. And, oh, what a prize this village would be to loot!

"Steady there!" shouted Delargy. "Don't fire, not any of you! I want peace here, not fight."

Deliberately he laid down his arms before him on the sand, then turned to his men. "Wait here," he ordered. "Don't fire unless they shoot at me! If any man shoots an arrow at me, then fire quickly - and all together!"

Casually he walked up the beach to the waiting warriors, keeping his eye on the chief. Walked right up to the big savage, smiled, made signs of peace and-trade!

Fortunately, he had brought plenty of trade goods in the boats, anticipating that he might have to bribe natives in searching for his lost men.

The Saibai warriors were eager indeed to trade for these wonderful goods and peace was quickly made. The warriors relaxed, all smiles now, eager to hurry to the gardens and gather fruits and vegetables for trade. Delargy shouted to his men to ground their arms, an order grudgingly obeyed. The warriors in turn laid their bows and arrows, clubs and bone and bamboo knives at their feet, then all hands hurried up into the village, the women appearing as if by magic at reassuring shouts.

What attracted the eyes of the South Sea men as a magnet was the solidly built Zogo House, riotously ornamented with skulls, a score or more obviously freshly cleaned and painted. Delargy estimated later there must have been one hundred and fifty skulls there. Delargy estimated later there must have been one hundred and fifty skulls there. Grimly he glanced at the puckered faces of his men, knowing those freshly cleaned trophies would be somewhat of a curb on their amorous intentions towards these comely village maidens.

While a huge feast of roast pigs, dugong, yam and taro, manioc and banana was being prepared the chief pridefully conducted the white captain on a tour through this, his main village. His great pride, of course, was the Zogo House, and as a very special favour the white man was allowed to climb up on the platform and peer inside at the gloom of cubicles divided by palm matting. Delargy saw shadowy things, including the savage eyes of two witch-doctors, grotesquely dressed. He was only allowed the merest glimpse at the shadows within this holy of holies. Thankfully he climbed down, praying his blood-lusting crew would not start anything during his absence.

Away from the Dead House, in the village, scrupulously clean everywhere under the groves of palms, Delargy admired with surprise solid, two-storeyed houses neatly built of bamboo poles and mangrove timber beams, with sides and roof sheathed with beautifully plaited palm-leaf matting. Carved weapons and cooking utensils of gourds, wood, and huge shells were plentiful. Beyond the village the captain caught a glimpse of green plains inland, watered by small streams, of large, well-cultivated fields of taro and yam, of numerous tropic vegetables and fruits. He was disappointed, though, that he could see no hills, for like many of the early adventurers he had gold at the back of his mind.

At a grand feast, the warriors put on a realistic war-dance, watched with mixed feelings by Delargy's own savage South Sea men. He did not like the glint in their eyes when they looked at the shapely, tantalizingly laughing girls. Every now and then he felt compelled to growl an angry warning, reminding them of the onlookers at the feast grinning down from the Zogo House. He was glad indeed when feast and ceremonies were over and he could stroll back to the beach for the great event-the trade. There he stood, gravely talking as best he could with the eager chief, while his men quietly picked up their arms and waded out to the boats as hundreds of men, women, and children, laden with their goods, crowded round to trade. And again he blessed the foresight that had made him put a goodly supply of trade goods into the longboats.

Thus a schooner captain found a new island, overcame a tricky position, made peace with a particularly virile and pugnacious tribe, and made allies and workers to collect *beche-de-mer* for him when in two moons' time he would return with the schooner. Similarly many an island was found in the island sea, for it was not always a tale of bloodshed.

But such an incident was merely in the day's work for many of those early adventurers. It was what this one eventually led to that made it notable; For during the *Active's* voyage back to Sydney, this simple experience, casually mentioned over the dining table at the Residency at Somerset, and followed by numerous stories of other islands and of that huge mystery of all of them, New Guinea, drawn out of the captain by the eager Chester, was to mean the birth of a great idea.

Could he - would it ever be possible - could he, Chester, "plant the flag" in New Guinea?

He had chafed at the seeming hopelessness of ever doing anything big under the conditions existing at Somerset. Was the end of his frustration in sight?

A dance ornament from the Torres Strait, 1880.

35

THE CHIEF KEBISU'S HOUSE

MEANWHILE Jardine, while he was in Brisbane, had found that the Colonial Secretary's Department was with him to the hilt in the development of the farthest north and the Coral Sea. Several far-seeing statesmen were in power, but the resources of such a huge[49] even then partly unexplored colony, with its scanty population[50] were strained to the uttermost. There was nothing left with which to develop the hazy north a thousand miles away, and an unknown sea over which Queensland had no official control. And there was no help from overseas. The second Singapore had not yet materialized. The Colonial Office was not interested, but the Queensland Government certainly was doing the very best it could and would continue to do so. Moreover, ambitions were big. Queensland wished to annex all the islands of Torres Strait, known and unknown, from the Queensland coast right to New Guinea. Besides this, oversea shipping, rapidly increasing, was more and more beginning to use the Inner Passage charted by the survey ships. This must surely result in that long-desired connection with the East, which would greatly enhance the value and importance of Somerset. Incidentally, such deep-sea ships would be offered every incentive to call in at Queensland coastal ports for cargo. For the Government was absolutely convinced that with time such ports would inevitably develop. Throughout the years the little *beche-de-mer* vessels, for so long following the routes of the early exploring ships, had now almost made the inner route plain sailing for deep-sea ships from overseas. The opening up of the far north by land would surely come with time. Jardine was assured that the Queensland Government would continue to do everything possible for the Settlement, and the Resident.

Jardine had arrived back at Somerset with supplies and reinforcements on 30th August 1870 in the schooner *Louisa Maria.* This enabled him to do a good turn to the ambitious and disappointed Chester, for he could truthfully describe the schooner to the Colonial Secretary as "a ship in which I had every possible service, but not a fit vessel for the Acting Resident to take his wife back to Brisbane in. The schooner has not proper accommodation for female passengers. A constable and his wife who were aboard for Somerset had berths provided for them in the hold with no bulkhead to divide them from the cargo, and no provision for the common decencies of life."

To Jardine's intense satisfaction, he gained something concrete out of his Brisbane trip, a smart little cutter, the *Lizzie Jardine.* Manned by water police, this little vessel was to do great work during the hectic years now commencing. For all his local knowledge, neither Jardine - nor anyone else - had the faintest idea how hectic those years were to prove.

Captain Banner's brig, loaded with pearlshell, was an *Argo* sailing into Sydney. *The Golden Hind,* sailing into Portsmouth loaded with Spanish treasure, set the bells a-ringing, the guns a-booming, and crowds hurrying to the foreshore. No such reception, of course, greeted the *Julia Percy,* though she came sailing into Sydney Cove with news of the discovery of a "Sea of Pearls", a discovery of infinitely more value to this country than a dozen ships laden with gold stolen from the Incas. There was excitement along the waterfront, in the growing city, and in little Brisbane also. Huddle of heads as commercially minded men interested in produce of the sea arranged business ventures, busy fitting out of the few vessels available - schooners, barques, brigantines, ketches, in sudden demand, luggers, cutters - all in a hurry to be fitted out ready for the coming sou-east trades. There was great demand for those so few sailormen experienced in this rough-and-ready sailor work among the islands. And then the first flotilla sailed, the vanguard of the coming first pearlshell rush. Nearly twelve months would drift by before the eagerly awaited results from these first ships reached Brisbane and Sydney. And it would be several years before the news really spread throughout the far-flung Island World. When it did sails would spread from unheard-of islands throughout the South Seas, all hastening towards this rumoured "Sea of Pearls". The years of the opening up of Torres Strait and the waters within the Great Barrier Reef would bring ships with names becoming familiar as a man's daily friends. The *Bluebell* and others were already familiar in the first roughly organized development of the *beche-de-mer* beds; there would come the *Storm Bird, the Australian Packet, Margaret* and *Jane, Susannah Booth, Crinoline, Krishna, Three Brothers, John Bell, Root Hog or Die, Hit or Miss, Pakeha, Woodlark, Freak, Georgina Godfrey, Active, Crown, Black Dog, Woodbine, Challenge* - these were but a few of the early birds. The Coral Sea had come alive with a vengeance, but not with oversea ships seeking trade with the Indies and China.

Jardine, frowning from the Residency veranda as he watched sail after sail go scurrying by, ignoring Somerset, sat him down to write the Colonial Secretary of the day.

Somerset, 1870

"... brigs, barques, schooners arriving to share the good fortune of the *Pakeha.* The schooner *Kate Kearney* in port awaiting the arrival of schooner *Melanie,* both bound for New Guinea. God knows what is going to happen in these wild seas with this rush of all manner of vessels and crews and no power to hold them in check."

The crew of the *Pakeha* cared not one whit about the woes of Authority at Somerset. In fact, some passed ribald remarks as the good ship sailed merrily along to seaward of Albany Island. They had painted Sydney red, and were lusting with desire to load up with pearlshell and return and do it again. The skipper was a happy man as the schooner neared Warrior Island and he saw the canoes loaded with people excitedly racing out to greet them. Banner had many presents aboard for Kebisu's men - and women, too! Great divers, those women! And what presents for little Maino! A whole sea-chest full!

The black-bearded captain chuckled aloud at thought of the boy's eyes popping out in speechless wonder. How he and his boy friends, and girls, too, would cluster round that sea-chest when he laid it before them upon the beach! He could see the mass of their little brown heads all around it, once they dared to touch it. The skipper knew it would be quite a time before he could prevail upon Maino to open the lid of that magic chest!

For the Sea Chief himself, though, he had such a present as no islander in all the seas could possibly have dreamt of.

A house - a house of *toorook*! An iron house!

Maybe that "house" was the first prefabricated house erected in Australia. Only a few sheets of iron, to be sure, but the effect on the islanders was one of incredulous amazement, as the news spread-according to the islanders themselves, through mental telepathy by members of their Zogo-le-and from islands up to one hundred miles away canoes came speeding to see for themselves this amazing sight. On that Bat islet bare except for its scraggy pandanus-trees, a Lamar house built of that treasure, *toorook!* A house of iron - to the islanders, it was a house of gold - for the great Chief Kebisu.

Kebisu squatted in state; all of him seemed one big smile as queues of islanders shuffled up in tum for a peep at this mightily proud chief inside his house of *toorook,* surrounded by many presents besides.

What had inspired Banner to procure such an unheard-of gift to "keep sweet" this fiercely uncertain, warlike chief? Apart from a slain warrior's skull, the most prized possession any warrior could possess was a Lamar tomahawk; he would have given all the gold in the world, had he possessed it, for such a priceless thing. Any scrap of iron from which to fashion axe-head or knife, harpoon head or spear-blade was precious. And here was the Chief Kebisu sitting within a great house of *toorook*! In amazement they gazed at it, came unbelievingly up, reverently touched it.

Yes, it was true! A house of *toorook*!

In the course of history, an occasional puffed-up potentate, out of tears and blood, has built for himself a "golden palace", meaning that his own rooms within were lined and adorned with gold, as was the bed upon which the poor fool gasped his life away. But no barbaric potentate ever owned a palace of gold to compare in his people's minds with that House of Iron of the savage Sea Chief Kebisu, Mamoose of Warrior Island, though it was but a hut upon a desolate strip of dead coral, lapped by a "Sea of Pearls".

Thus the stage was set for another fifty years of adventure and romance both by land and sea, with the Fingerpoint of the huge Peninsula pointing out into the Strait directly towards that mysterious New Guinea, as if silently claiming it as Australian land, which once it truly had been.

NOTES

1 He did, this very year 1827. He ordered Major Lockyer to form a settlement three thousand miles west at King George's Sound (Albany), and officially claimed British Sovereignty over all this continent of Australia. This was soon followed by settlement on the Swan River, destined to grow into the City of Perth.

2 The southernmost limit of the Reef (which is really a series of reefs) is Lady Elliott Island, just south of Swain Reefs, and it stretches northward for 1250 miles, enclosing the waters of Torres Strait to within a very few miles of the south-eastern coast of New Guinea. The inner sea between the Reef and the mainland varies in width from about fifteen to a little over a hundred miles.

3 In these days the varieties of scientist are about as bewildering as the Atomic Bomb to the ordinary human. In this case, I believe the correct term is marine biologist.

4 These were the most highly "cultured" islanders, inhabiting only a few of the islands actually in Torres Strait; but this fact, of course, would not be known at the time.

5 In 1803 she struck Wreck Reef on the Great Barrier, sailing in company with the Bridgwater and Porpoise, which Matthew Flinders was aboard.

6 A spirit in human form.

7 There existed a definite inter-communication system between the different, often warring, island groups.

8 Forbes, when rescued, was brought to Sydney and hospital. Soon familiarly known as "Timor Joe", he settled at Williamstown in Victoria. He died there in 1876. It could truly be said of this much battered man that he was "tough as they make them".

9 Actually, this cargo of *beche-de-mer* came from Torres Strait, at the entrance to the Arafura. But it was all the same sea to all but a handful of navigators.

10 The tribulations of the early Sydneyites over their water supply seem rather quaint to us now, when we are building a dam above the Warragamba which would be capable of filling Sydney Harbour with fresh water in a day.

11 After Governor Brisbane, since it was in his time that Lockyer, then Cunningham explored the river.

12 January 1829.

13 During the great Spanish Influenza epidemic just after the First World War saw some hundreds of aborigines lying dead upon the beaches of the Cape York Peninsula coast. They had lain in the water to "cool away" their burning temperatures, and their last strength was used to crawl back up the beach to high-water mark, to die. The same thing happened on Western Australia's far Kimberley coast, three thousand miles west of Cape York Peninsula.

14 The full story of the Charles Eaton has been told in *Headhunters of the Coral Sea* (ETT Imprint).

15 May 1836. Among this maze of reefs, the particular reef upon which the Stirling Castle struck was later named Eliza Reef, after Captain Fraser's wife. Thus the tragedy left to man and wife the name of a reef and the name of an island - which was no consolation to the unfortunate couple.

16 Known as Tursior Tallboy to the Aboriginals. For further information about Graham and the rescue of Mrs Fraser, see the next chapter.

17 Known "wild white men" in the Moreton Bay District about this time were "Boralchow" (Baker), "Tursi" otherwise "Tallboy" (Graham), "Wandl" (Bracefield), and "Durramboi" (James Davis). Yet others have been recorded.

18 Thereare two stories of the rescue of Mrs Fraser, Bracefield's account, and Graham's. I lean towards the records of Petrie and Stuart Russell, who after all were on the spot only a few years after the rescue, and who were sent out from Moreton Bay to find Bracefield and the burial places of the castaways if possible. These two men took the story from Bracefield when they found him. They have left voluminous records of those years. They held responsible positions, and have left names that stand high in Queensland's pioneering history. However, to any reader who is interested, Graham's story is very well told, and well authenticated it seems to me, in *John Graham, Convict* by Robert Gibbings.

19 The 20th October 1838.

20 Malarial prevention and cure was not discovered in those days.

21 1839-42. From 1837 she had been doing great work surveying the far north-western coastline.

22 He was probably gazing out towards the Barkly Tableland.

23 Actually approximately 112 miles south-east of Peak Point.

24 May Heaven protect me from the wrath of sailormen for comparing this deep-sea manoeuvre to the riding of the homely prad!

25 This means the "outer" wall of the Great Reef, which is exposed to the open Pacific.

26 J. Beete Jukes, *Narrative of the Surveying Voyage of H.M.S. Fly.*

27 1844-5.

28 February 1846.
29 On a clear moonlit night she had struck upon a coral reef off Cape Tribulation. By the greatest of good fortune, almost it seems as if Fate had decreed it, not only did she strike in calm weather, but a big coral block plugged up the hole as the ship was wrenched off the reef. But for this miraculous happening, the *Endeavour* must certainly have sunk, and quite probably Captain Cook and his ship and crew would never have been heard of again. Thus the whole course of our Australian history would have been changed, had it not been for a coral block plugging up a hole in a ship.
30 172 tons.
31 The full story of Barbara Thompson has been written in *Isles of Despair.*
32 The renegade, of course, had no knowledge that convictism was now a thing of the past in eastern Australia.
33 The Australian aborigines feared the horses of the early settlers, just as the Aztecs feared the horses of the Spaniards.
34 As had in 1846 the castaways from the wreck of the schooner *Thomas Lord.*
35 The same idea had occurred to Surgeon Hamilton during the open boat voyage to Timor of the survivors of H.M.S. *Pandora*, seventy years before.
36 10th December 1859.
37 Or use the cloth lava-lava as the case might be.
38 Another pioneering mystery that was never solved.
39 And an army did. But not until our day, during the Second World War.
40 The story of the Jardine boys' great adventure has been told in *The Great Trek.*
41 The Resident's words were deciphered from a white-ant-eaten old record.
42 Late in 1867. The battling colony was to be increasingly helped now by the fast developing sugar-cane industry.
43 In his report on the attack (1792) Bligh described the men of Tudu as "dexterous sailors and formidable warriors". Hence the name "Warrior Island".
44 In time coming, they would be forced to do this very thing. Many a young girl was saved this way.
45 The war-canoes were built by specialists among tribes of the Auwo Oromo from timber from the Dibiri (Bamu).
46 Few of the pure race remain today; their blood is intermingled with that of South Sea men and the kanakas of the Queensland sugar plantations.
47 Only one shell in from 800 to 1000 would contain a pearl.
48 1897.
49 666,497 square miles.
50 At this time about 100,000.

www.ingramcontent.com/pod-product-compliance
Ingram Content Group Australia Pty Ltd
76 Discovery Rd, Dandenong South VIC 3175, AU
AUHW020904290725
414507AU00002B/42

9 781923 205673